Thomas Pattison, John George Macneill

The Gaelic Bards

And original poems

Thomas Pattison, John George Macneill

The Gaelic Bards
And original poems

ISBN/EAN: 9783337329150

Printed in Europe, USA, Canada, Australia, Japan

Cover: Foto ©Thomas Meinert / pixelio.de

More available books at **www.hansebooks.com**

THE GAELIC BARDS,

AND

ORIGINAL POEMS,

BY

THOMAS PATTISON.

EDITED, WITH A BIOGRAPHICAL SKETCH AND NOTES,

BY THE

Rev. JOHN GEORGE MACNEILL,

CAWDOR.

SECOND EDITION

GLASGOW:
ARCHIBALD SINCLAIR, PRINTER & PUBLISHER,
62 ARGYLE STREET.

1890.

ARCHIBALD SINCLAIR, PRINTER AND PUBLISHER,
ARGYLE STREET, GLASGOW.

PREFACE TO THE SECOND EDITION.

THE First Edition of "The Gaelic Bards" having been exhausted, a new edition was called for. The work, in its two sections of Modern Gaelic Bards, and of Ancient Gaelic Bards is practically unchanged. A few vague and uninteresting original poems have been omitted, but other characteristic and popular pieces, such as "Captain Gorrie's Ride," "The Praise of Islay," and "Haste from the Window," have been inserted. Some distinct additions have been made to the present edition, in the shape of a biographical sketch, and appended illustrative notes by the Editor. A portrait of the Author is also given.

In introducing the Second Edition to the public, the Publisher and the Editor are confident that it will be welcomed by their brother Celts at home and abroad, as an acceptable contribution to the ever increasing important department of Celtic Literature. The labour bestowed on this Edition by the Publisher and the Editor, was ungrudgingly given in the midst of the whirl and worry of daily duty.

PREFATORY NOTICE TO THE FIRST EDITION.

THOMAS PATTISON was a native of Islay. He was designed for the Church, and after receiving a fair elementary education at the Parish School of Bowmore, was sent to the University of Edinburgh, and afterwards to that of Glasgow. In the latter he completed his studies, and became thereafter a licentiate of the Church of Scotland. His excellent attainments, enthusiasm in various departments of literature, and singular modesty of character, endeared him to his family and friends; and his death, at an early age, was profoundly mourned.

The friends of MR. PATTISON, on whom devolved the duty of ushering the Metrical Translations and other Literary Remains into the world, are indebted to one who was his early school companion and dear friend, now a clergyman of the Church of Scotland,* for the following truthful and eloquent tribute to his sweet and gentle memory:—

"Without pronouncing an opinion on the merits of his work as a literary composition, I am disposed to think that those who are capable of estimating the difficulties that surrounded the task of which these Translations are the performance, will hail them as at least a valuable contribution to a branch of study which has hitherto received but scant measure of consideration. Perhaps it

* Rev. M. C. Taylor, D.D., Professor of Church History and Divinity, Edinburgh University.

may be questioned whether MR. PATTISON did not attempt too much in the task which he set himself, and whether the result at which he aimed was not beset by unnecessary hindrances to a felicitous poetical translation. In presenting his readers with a version of Gaelic Poems, that conveys not only the substantial but the literal meaning of the originals, and that combines the original metres, line for line, with the English element of rhyme, it is plain that he had one fruitful source of embarrassment to contend with from which the *Bards* were free. At the same time, such as can compare the Translations with the originals, must acknowledge the remarkable fidelity with which even the most difficult passages have been rendered; and, although they may censure the plan on which the Translations were projected, they will not fail to make allowance for the difficulties it entailed. Even in this particular the Translator's aim was high.

"But while anticipating for the volume a hearty welcome at the hands of all for whom the poetry and literary activity of an ancient and kindred people have attractions, I fear it will give the reader little insight into the fair proportions of the Translator's mind. Those who knew his devotion to English Literature, his accurate and profound acquaintance with its history, his severe study of its greatest Masters, and the fine combination of strength and culture with which he latterly approached it, will feel with me that the translation of Gaelic Poetry was not a fair test of his literary powers, and that no amount of success in it can indicate the full extent of the loss sustained by us in his death. All who enjoyed his private friendship, are aware that his work on "The Gaelic Bards," was little more than an effort in a bypath of his studies and pursuits. If I am not mistaken, the impulse to it may be traced, in a great measure, to the "Highland Tales," published by Mr. John Campbell, of Islay. Being asked to assist in the collection of materials for that work, MR. PATTISON responded by giving his cordial co-operation. The result was an enthusiasm in the cause of Gaelic Literature and Antiquities; an enthusiasm that gave a certain permanence and character of real lifework to a pursuit accepted in the first instance as a recreation. It led him step by step, insensibly, away from his first intention. The search for fugitive Gaelic lore in prose and verse, languishing in every remote glen of his native Highlands, led to independent researches, and a careful perusal of the compositions of the Bards known to be in print. With a feeling of sadness, pardonable in a Highlander, he saw that the men of Celtic blood were being rapidly absorbed into communities of Anglo-Saxon lineage—and to rescue the poetry of the Clansmen from dying with the Clans, he set himself the task of transfusing it into the English tongue. The field was new to him, but he entered on it with the ardour of one who was engaged in a labour of love. It brought him once more in contact with the scenes and associations of his boyhood. It opened up glimpses of a national life which had for him the freshness of the sea-breeze and the scented heather, in the rambles of a long vacation. The student of Dante and of Shakespeare, of Goethe and of Burns, felt that it was indeed holiday-time with him on *Ben-Dorain* and in *Coire-Cheathaich*, with *Duncan Ban*, or with *MacDonald* and his boatmen aboard of the famous *Birlinn of Clan-Ranald*.

"It was a vigorous and patriotic effort; a right pleasant recreation to begin with, conducted with infinite spirit and very rapidly completed. If it bears on it, as we see it now, in a posthumous volume, the marks of haste, I am convinced it is because he felt that the fruits of more important avocations were ripening, and that the claims of larger plans were pressing. Although, therefore, the subject to which he devoted himself thus heartily for a time, was congenial to his sentiments and feelings, it certainly was not what he himself would have regarded as most in harmony with the natural bent and development of his genius, or as the proper fruit of his life's true work.

"At the time when these Translations were commenced, his health indeed was such as might well justify him in making a digression from the main course of his pursuits, for in youth he possessed the strength and litheness of an athlete; but, alas! the hand of death stayed him, so that he returned not to the old paths. It may be said that in what was but an interlude in the great game of life, for which he had trained himself with rare patience and fortitude, he sank upon his shield. In this volume, hastily prepared, we have at once his salutation and farewell: *Moriturus nos salutat.*

"We looked for his speaking to us from the heart of *English Literature*, with which few men of his years stood in such close relationship of thought and feeling. Old letters are beside me still, indicating a genuineness of discipleship to the leaders of thought in English speech, from Chaucer to Wordsworth and Tennyson, such as warranted the hope that he would, one day, himself become a master, the influence of whose teaching would be felt.

"He wrote much, that must still be accessible, during the years in which his reading was most extensive and his plans were being matured. Even his letters alluding, as they do, from time to time, to the subjects on which he was engaged, are themselves full of critical notices and discussions of points of literary interest, with sonnet or song, or stanza in heroic verse, interspersed by way of offset to the prose, many of which are worthy of being recast in a form of greater permanence. Must we despair of seeing a selection made from these remains by a kindly and discriminating hand? I cannot but believe that some such selection would amply justify the expectations of his friends, if it would also embitter the poignancy of their regrets. Feelings of regret are already strong in the breasts of those who knew him best;—they feel that his sun went down, not while it was yet day, but before the radiant promise of the morning had broadened into noon. They could wish that years had permitted him to vindicate his devotion to letters, and his choice of a secluded and studious life, as well as to prove to a wider circle, than that of friends, that he had rightly estimated his powers and understood his mission. Some of those who began life with him, may have made more of it in a way, and succeeded better in the world, as the world goes. Some, no doubt, regarded him as unpractical, dreamy, perhaps even indolent; for his life was a hidden life to such. They and he dwelt far apart. Yet few men were more sagacious, or less visionary, making allowance for difference of pursuits, and fewer still could have resisted for so long a period the drain made by protracted vigils and incessant mental effort on the vital powers. Few of the busiest, in your busy city, worked harder in his own way, or knew less of idleness. A disposition naturally retiring, joined to a sensitive and gentle spirit that was too just to take advantage of the weakness of others, and too proud to stoop to anything that partook of artifice, was somewhat out of joint, perhaps, with the usual conditions of success. There were others, however, who knew how to hold such a man in estimation. In their eyes, he was a man who had deliberately made choice of his vocation, and was following it out, in the spirit of an earnest faith; but a man, besides of genial temperament, who was sincere in his friendship, and honourable in all things. To them, his life—grand in the simplicity of its taste, and the nobleness of its aims—seemed to move bravely on, in an orbit of its own, till it 'shot on the sudden into the dark.'

"It would seem as if men passed from the midst of us at intervals, whose moral and intellectual worth, after covering their own lives with its beauty, and bidding fair to make lovelier the lives of many, were suddenly restrained by stern inscrutable decree from wider influence. It is as if the stream that had worn its way from the bosom of lone hills, and made beautiful its narrow course through glen and gorge, were of a sudden to slip underground, disappearing at its broadest and strongest, where the wild flowers and grasses of the uplands give place to the green verge of tilled and peopled plains. Their natural genius, and the discipline they willingly undergo, because the eye is fixed on some farther goal, having served to trim their own *life's bark*, these men quit us on a voyage in which we may be borne to them, but from which they cannot return to us. Such men are understood only by the few who feel their power and influence, as those of a life rich in its own gifts, and moving altogether, with its faith, hopes, aims and labours, in a plane higher than that on which the traffic of ordinary minds is driven.

"It is fortunate for men of this order, especially fortunate for those of them whose lot is cast in these exceeding practical times of ours, that they have found a champion whose shield protects them from the unfeeling *pity* of that portion of the world that is busied only with material interests, as well as from the taunts of all who measure themselves and others by small successes in ignoble spheres. Of this order Arthur Hallam may now be regarded as the Representative, and "In Memoriam" as the enduring Vindication. To that same order of minds, and that same band of pure, high-souled, devoted men, whom "God's ordinance of Death" withheld from the achievement of a distinction commensurate with their powers, belonged THOMAS PATTISON.

> "'Sleep sweetly tender heart in peace:
> Sleep till the end, true soul and sweet.'

BRIEF BIOGRAPHICAL SKETCH.

THOMAS PATTISON, the translator of the "Gaelic Bards," and the author of these Original Poems, was the son of Mr. Peter Pattison, tenant of the farm of Skerrols. His mother's name was Bethia MacLean, daughter of Mr. Lachlan MacLean, who occupied the farm of Cladach in the neighbourhood of the village of Portnahaven. It was a memorable event in the quiet annals of the parish of Kilchoman, when on the same day, Lachlan MacLean, Cladach, and Samuel Crawford, Ealabus, married the two sisters, Lucy and Peggie, daughters of Mr. James Campbell, of Balinaby. Crawford was a vigorous pluralist who exercised the threefold functions of Medical Practitioner, of Factor of the Islay Estate, and of Miller. During the minority of W. F. Campbell, Esquire of Islay, who in 1816 succeeded his grandfather, "Old Shawfield," Mr. Peter Pattison rented for a few years the Home Farm of Islay House, where his father Mr. Thomas Pattison was gardener. After that, he took the farm of Skerrols, and married Bethia MacLean. All their children were born during his occupancy of this farm. The farmer of Skerrols was no less distinguished for his physical energy, than for his mental ability. It was he who wrote the spirited and crushing reply to the ill-founded attack which Dr. MacCulloch made upon the character of the Highlanders. An entry in the Baptismal Register of the parish of Kilarrow is in these words,—"Peter Thomas Pattison, son of Peter Pattison and Bethia MacLean, born 27th August, 1828."

After Mr. Pattison's death, the widow and family removed from Skerrols to Bowmore, and thence to that charming sea-side villa, Fern Cottage, on a farm called in Gaelic *Rainneach Mhòr*. The predecessor of the Pattisons in this cottage was Mr. Soutar, the father-in-law of the late Rev. William Barclay, M.A., Free Church minister of Auldearn, Nairnshire. The Parish School of Bowmore was about a mile from Fern Cottage. This school has been successively taught by competent and successful teachers, such as Dr. MacKintosh MacKay, Mr. — Russell, M.A., Mr. John Taylor, and Mr. David MacBean, whose son the Rev. John MacBean, M.A., is the Free Church minister of the well-known Gaelic parish of Killin, Perthshire. Special reference may be made here to two of them. 1. The Rev. M. MacKay, LL.D., who afterwards rose to be one of the Moderators of the Assembly of the Free Church of Scotland, was the literary friend of Sir Walter Scott, and of that premier of biographers, Mr. John Gibson Lockhart. Dr. MacKay is widely known for his accurate knowledge of the Gaelic language. When he was minister of the parish of Laggan in Inverness-shire, he acted as tutor to Mr. William Forbes Skene, who afterwards became the celebrated historian of "Celtic Scotland." Dr. George MacDonald, poet and novelist is a near relation of Dr. MacKay. 2. Mr. John Taylor, the learned teacher of the Greek and the Latin classics, whose two sons, the Rev. M. C. Taylor, D.D., the cultured Professor of Church History and Divinity in the University of Edinburgh, and the Rev. Duncan Taylor, Avondale, are honoured names in the Established Church of Scotland. Thomas Pattison was one of Mr. Taylor's favourite pupils. First at the University of Edinburgh, and afterwards at that of Glasgow, the gentle, sensitive, and shy student prosecuted his studies with diligence and zeal. With his devotion to ancient and modern literature he gradually became well acquainted with the princes of poetry from Chaucer to Tennyson, and with the peers of prose from Bacon to Carlyle. The father of the writer loves to speak of the day on which he drove Mr. Pattison and Mr. Taylor to the meeting of the Presbytery of Islay at which the former was licensed to preach the Gospel. It is a curious occurrence, that the driver of that day, and his family afterwards resided in Fern Cottage, and that a son of his was also one of Mr. Taylor's scholars, and that this son, and his wife, a daughter of the publisher of the first edition of the "Gaelic Bards" passed the first night of their married life in Islay, in this cottage, which was once the weird habitation of mysterious Dr. Brash, and after that, the fancy-inspiring abode of the wooer of the Muses, Mr. Pattison. Thomas Pattison in his youthful days frequently walked to Skerrols to hear the Rev. Jas. Pearson. Was this because that like Mr. Donald Mathieson, a well-educated farmer of Kynagarry, and the author of a series of interesting letters, "he found relief and comfort under the ministry of Mr. Pearson?" Had Mr. Pattison at the date of his license been able to read and to preach Gaelic fluently, he might have been settled as pastor of one of the vacant charges in his native island. It was then he visited the Pious Labourer who "lived in a small cottage, thick with heather thatched." In this lonely, rustic house, built beside *Loch na Crannaig*, Laggan, the young divine and the aged pilgrim perused together the Volume of Life in the soul-thrilling tongue of the Gael. Pattison might well say:—

> "Isaiah here hath rapt my soul
> And Job hath thrilled me through."

Again, in his eloquent tribute to the moral worth of his saintly friend, there occurs this touching thought, "And I'm persuaded Angels may have caught themes for their praises from this cottar's acts."

The democratic tone of Pattison's writings touches a sympathetic cord in the Highland heart. This appears and re-appears all through his productions. This very much accounts for the popular appreciation of his work. His instinctive adoption of the ennobling principle of universal brotherhood, that "A man's a man for a' that," is evinced by the innumerable tributes his literary labours called forth. In any correct estimate of his work, the range of his imagination, and the intensity of his emotions should be carefully considered. This gifted son of Islay, as a co-worker with other true yokefellows, wrought nobly for the intellectual awakening, and for the social advancement of his beloved Celts. "Man's inhumanity to man" moved his soul to its depths. Had he lived to our day, he would certainly have stepped forth as the unflinching advocate of the people's rights. This trait of his character very much endeared Mr. Thomas Pattison to his admirer and publisher, Mr. Archibald Sinclair. With his enthusiasm in the cause of Celtic literature and antiquities, Mr. Pattison, if his life had been spared, might, like his contemporaries Mr. William Black and Mr. Robert Buchanan, have achieved renown in the departments of creative effort. In his prose writings he shows no strivings after the graces of a literary style. But his Translations of "The Gaelic Bards" into English verse, although beset by enormous difficulties and embarrassments, have been executed with marvellous fidelity and success. They are good specimens of the author's literary deftness.

Pattison's life-like pen-portraits, in the best pieces of his Original Poems, remind me of the graphic and vivid pictures of persons and of places in Pollok's "Course of Time." Pattison, like Pollok, clearly rings out the heart-consoling notes of steadfast faith, of fadeless love, and of deathless hope. The Gaelic Bards, such as Alexander MacDonald, Duncan Ban MacIntyre, Dugald Buchanan and others, besides largely enriching Gaelic Literature with admirable original creations of their rich and well-balanced imaginations, caught by their musical ear the melodious airs and the vibrating strains of Celtic melodies and their tuneful soul wedded them in their respective works to matchless Gaelic verse. Their historic faculty seized upon the popular aspects of Highland scenery, story and romance, and these their artistic eye painted in unfading colours on the canvas of descriptive song. Their work is deeply rooted in the hearts of the Gaelic people. Like the great masters of religious poetry, Dante and Milton, our Gaelic Bards hold to the central truths of our religion and to a belief in the glorious resurrection of the body, and in the joyful ennoblement of life beyond the grave. In the words of Robert Browning our Gaelic Bards,

> "Never doubted clouds would break,
>   Never dreamed, though right were worsted,
>   Wrong would triumph,
>   Held we fall to rise, are baffled to fight better,
>   Sleep to awake."

Of the broad sympathies and deep yearnings of the human heart expressed with genuine feeling and real poetic power in the Gaelic Originals, Thomas Pattison became the faithful interpreter in his felicitous English Translations.

Peter Thomas Pattison died on the 16th day of October, 1865, at 28 Florence Place, Glasgow: aged, 37 years.

J. G. MACNEILL.

FREE MANSE, CAWDOR, 1890.

CONTENTS.

MODERN GAELIC BARDS.

	Page
INTRODUCTION,	XXIII
ALEXANDER MACDONALD,	1
Manning of the Birlinn,	8
The Sugar Brook,	28
Hail to the Mainland,	34
Flowers (from the Ode to Summer),	35
Birds (from the Ode to Winter),	36
The Grouse Cock and Hen,	37
Morag and other Belles,	38
Song of the Highland Clans,	39
The Praise of the Lion,	42
DUNCAN BAN MACINTYRE,	49
Introduction to Ben Dorain,	54
Ben Dorain,	55
Introduction to "Coire Cheathaich,"	60
Coire Cheathaich,	61
Introduction to "Màiri bhan òg,"	66
Song to his Spouse, newly wedded,	68
The Praise of Dunedin,	73
From the Song of Glenorchy,	77
A Rhyme to Thirst,	79
Introduction to "The Last Farewell to the Hills,"	80
The Last Farewell to the Hills,	82

DUGALD BUCHANAN,	85
The Skull,	91
From the Ode to Winter,	94
From the Day of Judgment,	95
ROB DONN,	99
The Greedy Man and the World,	100
The Shieling Song,	102
The Death-Song of Hugh,	105
WILLIAM ROSS,	107
The Cuckoo on the tree,	109
MARY MACLEOD,	111
MacLeod's Ditty,	112
MACGREGOR'S LULLABY,	116
Gregor MacGregor's Lament,	117
Sorrow now fills me,	121
The Braes of Ccathach.	124
FUGITIVE SONGS,	126
Och mar tha mi,	127
The "Gille dubh, ciar dubh,"	130
Hoog orin O!	132
Sick! Sick!	133
A Maiden's Lament,	135
The Boatman,	137
Monaltri,	139
Mali Bheag Og,	141
Breigein Binneach,	144
Màiri Laghach,	145
The love that will not fade,	147

ANCIENT GAELIC BARDS.

OSSIANIC POETRY,	149
The Sweetest Sound,	157
The Banners of the Feinne,	162

Ossian and Evir-Alin,	165
The Death of Oscar,	170
The Lay of Diarmad; or Fingal's Revenge,	177
Ossian's Address to the Rising Sun,	184
Address to the Setting Summer Sun,	188
Dàn do'n Ghréin,	191
Translation of the same,	192
A Sail in the Hebrides,	194
The Bed of Gaul,	196
Fingal going to battle,	198
The Four Wise Men at Alexander's Grave,	200
The Aged Bard's Wish,	203
Verses addressed to Mr. E. Llhuyd,	212

ORIGINAL POEMS.

A Fair Day,	219
Loch-in-daal,	227
Sir Lachlan Mòr,	230
The Pious Labourer,	235
Captain Gorrie's Ride,	239
The Haunted Water of Dubh-thalamh,	244
Knowest thou the Land?	250
The Islander's Guiding Star,	251
Dear Islay,	253
Hollow Friendship,	255
Little Emmeline,	256
Oppressors and the Oppressed,	258
Old Memories,	259
Farewell of the Emigrant,	261
Haste from the Window,	262
Bi falbh o'n Uinneig,	263
The Praise of Islay,	264
Moladh na Landaidh,	265
Notes on the Original Poems,	268

INTRODUCTION.

In the introduction to a small work which assumes the flattering title of "The Book of Scottish Song," I find the following sentences:—"Nearly all the beautiful music, and delicious snatches of song, commonly considered to be Scottish, belong to that section of Scotland known as the Lowlands, and a country in which the people speak one of the many 'Doric' dialects of the Saxon English language." ... "If a line be drawn from Greenock on the Clyde north-east by Perth to Inverness, it will be found that by far the greater portion of the songs and melodies which are known as Scotch, to Scotchmen and to the world, and of which Scotchmen speak and write with the highest pride and enthusiasm, have been produced to the south and east of it." . . . . "North-west of that line is the land of the Gael—of the semi-barbarous and imperfect instrument the bagpipe, of wild pibroch tunes, of rude melodies, very little known and still less admired, and of a species of song which has rarely been considered worth the trouble of translation. But on the south-east of the line, and all the way to the English Border, where the Saxon tongue prevails, and where the minds of the people have for ages had access to English literature, the land is vocal with sweet sounds." . . . . "The Highlander who has no right or title to this music or song, is as proud of both as the

Lowlander; and not unfrequently claims for his own wild melodies and for his rude attempts at lyrical poetry in the language of the Gael, a large portion of the admiration lavished upon compositions of a totally different origin and character. The Lowlanders, while they admit the claim of the Highlanders, take to themselves the little that is good in Celtic music and song, in order that with it they may swell the triumphs of a land, that not being geographically English, is considered to be Scotch."*

When such utter ignorance, and such absurd misstatements, are found in a book which, both from its title and its subject, ought to show better things—when we know, moreover, that not merely strangers, but the Scottish people themselves—many even of the Highlanders, and almost all the Lowlanders are quite unaware of the immense mass of popular poetry belonging to their country, which is treasured in the Gaelic Language, and do not frequently so much as know the names of poets whose admirable works should do so much to raise the

---

* The following letter from Dr. Charles MacKay, who wrote the introduction to "The Book of Scottish Song," appeared in the *Highlander*, May 31, 1873.

REFORM CLUB, LONDON, MAY 24, 1873.

SIR,—The Edinburgh correspondence of the *Highlander* contains a mention of me, which requires a word, not of contradiction, but of explanation on my part. It is true that twenty years ago I wrote the sentences which your correspondent quotes with good natured condemnation. I have only to plead ignorance in excuse for the heresy of which I was guilty; and to confess that at that time, I knew nothing of the venerable and beautiful language of my ancestors, and had imbibed erroneous ideas from the ways of Dr. Johnson and other prejudiced and incompetent critics. I am wiser now, and every day discover new beauties in the Gaelic, and widely spread proofs of its influence over all the languages now spoken in Western Europe, as I hope to be able to prove in my forthcoming volume.

lyric glory of Caledonia, it is surely time for those who, happening to have been more favourably circumstanced, are on this point better instructed, to endeavour to show their countrymen how much they have been neglecting— how unfair they have been to the Highlands and their inhabitants, when they believe on the worst, or on no authority at all, that the lyric genius, which has made Scotland so famous, has been bounded by an imaginary geographical line, and that the descendants of the people who have given the northern half of the British Isle all the names by which it ever has been known, have used a language always unblest by the spoken music of sentiment, and have done nothing to add to the glory of their land, except what was reaped on the fields of battle by their strong arms and their hardy valour. This shows the folly into which people will stray, who take upon themselves to dictate with regard to things they do not even endeavour to understand. Of the Lowland Scottish Language, and its claims to be considered something different from, and higher than the provincial dialects of the English counties, we have nothing to say at present, neither does it come in our way to speak of Scottish Music, or of its origin, Highland or Lowland, Celtic, Scandinavian, or Saxon, or a union of them all; but we make this one remark in passing, that Highland music is very unfairly characterised when it is termed "rude and wild," meaning thereby, not that it has never received any scientific culture, which is quite true, but obviously that it is destitute of beauty, of natural grace and artistic feeling, to affirm anything like which is to assert something outrageously false. Whatever of tenderness, of freshness of natural elegance, of depth of sentiment there is in the Lowland Scotch Music, any one who goes about such inquiry, in an unprejudiced spirit, will find in the Highland melodies too, and not in a inferior degree. I remember hearing a gentleman, himself a musician, well acquainted with music in its highest and most elaborate departments say, that Highland melodies, when properly played or sung—that is with their own simple and peculiarly expressive character—thrilled him through with an amazing power. He felt as in a moment surrounded with Highland scenery, its lofty mountains and sweet glens, its sounding winds and waters, its mists and varied skies, and old historic associations, and he was accordingly profoundly affected. I can well understand this, for no music can be more like a living wail of sorrow, or a living laugh of joy, than that which melts our hearts, or makes them dance beneath its magic influence in the sweet wild notes of the mountain melodies of the Highlands. For my own part I will yield to no Scotchmen whatever in admiration of everything that is good and beautiful, and distinctively characteristic in Scottish poetry, no matter where or by whom produced; but I believe there is a chapter, and that not the worst in it, yet to be added to "The Book of Scottish Song;" and I believe, when that chapter is added, this book will contain a treasure of popular national lyrics such as is possessed by no other nation in the world.

In the following pages I attempt to show, not only that there is as much Highland poetry, in proportion to the population, as there is of Lowland poetry, but that it possesses as much variety, and as high excellence of its own, as the Lowland Scottish poetry, of which we are all so justly proud. With regard to the poetry current at one time or another in the Highlands, a simple statement of one or two well-known facts will be sufficient to render that strikingly evident, and to prove that poetic genius was abundantly possessed by the inhabitants of the mountain and insular districts of Scotland. In Reid's "Bibliotheca Scoto-Celtica, an account of all the books that have been printed in the Gaelic Language," there is a list given of fifty-eight different volumes of Gaelic poetry, containing the words of well-known bards, or the result of collections made orally throughout the Highlands.

INTRODUCTION. xxvii

Reid's book was published in 1832. Since then very important additions have been made to the poetical literature of the Highlanders. Besides many minor publications, a collection of Gaelic poetry, made by Sir Duncan MacGregor, Dean of Lismore, more than three hundred years ago, and containing selections from the compositions of fifty Gaelic bards, none of whom is included in the fifty-eight volumes already mentioned, has been published in 1862. About twenty-five years ago MacKenzie's "Beauties of Gaelic Poetry" was published. This work, without interfering with the Ossianic poetry at all, gives specimens of the productions of thirty-six noted Gaelic bards, along with a rather limited selection of fugitive Gaelic lyrics, among which, it may be interesting to notice, there is a song by the grandfather of the late Lord MacAulay, so that there is no difficulty in guessing whence that distinguished writer inherited his poetical genius. The "Beauties of Gaelic Poetry"* is a large book, with small print and double columns. It contains more than thirty thousand lines of poetry, in many different kinds of rhyme and rhythm, and on a vast variety of subjects. These poems are in point of style quite as polished, and in point of structure quite as complete, as elaborate, and as finished as any such

---

* To the excellent publications of Reid and MacKenzie may be added:—(1) Campbell (J.F., of Islay)—*Leabhar na Féinne;* Heroic Gaelic Ballads, consisting of 54,169 lines, collected in Scotland chiefly from 1512 to 1871, copied from old manuscripts, preserved at Edinburgh and elsewhere and from rare books; and orally collected since 1859 with lists of collections, and of their contents; and with a short account of the documents quoted; and published in 1872. And (2)—Archibald Sinclair (of 62 Argyle Street, Glasgow)—*An t-Oranaiche;* The Gaelic Songster, a valuable collection of 290 Gaelic Songs, composed by nearly as many different authors, and published in 1879. There is also a vast mass of unsystematised and uncatalogued religious poetry in Gaelic.—*Ed.*

collection has ever been or ever can be, although they are, in a great measure, the compositions of authors who were quite uneducated, many of whom could neither read nor write. I am far from saying that they are all equally good, or that they are all worthy of being translated; but I can safely assert, that none of them is altogether bad, and that a good many of them are really of the first excellence in their class. They range in length from the heroic or descriptive imaginative chant, sometimes eight or nine hundred lines long, down to the little lay of three or four stanzas.

I know that he who would translate from the Gaelic must brace up his faculties for the work, or else he had better let the thing altogether alone. It will not be sufficient to give a feeble echo of the Highland sentiment, in dawdling slipshod English, or to dress it in some shabby threadbare Lowland garb. In every Gaelic song that deserves translation, there is not merely something that is good, but something that is characteristic of its birth-place, and that is not therefore in the English or Lowland lyric. The air and sun of the great mountains, and the tuneful sea-lochs, have breathed and shone upon the poetry of the Highlands, and given its every feature their own peculiar tan. The translator's difficulty is to preserve this, and it is no small one. I am well aware of that; but yet I trust, the Highland Poems here rendered, will be found to retain something of their own look. I hope that no one who knows them in the original, will feel that they have lost all that is good in their old expression, when I present them with an English face.

THOMAS PATTISON.

GLASGOW, 1866.

MODERN GAELIC BARDS.

ALEXANDER MACDONALD.

ALEXANDER MACDONALD, always styled by his own countrymen, *Mac Mhaighstir Alastair*, *i.e.* the son of Mr. Alexander, a man of very vigorous parts, and to say the least of it, unexcelled in point of general ability by any of the Gaelic Bards—was the son of the Episcopalian clergyman for the parishes of Ardnamurchan and Moidart—at the end of the seventeenth, and beginning of the eighteenth century.

His father resided at Dalilea in Moidart, and would appear to have united the pleasant calling of the Highland Tacksman with the functions—not over-burdensome probably in a Presbyterian country, of the Episcopalian clergyman.

This gentleman is said to have been a man of immense bodily strength—nor is it strange that this quality is not forgotten, even in a man who exercised his sacred vocation; for it was a gift not superfluous in his circumstances: not one which the habits of his Christian flock allowed to rust in him unused. For instance, he had to walk to his church many miles every Sunday, over a rough country, at that time, without roads; and then, after conducting the service, back to his home in the evening.

Again, the funerals, which, in his clerical capacity, he attended, were not always decorous scenes. His parishioners, on such occasions, used to bring with them a quantity of whisky—which being freely dispensed to the mourners, caused a good deal of excitement that did not always pass peaceably away.

When the war of words changed into actual conflict, and the voice of reason could no longer be heard in the tumult, then the clergyman dashed in person into the fray, and settled the disputes on which his pastoral advice was wasted, by the strength of his right hand—the stoutest combatant, it is affirmed, seeing more than he quite cared to face, when he found he had to reach his antagonist through the intervening prowess of his minister. This strong pacificator, however, laid himself open to the charge of not dealing with perfect impartiality in his interference when the men of Moidart, who were his friends and relatives, happened to quarrel with the neighbouring men of Suainart; who were comparatively strangers to him, and to his flock. His hand was heavier on the men of Suainart than on the men of Moidart. Such was the well-known "Mr. Alexander," as the son of whom, their distinguished poet, Alexander MacDonald, is always spoken of by the Highlanders.*

Of the poet's own life, very little more than a few dates, is recorded. Even the date of his birth is nowhere mentioned; nor do we hear much of his education, though he was almost the only one of the Gaelic Bards who received anything like a scholastic training. Not that

---

* A kindred soul with the above, and also a contemporary of his, was a Rev. Mr. Stewart, who followed Viscount Dundee's army, in 1689. When the Highlanders made their impetuous and decisive charge at the battle of Killiecrankie, this gentleman, accompanied them wielding a heavy broad-sword. He used his weapon with such effect in the battle and pursuit, that eleven of the Royalists sank beneath its sway. When his excitement cooled down, however, he found that he could not draw his hand from the basket-hilt of his sword; nor was it till a friend had cut through the net-work, that the warlike ecclesiastic was able to resume his ordinary appearance.

the influence of his scholarship, whatever its extent might be, leaves any decided trace in his writings Far from it. There he is always the pure Highland singer; with the exception, at most, of the occasional use of an English word; or of a proper name like Phœbus, borrowed from the Greek mythology. His masters in poetry were those of his own countrymen, who were his predecessors; and the inspiration which his country itself, with its history, sentiments, and scenery, afforded him, as well as them. With regard to his tuition, we are told that he studied first under his father's superintendence; and latterly, for a year or two, at the Glasgow University. According to one account, his father intended him for his own profession, but discovered something in his character, or conduct, that did not suit well with this idea.

According to another account, the Clan-Ranald of the day, being fond of patronising young men of merit, wished to educate him for the bar; but an early marriage, imprudently contracted by the poet, interrupted his studies before he was qualified for a profession. To support his family, MacDonald was obliged to leave college, and retire to Ardnamurchan; where he lived, teaching and farming, and composing poetry—a Presbyterian, and an elder of the Established Church, till the year 1745: when, he not only forsook his all to join Prince Charles, but even changed his religion, and became a Catholic. The fiery and warlike songs with which he roused his countrymen, and animated their devotion for the unfortunate Stuart cause, show how true a Jacobite, and how good a poet, the son of Mr. Alexander was. He held a commission in the Highland Army, but whether he actually served in the field or not, does not clearly appear. After the battle of Culloden, he lived in hidings, in the wood and caves of *Ceannloch nan Uamh* in the district of Arisaig, and was exposed to considerable hardships for some time. On one occasion, when lurking about with his brother Angus, the cold was so intense, that the side of MacDonald's head, which rested on the ground, became quite grey in a single night.

After this, he lived a short time in Edinburgh, teaching the children of some of his Jacobite friends. But he soon returned again to the Highlands, where he remained till his death, which happened (in what year is not stated), when he had reached "a good old age."

Reid, in his "Bibliotheca Scoto-Celtica," gives a description of the poet's personal appearance and habits, which is certainly very far from flattering.

"In person," Mr. Reid says, "MacDonald was large and ill-favoured. His features were very coarse and irregular. His clothes were very sluggishly put on, and generally very dirty. His mouth was continually fringed with a stream of tobacco-juice, of which he chewed a very great quantity. His manner of composition was to lie on his back, in bed in winter, or on the grass in summer, with a large stone on his breast, muttering to himself in a low whisper his poetical aspirations."

It is in reference to this and other parts of Reid's notice of MacDonald, that MacKenzie in his "Beauties of Gaelic Poetry" says, "Like most men of genius, who have made some noise in the world, *Mac Mhaighstir Alastair* has been much lauded, on the one side, by the party whose cause he espoused, and as much vilified, and as much falsified, by the other party. Mr. Reid in his book, 'Bibliotheca Scoto-Celtica,' seems to have had his imformation from the last mentioned source."

The grotesque description of MacDonald then, just quoted, is probably a total fabrication; or at any rate, a gross caricature by one of his enemies. Who ever heard of a poet, or any sane man, lying on his back in his bed, or on the grass, with a stone on his breast when he was composing! A small spice of malice, or a drop of envy to anoint the eyes, and a description of Burns might very readily be given about as bad as the above; substituting the smell of whisky for tobacco-juice, and the wet bundle of straw on which he composed "Mary in Heaven," for the stone on the breast when he was composing.

MacDonald's first work was a Gaelic and English Vocabulary, published in 1741. His poems were published in Edinburgh in 1751. They formed one of the earliest volumes of original poems ever published in Gaelic. A second edition appeared in 1764. This little book contained only thirteen poems; but a good many more were added to it, after the Author's death. It is supposed, however, that not more than a tenth part of his Songs and Poems have been given to the world: a number of his MSS. having been torn, tossed about, and lost in the house of one of his sons. So his poetry, though in respect to quality, it holds a very distinguished rank, is in regard to its quantity, far from being in the first place among the works of Gaelic Bards.

Alexander MacDonald displays a great command of the Gaelic language, and a vast deal of talent and energy. He is a vehement, rapid, and exciting singer, as a general rule; but yet, he is by no means deficient in tenderness and grace; especially in his many sweet and pastoral descriptions of Nature. He is the most warlike, and much the fiercest of Highland poets, indeed almost the only one of them all, at least for three centuries back, to whom this trait can with any truth be ascribed.

Although his poems are few in number, only thirty-one altogether, they exhibit more variety of excellence on the whole than those, perhaps of any of his fellow singers. While, although not so smooth and equable as Duncan Ban MacIntyre, he is equalled by no other when at his best.

The poem which follows, is considered by many Highlanders to be the most important production in their language. No poem is ever spoken of in the same breath with it, except the "Coire Cheathaich" or "Ben Dorain" of Duncan Ban; and, even these, are perhaps not always looked on, with quite the same pride; though, being easier understood, and composed altogether in a more elegant style, they probably impart fully as much pleasure, both to hearers and readers. Yet, if all Gaelic poems were to be destroyed, and one only excepted from the general ruin, I believe the voices of the majority of Highlanders would fix on "The Birlinn of Clan-Ranald," as that one. The reason of this preference, however, may be those very peculiarities of style and structure, the tendency of which will be, perhaps, as much to repel as to attract a stranger, at least, in the outset. I think, however, no one can read this poem with attention and intelligence, without deeming it, in every respect—as regards expression, arrangement, conception—singularly original; without finding in it much graphic painting— and feeling it to be emphatically lively and energetic. Such a reader will discover many minute touches in the poem to please him, though they might escape a more careless eye:— such for instance as the incitement to the rowers to

"*Wound* the huge swell on the ocean meadow,
   Heavy and deep."

Or this other,

"Let your fists' *broad grasp be whitening*
   In your rowing!"

Or how the effect of the cry "Suas oirr'!".

"*Hurls* the Birlinn through the cold glens,
   Loudly snoring."

Or again when they are told in the Boat-song to

"Let the grey sea ever foaming,
 Splash her forward pressing shoulders,
 And the currents groan and mingle
   Far behind her."

Or the description of the steersman, who is to be,

> "A well set prop full of vigour,
> Broad-seated, thick,
> Stout and sure, and skilful and wary,
> Cautious, yet quick."

Or that of the balesman,

> "His trust he'll rigidly discharge it,
> Neither faint nor slack,
> Nor straightening, while a drop remaineth,
> His bending active back;
> 'Though her boards should all get riddled,
> He must keep her snug,
> As a well made lid, close fitting,
> Keeps a polished jug."

Then, there is the description of the storm, in which the Birlinn made her first entry on the open sea. This, as a more elaborate and sustained effort of the poet's imagination, cannot fail to attract the notice of a discerning reader. The elements are let loose in their wildest fury, and terror is heaped on terror round the good ship of Clan-Ranald, as she courses on her perilous way from Uist to Carrickfergus; and not until all her sails are rent, and every board and plank in her are strained, does the poet flag or stop to draw breath, or let "the rough wind bitter boaster"—"ruffle round her fair."

But though possessing many such notable points as the preceding, though altogether so remarkable a production, so very vigorous, so very characteristically Highland, "The Manning of the Birlinn" may not possibly abound in some other qualities, which are perhaps more attractive to the general reader than the lavish display of strength, the mere powerful exertion of energetic and robust faculties can ever be.

"The Manning of the Birlinn" is here translated line for line, with the original. It is the longest poem in Gaelic, except such as are Ossianic.

THE MANNING OF THE BIRLINN.

THE BLESSING OF A SHIP;

Along with an incitement for the sea, that was made for the crew of the Birlinn of Clan Ranald.

May God bless the ship of Clan-Ranald*
   This first day it floats on the brine,
Himself, and the strong men who guide it,
   Whose virtues surpassingly shine!
May the Holy Trinity temper
   The stormy breath of the sky,
And sweep smooth the rough swelling waters,
   That our port we may draw nigh!

Father! Creator of ocean,
   And each wind that blows from on high!
Bless our slender bark and our heroes;
   Make all ill things pass them by.
O Son! bless thou our anchor,
   Our tackling, helm, and sail;
Everything on our mast that is hanging,
   Till our haven at last we hail.

*In Bishop Carswell's Gaelic Prayer-Book, published in the year, 1567—the first book ever printed in the Gaelic Language—there occurs a prayer somewhat similar to this one, to be used by mariners going to sea. It, too, is a prayer to the Trinity; very well arranged and expressed, and full of devotional feeling. It could hardly have been used or appreciated by a wild and savage people, such as we are sometimes, I think, very incorrectly, taught to regard the Highlanders of three hundred years ago.

[This Prayer Book was reprinted under the editorship of the late Dr. Thomas MacLauchlan in 1873. Only two copies of the first edition were known to exist then.]

ALEXANDER MACDONALD.

Bless our yards and all our mast-hoops;
    Our masts and ropes, one and all;
Our halyards and stays keep unbroken—
    Let no ill through them befall.
May the Holy Spirit be at the helm,
    And guide to the proper place;
He knows each port beneath the sun,
    We cast us on His grace.

THE BLESSING OF THE ARMS.

May God bless all our weapons—
    Our blades of Spain, sharp and grey,
And our massy mails which are able
    The keenest edge to stay;
Our swords of steel and our corslets,
    And our curled and shapely targets—
Bless them all without exception—
    The arms our shoulder-belts carry.

Our bows of yew, well made and handsome,
    Bent oft times in the breast of battle;
Our birchen shafts not prone to splinter,
    Cased in the sullen badger's hide.
Bless our poinards and our pistols,
    And our tartans fine and folded,
And every implement of warfare
    In MacDonald's bark this hour.

Be you, our crew, not soft or simple;
    Hardily brave deeds encounter;
While four boards shall hold together,
    Or one plank to plank be tied—
While beneath your feet she welters,
    Or one knob remains above,
Oh! defy each sight of terror
    Your strong hearts to melt or move.

If you only battle it well,
    And the sea does not feel that you quail,
She will humble herself in that knowledge,
    And her pride to your might will she vail.
Thus confront thy spouse on the land ;
    Let her not see thee get weak,
And the chance is she yields in the strife,
    Nor such contests will rashly re-seek.

Even so is the mighty deep,
    Tho' fierce frenzy her bosom fills ;
She will yield to your might none the less,
    As the King of the Universe wills.

THE INCITEMENT TO ROW TO A SAILING PLACE.

To bring the barge so dark and stately,
    Whence we'd sail away ;
Thrust out those tough clubs and unyielding,
    Polished bare and grey ;
Those oars well made, smooth-waisted,
    Firm and light ;
That row steadily and boldly
    From smooth palm to foam white ;

That send the sea in splashing showers
    Aloft unto the sky,
And light the brain-fire bright and flashing,
    As when coal sparks fly.
With purpose-like blows of the great heavy weapons,
    With a powerful sweep,
Wound the huge swell on the ocean meadow,
    Rolling and deep.

With your sharp narrow blades white and slender,
    Strike its big breast ;

Hirsute and brawny, and rippled and hilly,
    And never at rest.
Oh stretch, and bend, and draw, young gallants!
    Forward going!
Let your fists' broad grasp be whitening
    In your rowing!

Ye lusty, heavy, stalwart youngsters!
    Stretch your full length;
With shoulders knotty, nervy, hairy,
    Hard with strength;
See you raise and drop together
    With one motion
Your grey and beamy shafts, well ordered,
    Sweeping ocean.

Thou stout surge-wrangler on the foremost oar,
    Shout loudly, "Suas oirr'!"*
The song that wakes the arm's best vigour
    In each cruiser,
And hurls the Birlinn through the cold glens,
    Loudly snoring;
Or, climbing, cleaving the swollen surges,
    Hoarsely roaring.

When hill-waves thus are flung behind,
    By your stout shoulders;
"Hugan" will the ocean wailing shouting say,
    And "Heig" groan the oar holders.
From the strong surge a thud—a dash of spray,
    Goes o'er each timber,
But still oars creak, though blisters rise on fingers,
    Strong and limber.

---

* "Suas oirr'" "Up with her"—*i.e.*, the Birlinn. "Suas e," is a common cry of encouragement. Whoever has seen Higlanders dance their reels, must have witnessed the effect of "Suas e."

For the stout, stiff, manly heroes
    Must work untiring,
Should every board of her be quivering,
    Round oaken post and iron;
While oar blades splash among the water,
    And knobs clank on her side,
On with such force, you'll make her course,
    With fearless pride.

Strong arms can drive this slender bark
    Through the wide deep,
Right in the face of the blue billows'
    Rising, bristling heap.
Now for such mettled manly crew,
    Our oars to sweep;
To make the grey-backed eddies whirl
    Where their strokes press'd,
And flag not, tire not, drowse not, bend not,
    In the storm's rough breast.

    Then after the six men and ten are seated at the oars, in order to row under the wind to the sailing place, let stout Callum, son of Ranald of the Ocean, shout the Iorram* for her and be seated on the foremost oar, and let this be it:—

Now since you are rank'd in order,
And seem all to be well chosen,
Give her one good plunge, like champions,
    Brave and boldly.
    Give her one good plunge, &c.

---

    * Iorram (pronounced, Yirram) is a boat-song, or an oar-song, and sometimes a lament. This double meaning it acquired from the fact of the Iorram being so often chanted in the boats that carried the remains of chiefs and nobles over the western seas to Iona.

Give her not a plunge imperfect,
But with right good will and careful,
Keep a watch on all the storm hills
  Of the ocean.
  Keep a watch, &c.

With a mighty grasp and manful;
Stretch your bones and stretch your sinews;
Leave her track in light behind you,
  Stepping proudly.
  Leave her track, &c.

Give a gleesome bout and lively;
Stoutly rousing one another,
With this dainty boat-song chanted
  By your fore-oar.
  With this dainty boat-song, &c.

Raise the foam-bells round the thole pins,
Till your hands are bare and blister'd,
And the oars themselves are twisted
  In the strong waves.
  And the oars themselves, &c.

Let your brows be hotly lighted;
Heed not should your palms get skinless,
And the huge drops from your forehead
  Fast be falling.
  And the huge drops, &c.

Bend, and stretch, and draw, young gallants,
Your shafts of fir, in hue light grey;
And pass with heed the wild rough currents
  Whirling briny.
  And pass with heed, &c.

Let your set of oars, full sweeping,
Mash the great sea with their vigour,
Going splashing in the wild face
    Of the billows.
    Going splashing, &c.

Row together, clean and steady,
Cleaving the great swelling water,
Work with life and work with spirit,
    No delaying.
    Work with life, &c.

Give a graceful and a strong pull,
Looking oft on one another;
Wake the force that's in your sinews
    All so strongly.
    Wake the force, &c.

Be her ribb'd and oaken body
In the wild glens moaning sadly,
And her two thighs ever pounding
    Down the surges.
    And her two thighs, &c.

Let the ocean, crisp and hoary,
Rise with rough and deep-toned heavings,
And the lofty wailing waters
    Shout and welter.
    And the lofty, &c.

Let the grey sea, ever foaming,
Splash her forward pressing shoulders,
And the currents groan and mingle
    Far behind her.
    And the currents, &c.

Stretch, and bend, and draw, young gallants!
Your shafts, with smooth waist painted red;
Work them with the pith and marrow
  Of strong shoulders.
  Work them, &c.

Sweep around yon point before you,
Till your brows are streaming moisture;
Thence, with full-spread sail, leave Uist
  Of the solans.
  Thence, with full-spread sail, &c.

THEN THEY ROWED TO THE SAILING PLACE.

And they hoist up the new-blessed sails
  Tauntly on high,
And rattle in six oars and ten
  And lay them by,
Clear of the pegs that hold the sails
  Along her thigh;
Then, Clan-Ranald from his nobles order'd
  Good ocean skippers to sail by—
Men who fear'd not any spectre,
  Or sight of terror came them nigh.*

---

* The Birlinn having arrived at the sailing place, we have here to suppose that Clan-Ranald himself, or some one else deputed by him for the purpose, placing himself in a conspicuous situation, calls out the men, one by one as they stand grouped before him, waiting for their instructions. He singles them out, however, not by name, but by a description of some of their personal characteristics, and of their capacity for making themselves useful on board the untried Galley, which they had just been rowing. The poet had possibly a real personage in his eye for every picture he draws, and assigned to each good boatman of his acquaintance the post he would have been fitted to fill in the circumstances imagined; describing at the same time his appearance so accurately, that he might readily be recognised by those who knew him.

Then was it ordered, after choice had been made, that every man should look after his own particular charge. Immediately on this, there was a shout raised for a steersman to take the helm, in these words:—

Let this broad heavy hero sit at the helm,
    Powerful, ready;
No dash of the rising or falling sea
    Must make him unsteady;
A well-spread prop full of vigour,
    Broad-seated, thick—
Stout and sure, and skilful and wary,
    Cautious, yet quick.
Never once hasty while watching the canvas,
    Which swift winds unfurl.
When he hears the shaggy ridge of the waters'
    Roaring whirl,
He'll smartly keep her narrow head
    Against the swirl.
He'll guide her so that she rocks or reels not
    In her tack.
Ruling sail and sheet with eye that windward
    Glances back;
He must not lose one finger's fore-joint
    Of the right course,
In spite of all the tumbling surges,
    And their force.
He'll beat so boldly, when there's need,
    In the wind's eye;
He'll make each oaken plank and fastening
    Creak and cry.
He must not blanch or get confused
    With doubts and fears—
Not should the sea's grey-headed swell
    Rise round his ears.
This stalwart seaman every terror
    Must withstand;

Nor stir, nor move, but keep his place
    With helm in hand;
And, watching the old hoary ocean,
    Stern though it be,
Must loosen or draw in the sheet,
    As need he'll see,
And make her battle, run, or beat,
    With full-sail'd glee.
Thus he'll keep her stiff and stubborn,
    On top of the wild wave—
Straight and sure into her harbour,
    Let storms howl and rave.

THE MAN WHO WAS TO WATCH THE RIGGING ORDERED OUT.

Place this shrewd man—great-fisted—there,
    To watch the rigging,
Who'll be sedate and full of care,
    With huge grasp—strong-finger'd;
Who'll haul the yards with right good will,
    When the ship needs it;
And watch the mast and tackling still,
    And bind and loosen.
And he must know the winds that blow,
    What course best suiting;
And he must work in harmony
    With him who holds the sheet,
And guide the tackling manfully,
So long as his stout ropes and high
    Shall hold together.

THE MAN SET ASIDE FOR THE SHEET.

Let this man with mighty shoulders,
    Sit on the thwart;
Who is so sinewy and hairy,
    With his bones big—

A thick-set, broad, and craggy champion,
    With fingers huge.
The sheet he must be ever guiding
    With scrambling force;
When the winds come fiercely blowing,
    Pulling well in;
But when it slacks, and lags, and flutters,
    He lets free.

THE MAN ORDERED OUT FOR THE EAR-RING.

Let this man who is tight and sturdy,
    Handy, nice, and fine,
Work the jib-sheet without flinching,
    When she nears the wind;
Bring it up and down in order,
    To each fitting hold,
As the wind may chance to follow,
    Or the high topp'd wave;
And if he find the tempest rising,
    Or loud groaning come,
He'll bring it, with good grasp heroic,
    To the gunwale down.

THE LOOK-OUT ORDERED TO THE FORE.

Now, rising, let this slow man go
    Up to the prow;
Our harbour with unerring knowledge
    He must show;
Every art descrying keenly
    Whence the wind can blow,
And telling to the steersman surely
    The right way to go.
Each landmark he must note and gather
    From afar,
Since it, with Him who rules the seasons,
    Is our guiding star.

THE MAN SET ASIDE FOR THE HALYARD.

At the halyard place this wight
    Who is no sloven,
But athletic, full of might,
    Skilled and well-proven.
Careful ever, free of haste,
    With dark frowns ready;
And to guide his rope well placed,
    Dainty but not heady.
With a tug and with a twist
    The sail restraining,
Bending downward on his fist,
    And strongly straining,
Hard and fast he must not tie
    The tough tight rope;
He only dares a loose loop try,
    Giving it scope
To run freely and to fly,
    And murmur hoarse
Round the peg, with hum and cry,
    So swift its course.

    The reporter of the waters about to be set aside, and just then the sea getting too rough, the steersman says of him:—

Let a man to watch the rain-squall
    Quick, come nigh;
And sharply on the weather's heart
    Let him keep his eye.
Choose me a man half-frighten'd,
    Cautious, sly;
But not a coward out and out,
    And let him pry,
With curious watch, until the shower,
    He rippling spy;

Then mark keenly if the gusts
    Before, or behind it, fly;
Nor must he let my heedless thoughts
    Securely lie,
But wake me up at sight of danger
    With an eager cry,
When towards us the drowning waters
    Wailing hie;
He must say, "The beam's thin head
    Quick put about!"
"A breaking wave!" with thunderous accents
    Must he shout.
He must thus inform me duly
    When danger is nigh;
But let no other weather-watcher
    But himself be by,
Nor make confusion, doubt, and tumult,
    Through the whole crew fly.

A balesman is ordered out; in case the sea rush over her behind and before:—

To bale her let this strong man rise,
    Active and brave,
Who will not blanch, or yield, or tremble
    For the shouting wave;
Who will not quail, who will not soften
    For cold sea or hail,
Though they lash and splash his neck and breast
    On the strong gale.
With a thick, round, wooden vessel
    In his horny hand,
He'll let not the inpouring water
    One moment stand;
His trust he'll rigidly discharge it,
    Neither faint nor slack,

Nor straightening while a drop remaineth
 His bending active back;
Though her boards should all get riddled,
 He must keep her snug,
As a well-made lid, close-fitting,
 Keeps a polished jug.

Two are ordered to watch the ropes behind the canvas, should there be any appearance that the sails will be swept from her with the roughness of the tempest:—

Now let this pair of strong and raw-boned men,
 Rough and hairy,
Be set to watch the ropes behind the sail,
 Well and wisely.
With pith and marrow, and great bone and brawn,
 And tough sinews,
To draw well in when time of danger comes,
 Or else let free;
Careful to keep it always with smart hand
 In the right middle.
Donald MacCarmaig let us choose for this,
 And John MacIain—
Two most audicious fellows and expert,
 Of the men of Canna.

Six are chosen as a reserve, in case any of those I have spoken of should fail, or that the fury of the sea should pluck him overboard, then one of these could take his place:—

Now let these six agile men be ready,
 Handy, lively,
To get up, and leap, and run
 Fore and aft her,

Quick as a hare upon the hill-tops,
    And the hounds near by.
They must climb the hard smooth ropes,
    Fine and hempen,
Like a squirrel in the spring-time
    Up a tree side.
They must be skilful, hardy, active,
    Sure and restless,
And spring to rope, or chain or sail, or any
    Needful order,
Guiding the good ship, without weakness,
    Of Vic Dhomhnuill.

Now, when everything appertaining to the sailing had been got under famous regulation, and every gallant hero drew without softness, without fear, without trembling, to the exact place where he had been ordered to go, they raised up the sails about the rising of the sun on the day of the Feast of St. Bride, and they bore out of Loch-Ainneart, in Uist, looking southward.

The sun had opened golden yellow,*
    From his case,
Though still the sky wore dark and drumly
    A scarr'd and frowning face;
Then troubled, tawny, dense, dun bellied,
    Scowling and sea-blue;
Every dye that's in the tartan
    O'er it grew.
Far away to the wild westward
    Grim it lowered,

---

*Any one who has watched a threatening February morning in the Hebrides, will be at no loss to perceive that this vigorous description has been taken directly from nature. The varied colours of the sky, and the wild aspect of the sea, are particularly striking

Where rain charged clouds on thick squalls wandering
    Loomed and towered.
Up they raised the speckled sails though
    Cloud-like light,
And stretched them on the mighty halyards,
    Tense and tight.
High on the mast so tall and stately—
    Dark-red in hue—
They set them firmly, set them surely,
    Set them true.
Round the iron pegs the ropes ran,
    Each its right ring through;
Thus having ranged the tackle rarely,
    Well and carefully.
Every man sat waiting bravely,
    Where he ought to be;
For now the airy windows opened,
    And from spots of bluish gray;
Let loose the keen and crabbed wild winds—
    A fierce band were they.
And then his dark grey cloak the ocean
    Round him drew—
Dusky, livid, ruffled, whirling,
    Round, at first it flew;
Till up he swell'd to mountains, or to glens,
    Dishevelled, rough, sank down—
And the kicking, tossing waters
    All in hills had grown;
Its blue depth opening in huge maws,
    Wild and devouring,
Down which clasped in deadly struggles
    Fierce, strong waves were pouring.
It took a man to look the storm-winds
    Right in the face—
As they lit up the sparkling spray on every surge hill,
    In their fiery race.

The waves before us shrilly yelling
  Raised their high heads hoar,
While those behind, with moaning trumpets,
  Gave a bellowing roar.
When we rose up aloft, majestic,
  On the heaving swell,
Need was to pull in our canvas
  Smart and well.
When she sank down with one huge swallow
  In the hollow glen,
Every sail she bore aloft
  Was given to her then.
The drizzling surges high and roaring
  Rush'd on us louting;
Long ere they were near us come,
  We heard their shouting.
They roll'd sweeping up the little waves,
  Scourging them bare.
Till all became one threatening swell,
  Our steersman's care.
When down we fell from off the billows'
  Towering shaggy edge,
Our keel was well nigh hurled against
  The shells and sedge;
The whole sea was lashing, dashing,
  All through other.
It kept the seals and mightiest monsters
  In a pother.
The fury and the surging of the water,
  And our good ship's swift way
Spatter'd their white brains on each billow,
  Livid and grey.
With piteous wailing and complaining,
  All the storm-toss'd horde,
Shouted out "We're now your subjects;
  Drag us on board."

And the small fish of the ocean
    Turn'd over their white breast—
Dead, innumerable, with the raging
    Of the furious sea's unrest.
The stones and shells of the deep channel
    Were in motion;
Swept from out their lowly bed
    By the tumult of the ocean;
Till the sea, like a great mess of pottage,
    Troubled, muddy grew
With the blood of many mangled creatures,
    Dirty red in hue—
Where the horn'd and clawy wild beasts,
    Short-footed splay;
With great wailing gumless mouths
    Huge and wide open lay.
But the whole deep was full of spectres,
    Loose and sprawling
With the claws and with the tails of monsters
    Pawing, squalling.
It was frightful even to hear them
    Screech so loudly;
The sound might move full fifty heroes
    Stepping proudly.
Our whole crew grew dull of hearing
    In the tempest's scowl,
So sharp the quavering cries of demons
    And the wild beasts' howl.
With oaken planks the weltering waves were wrestling
    In their noisy splashing;
While the sharp beak of our swift ship
    On the sea-pigs* came dashing.
The wind kept still renewing all its wildness
    In the far west,

---

* Sea-pigs (muca-mara) are porpoises

Till with every kind of strain and trouble
    We were sore distress'd.
We were blinded with the water
    Showering o'er us ever;
And the awful night like thunder,
    And the lightning ceasing never.
The bright fire-balls in our tackling
    Flamed and smoked;
With the smell of burning brimstone
    We were well-nigh choked.
All the elements above, below,
    Against us wrought;
Earth and wind, and fire and water,
    With us fought.
But when it defied the sea
    To make us yield;
At last, with one bright smile of pity,
    Peace with us she seal'd.
But not before our yards were injured,
    And our sails were rent,
Our poops were strained, our oars were weaken'd,
    All our masts were bent.
Not a stay we had but started,
    Our tackling all was wet and splashy,
Nails and couplings twisted, broken.
    Feeshie, fashie.*
All the thwarts and all the gunwale
    Everywhere confess'd,
And all above and all below,
    How sore they had been press'd.
Not a bracket, not a rib,
    But the storm had loosed;
Fore and aft from stem to stern,
    All had got confused.

---

* Fise, faise! pronounced as above, occur here in the original. They are mere expletives, and have no meaning.

Not a tiller but was split,
    And the helm was wounded;
Every board its own complaint
    Sadly sounded.
Every trenel, every fastening
    Had been giving way;
Not a board remain'd as firm
    As at the break of day.
Not a bolt in her but started,
    Not a rope the wind that bore,
Not a part of the whole vessel
    But was weaker than before.
The sea spoke to us its peace prattle
    At the cross of Islay's Kyle.
And the rough wind, bitter boaster!
    Was restrained for one good while.
It rose from off us into places
    Lofty in the upper air,
And after all its noisy barking
    Ruffled round us fair.
Then we gave thanks to the High King,
    Who rein'd the wind's rude breath,
And saved our good Clan-Ranald
    From a bad and brutal death.
Then we furl'd up the fine and speckled sails
    Of linen wide,
And we took down the smooth, red dainty masts,
    And laid them by the side.
On our long and slender polish'd oars
    Together leaning—
They were all made of the fir cut by MacBarais
    In Eilean Fionain.
We went with our smooth, dashing rowing,
    And steady shock,
Till we reach'd the good port round the point
    Of Fergus' Rock.*

    * Fergus' Rock, or Carrickfergus.

There casting anchor peacefully,
    We calmly rode;
We got meat and drink in plenty,
    And there we abode.

THE SUGAR BROOK.†

Passing by the Sugar Brook,
    In fragrant morn of May;
When, like bright shining rosaries,
    The dew on green grass lay;
I heard the Robin's treble,
    Deep Richard's bass awake;
And the shy and blue-winged cuckoo,
    Shout " goog-goo " in the brake.

The thrush there threw its steam off,
    Upon a stake alone:
And the brown wren so blithesome,
    Had music of its own.
The linnet with a jealous bend,
    Tuned up his choicest string;
The black-cock he was croaking,
    The hen did hoarsely sing.

The trout kept leaping nimbly,
    With merry plunge and play;

† *Allt an-t-siùcair*, or the Sugar Brook, is a small stream in the north west of Argyleshire, that falls into the Sound of Mull.

Dimpling the burn with sprightly tricks,
    Warm in the sunny ray.
Their blade blue back and spotted gills,
    Gleamed with their gemlike scales;
When with a dash they snapt the fly,
    That careless wandering sails.

How sweet, and swift, and limpid,
    Fast whirling soft of sound;
The Sugar Brook's rough torrent wave,
    That sweeps and murmurs round.
All grasses, herbs, and wild flowers,
    Close to its borders rise;
Which, with the sappy source of life,
    Its pleasant stream supplies.

This clean transparent streamlet,
    That flows so bright and clear;
With the soul of growth and motion,
    Fills all the meadows near:
Where fly the yellow-red bees,
    And tickle golden flowers;
To fill with store of honey sweet,
    The wax-cell in their bowers.

A soothing sound is that which comes,
    From the loud-bellowing kye;
As to their speckled, giddy calves
    From the fold the dams reply:
Where the milkmaid with her buara,*
    Lists to the herdsman's tale;
When sitting by the brindled cow,
    She fills her foaming pail.

---

* *Buarach*, fetters made of horse hair, and used for those cows that were apt to kick while being milked.

The wailing swans their murmurs blend,
    With birds that float and sing;
Where joins the Sugar Brook the sea,
    Their tuneful voices ring.
Softly sweet they bend and breathe,
    Through their melodious throat,
Like the mournful, crooked bagpipe,
    A sad but pleasing note.

O! dainty is the graving work,
    By Nature near thee wrought!
Whose fertile banks with shining flowers,
    And pallid buds are fraught.
The shamrock and the daisy,
    Spread o'er thy borders fair,
Like new-made spangles, or like stars,
    From out the frosty air.

Ah! what a charming sight display,
    Thy ruddy, rosy braes;
When sunbeams dye their flowers as bright,
    As brilliants all a-blaze:
And what a civil suit they wear,
    Of rib-grass and of hay;
And gay-topt herbs o'er which the birds,
    Pour forth their pompous lay.

O Lily! king of flowers—thou
    The new rose hast outdone;
In bunches round of tender hue,
    And white-crown like the sun:
To keep the Sugar Brook from harm,
    As amulets are given,
Such stars to sparkle where it winds,
    Like guiding lights in heaven!

Green sorrel too and rushes,
  Sprout thick around its wold;
And slender waving stalks that look
  Like well turned work in gold:
Its brakes are full of mossy nests,
  Round wreathed for birds to stay;
Where boughs wave o'er the tassell'd grass,
  Or touch the curling spray.

'Twould med'cine any fading sight,
  That could the swift ships spy:
In white and swelling canvas drest,
  Close to thy banks go by:
Their fir-masts light and handy,
  With hempen ropes arrayed—
While down the cold torn Sound of Mull,
  The north blast keenly strayed.

The corry best in all the land,
  Of rich and sappy lea,
Is the corry of the Sugar Brook—
  The corry loved by me.
The corry rough and lovely,
  Where soft tufts thickly lie;
And water runs o'er sands that seem
  Crushed sugar to the eye!

The corry of the foals and lambs,
  Of kids and lonely cows;
The corry of the verdant glens,
  Where calves so early browse.
The wooded, rushy corry,
  Where the cockoo sings in March,
And the otters and the foxes' haunts
  The old grey cairns o'er arch.

The corry where the sheep in scores,
  Spread with their young away;
And stretch with fat their bursting skins,
  So warm, and white, and grey;
Thus, good for food and clothing,
  Through thy wild glens they go—
Thou lovely, lofty corry,
  That dost with grace o'erflow.

Thou corry where the ducks and drakes,
  And curlews haunt the shore;
Thou corry which the full grown stags,
  And heath-cock wander o'er;
'Tis time I ceased to number,
  Thy many a pleasant show;
Thine isles, and groves, and grassy plains,
  Where milk and honey flow.

Alexander MacDonald lived so long in the small Island of Canna, that he seems to have come to regard the mainland of Argyle, at one time, with the eyes and feelings of an Hebridean; as the following poem, "A Hail to the Mainland," shows.

The Island of Canna is thus described by Pennant, who visited it in the year 1775; when it could have changed but little, if at all, from the appearance it wore in MacDonald's day:—" As soon as we had time to cast our eyes about, each shore appeared pleasing to humanity: verdant and covered with hundreds of cattle; both sides gave a full idea of plenty—for the verdure was mixed with very little rock, and scarcely any heath. . . . . The length of the Island is about three miles, and the breadth, near one; its surface hilly. This was the property of the Bishop of the Isles; but at present, that of Mr. MacDonald of Clan-Ranald. His factor, a resident agent, rents most of the Island: paying two guineas for each *penny-land*; and these he lets to the poor people, at four and a half guineas each; and exacts, besides this, three days' labour in the quarter from each person. Another head tenant possesses other *penny-lands*, which he lets in the same manner to the impoverished and very starving of the wretched inhabitants."

According to Reid, MacDonald, when a young man, was ground agent or under factor in this little Island; and was very much in the company of the head factor, whose society, the same authority assures us, did him no good. For it was principally to gratify the depraved taste of this patron of his, that the poet, it seems, composed some of his pieces which are not very creditable now to his memory in point of good taste and right feeling.

An explanation of the lines in which MacDonald says of the Mainland or Mor'ir, that

> Blest with plenty, to thee never
> Comes the spring-time trying;

will be found in the following statement of Pennant's when speaking of Canna:—"The Isles, I fear, annually experience a temporary famine; perhaps from improvidence; perhaps from eagerness to increase their stock of cattle, which they can easily dispose of to satisfy the demands of their landlords, or the oppressions of an agent."

The Mor'ir, on account of the richness of its soil, or the beneficence of its landlords, was free from this periodical suffering. This little trait is worth mentioning, since it is pleasant to find MacDonald, notwithstanding his connection with the factor of Canna, showing his sympathies, however slightly, on the generous side of a question—as a poet ought always to do.

HAIL TO THE MAINLAND.

Hail to thee, thou bonny Mainland!
    In the Beltane glowing;
Golden, sunny, green-clad Mainland!
    Rosy burn-banks showing.

Blest with plenty, to thee never
    Comes the spring-time trying;
Bird-loved jewelled are thy hill sides,
    With green tree-tops sighing.

Thy woods so gay, are surely clad in
    Wedding garments fairly;
Straths and mountains here are lovely,
    Glens are tinted rarely.

When the sun-rise gilds the mountains,
    Then the bee goes snoring;
Ruddy bee that tickles flow'rets,
    And hums—honey storing.

Now the brisk trout leaps the eddies,
    And droll flies keeps chasing;
While a green flag o'er the fountains,
    Every knoll is raising

And buds are swelling, full of fragrance,
    Blue, and red, and paly:
Musical the slender sprays are,
    Where the birds dance gaily.

Cosy rushy beds the fold has,
    In the summer weather;

Foamy, creamy milk in beakers,
    Herdsmen quaff together.

Butter, curds, and whey, in streamlets
    Lappered milk they're sharing;
Drink unmeasured set before us,
    With no thought of sparing.

FLOWERS.

(FROM THE ODE TO SUMMER.)

O PRIMROSE! that growest
    So pallid and sweet on the brae,
In tender tufts blowing,
    In curly leaves flowing—
The hardiest flower art thou
    Sprung from the clay;
Thus wearing thy spring-dress
    While others still slumber away.

And wreath of Cuchulinn* of cairns,
    How pleasant the odour that's shed
Where tasselled and brindled,
    With legs long and spindled,
Rough clustered, modest hued,
    Yellow-tipt, high o'er-head,
Round the lone knoll we see thee
    With wood-sorrel spread.

Spiraea Ulmaria—Meadow-sweet, queen of the meadow, Gaelic: *eneas, or crios Chu-chulainn.*

BIRDS.

(FROM THE ODE TO WINTER.)

Sorrow lies on the earth all around,
   And the hill and the mountain grow bare;
Fast darkens the face of the ground,
   Shorn and bare, faint and withered with care.
All the speckled birds, tuneful and sweet,
   Erst that sang from the top of the tree,
Have their pleasant mouth's gagged when we meet;
   They have lost bow and string—lost their glee.

The winged folk now of the sky,
   Cease their sunny songs here for a space;
Nor their matins they carol on high,
   Nor with vespers the holy eve grace.
But in chill caves all sleepy they stay,
   And cow'r cold in the holes of the crag,
Where they miss much the warm glancing ray,
   Whose bright sheen made their summer songs flag.

There's a dark frown on Europe throughout
   Since the strength of the sun grew so wan,
Whose light spreads such solace about—
   The Lamp by which all things we scan;
But when to the Twins he comes back,
   And beams on these regions again,
A bright hue the rough hills shall not lack,
   Nor the gold gleaming heaps of the main.

And those psalmists, then spotted anew,
   In their close leafy pulpits shall stand,
Hymns and praises to sing as their due,
   Since the Summer time shines on the land

They have meetings the green boughs among,
  And rare pews in each soft tender spray,
And they pour forth the offering of song
  On their slender-tipt wings far away.

There is none 'neath the cup of the sky,
  But returns to his spirit once more,
When Phœbus that shines from on high,
  The might of their souls shall restore:
Then they rise up at once from the grave,
  Where the cold kept them chilly and dumb,
Saying, " gooly-dro-hidolo-haive,
  Winter's gone and the Summer has come."

THE GROUSE COCK AND HEN.

The grouse leaving the green buds,
  That dapple the spray,
Takes his short beaked and speckled spouse
  To the mountains away;
Like a courtier there wooes her,
  Where the shade of the heather is cool;
Though still she laughs hoarsely,
  " Pee-hoo-hoo, you're a fool!"

MORAG AND OTHER BELLES.

A face I never saw,
   Since my dawning days—
Not one so free of flaw,
   Full of glorious grace;
Though Mally still was mild,
   And her cheek like rowans wild,
As fickle as the wind she smiled,
   When it drones and strays.
Peggy had a slight
   Trace of age's blight;
Marsaly was light,
   Full of saucy ways.
Lilly's love was bright,
   Though a speck had dimmed her sight,
But they were all as tame and trite
   As washing suds to Morag.

It is unfortunate that from the nature of the Song in Praise of Morag—in many respects, a very beautiful one, from which this short extract is taken—a fair translation of it, as a whole, is a thing on which no one is very likely to venture. MacDonald was a married man when he saw the young girl, Morag, whose beauty he celebrates in a strain very impassioned, though not always very decorous or refined.

An idea of the poem he produced on the occasion, may be formed from some of Burns' Songs in which the rapture, though indubitable, is far from being of the highest kind—with this difference, however, that Burns' Songs consist of two or three stanzas only, while MacDonald's is an elaborate composition of about three hundred and fifty lines in length. It is in a sort of rhythm peculiar to the Highlands—of which a further account will be given under the head of MacIntyre's "Ben Dorain."

FROM THE SONG OF THE HIGHLAND CLANS.

O! LOVED and loyal Kindred,
    Choice homage now give ye;
Let no mote cloud your eyesight—
    Your heart from care keep free.
The health of James Stuart
    With welcome send it round;
Without reserve receive it—
    This holy pledge we sound.

Now fill a draught for Charlie—
    Rogue! let this cup o'erflow;
Ha! 'tis a balm to heal our hearts—
    Revive us when we're low.
Yea! should death's hand be laying us
    Weak, wan beside the grave,
Oh, Universal King! return—
    Return him o'er the wave.

Hard is the case of all his friends,
    Because of his delay;
They are like a callow orphan'd brood—
    Like garden bees, a prey
To the destructive fox, when faint
    They drop along the brae;
Come quickly with thy fleet, and drive
    Thy people's plague away.

MacDonald is said to have gone over the Highlands singing the Song from which these verses are taken, and rousing his countrymen with its energetic appeals to rise and join Prince Charles. The rest of the Song consists of an address to all the Clans successively, so very similar to that contained in the Clan Song in "Waverley," "There is mist on the mountain and night on the vale," that a reader of Sir Walter Scott's spirited imitation will be able to form an exceedingly correct notion, both of the nature of this and all other Clan Songs of the Highlands.

A species of Clan Song also, is MacDonald's poem entitled, "The Praise of the Lion," in which he celebrates so cordially the prowess, valour, and greatness of all the septs that bore his own distinguished name. It is, at the same time, no unfair specimen of those War-songs, or Battle incitements, as they were called, with which the bards, from very remote ages, used to animate their friends and kinsmen when about to engage in battle.

Some of these, of an old date, are still extant and well known. The most extraordinary of them, in every respect, is one composed by Lachlan Mor MacVurich Albanich, hereditary bard of Clan-Ranald, and chanted by him to his clansmen at the battle of Harlaw, 1411. This most unique production consists of three hundred and thirty eight lines; the theme of the whole being, "O Children of Conn of the hundred fights! remember hardihood in the time of battle." Round this theme the Bard has gathered no fewer than six hundred and fifty adverbial adjectives, arranged in alphabetical order, and all bearing a special and bloody reference to the subject in hand.

The Poem contains nothing else but these adjectives. There is not much that can be called poetry about them; but yet, when supplied without hesitation by a good memory in all their astonishing alliterative array, by a ready speaker, gifted with a strong and sensitive voice, they could not but have offered a rare opportunity for impetuous, vehement and effective declamation. A man of good presence, as Lachlan Mor probably was, hurling them forth in this way on his audience, with flashing eye and fiery, and appropriate gesture, must have created no small stir and excitement among the valiant children of

Conn: even with a string of sonorous adjectives—a good many of them too compounded by himself, with no little ingenuity for the occasion.

Alexander MacDonald, in his Song in Praise of the Lion, is sufficiently ferocious and complimentary to the MacDonalds to have pleased Lachlan Mor himself. Rather than leave out any portion of his Clan's due meed of praise, he has perhaps said nearly the same thing more than once over, in slightly different words. This, however, is not more than two or three times the case, and does not lessen the value of the lyric, as a spirited, energetic production—full of ardour and poetic fire. It will contrast pleasantly with those soft and tender descriptions of Nature that have just been given; and show, along with them, the variety of bardic power possessed by the author. As a piece of animated war-poetry, not unworthy of any lyric writer, may be cited the four stanzas in the succeeding Poem, following from, " Strong rock, and everlasting," down to, " Groaning hard and moaning, resound the site of battle o'er." These display, not merely vigorous composition, but genuine feeling. The Poet is describing what he really admired, and would have joined in himself. He is not like too many of our most martial poets, working up a safe effervesence, for the sake of effect; and crying, " Ha-ha!" amid a dim fancy of trumpet sounds—a proceeding not commendable, being so evidently the very reverse of their natural propensity.

THE PRAISE OF THE LION.

To the Air of "Caberfac."

HAIL ! thou rending Lion,
    Of matchless force and pompous pirde !
When up thy chieftains roused them,
    Gay banners fluttered far and wide.
All thy tribes would gather,
    With martial pace and manly grace ;
Then losses came and crosses
    On every foe that met with them ;
Their line so splendid, far extended—
    Fiery, flaming, furious ;
A stormful path, their joyous wrath,
    With gory blades carved curious.
With sharp rage, wild war wage,
    Heads, and limbs, and trunks they'd hack ;
No soft foe with swords could go
    To keep the haughty heroes back.

Wake yet, thou battling Lion !
    Wake and rise with sounding stir—
So tawny on thy white flag,
    With thy badge of heather, sir ;
Raise thy head so airily,
    In the blue sky restlessly,
And to the fray, as well 's I may,
    Will I go and fight for thee.
Oh ! let me raise the precious praise
    Of that head, so royal held ;
This realm is fair, but none hath e'er
    Throughout its bonds thy might excell'd :

In hardihood so firm and good—
   Lovely, free of fear and doubt,
With vigorous zest in terror's breast,
   Thee thy clansmen flock'd about.

Oh! who could taunt or tease thee,
   Or with mean things disparage thee,
Or venture to displease thee,
   Or once hope to discourage thee,
Thou kingly splendid creature?
   So fierce, full form'd, and fairly seen,
On thy silken pennon clean,
   With fine smooth mast of sapling green.
There thou flutterest, proudly, loudly,
   Flapping fast and saucily;
While a gallant host heroic
   Stand beneath thee gaucily:
Rage for bloodshed makes their brows red—
   Rage and wrath to follow thee;
Now slaughtering blades and death's cold shades
   Will come on all who sighted thee.

Ne'er backward nor inglorious—
   The noble race thou well dost grace;
But prosperous and victorious,
   In battle bright and great in might;
With guns, and swords, and shields of gold,
   And corslets—what a deadly set!
Their glaives they plied, and deep and wide
   The wounds they gave to all they met.
Powder blazing—war smoke raising,
   Till a cloud about them grew;
The lively, fair, and quick youths there
   Then cut ribs and marrow through:
With bitter blades—thick-back'd, dark blue—
   In every stubborn stripling's hand,

That cleft the sturdiest body through—
   My joy! I think their pride was grand.

Sufficient, strong, and manly—
   A daring band, and clannish all—
The race of Collai red hand—
   Full of might and spirits, tall.
Keen their ire as flames of fire,
   When March's wind put strength in them—
Without failing rust, or ailing,
   In the breadth or length of them.
With buoyant life they go to strife,
   No dread of wounds can hold them back;
They need no stain to make them fain,
   Hearts, and brains, and reins they whack;
Heads they sweep off—hands and feet off—
   In the smoke, with battle's mirth—
Each one so brave, with hardy glaive,
   So manly, sharp, and full of worth.

The lovely race—the daring—
   Well equipp'd in war array,
Their long, smooth muskets wearing,
   So deadly in the dread affray;
With lock, and flint and hammer
   Ready trimm'd to give the blow
That sends away the powder grey,
   In a bright and fiery glow.
Then bullets red in showers are sped,
   Through smoke and roar and lustre quick,
That smash and slay and crush and bray
   The cassock'd bodies short and thick;
With broken bones and piteous groans
   On the field they toss and kick,
When like wasps in your strong grasps
   You wield your blades, so sharp and slick.

Clan-Donald, I am saying,
    Right honourable race are they ;
Oft the conflict swaying,
    Their foes they grandly swept away ;
They are fearless, bright, and peerless,
    Full of stinging venom too—
Like serpents on the mountains bred,
    Their hardy blades so sharp and blue.
Smart and airy, wild and wary,
    With quick hands that nothing mars ;
Hard as rocks and swift as meteors,
    Their whistling strokes are heard afar :
My manly men, shamefast * and nimble,
    Solid, strong, and firm and sure ;
Like the flood's course that thunders hoarse,
    Or flames that light the mountain moor.

Strong rock, and everlasting,
    Hard, and old, and undecay'd,
High thy royal crest show,
    For thousands gather in thy shade,
With mirth, in their armour bright—
    The dauntless race that never yield—
The spectres that stir panic flight,
    When quick striking swords they wield.

---

* Shamefast ("nàrach," susceptible of shame.) This was a much esteemed quality in the Highlands, even in soldiers. The Highlanders, while fighting the battles of their country, and billeted among the various peoples, at home and abroad, were designated, "lambs in the house and lions in the field." There is another word something like this one in appearance—"nàisinn," implying a delicate and almost morbid sense of moral obligation—which is frequently heard still and always applied only when a man is commended. These two words are very characteristically Highland, and are both extremly creditable to the moral feelings of the people among whom they took their origin and are in constant use.

Many gallant youths beneath thee,
    With stout hands and shoulders great,
Go rushing on where honour's won,
    For wild fight they're never late:
With steady foot and agile hand
    To thrust or cut, each weapon gleams;
Red on the ground death gasps around,
    But gay o'er head the Lion streams.

Thou roaring, frowning Lion!
    Who fright and fear canst spread about—
Often proved where war has moved,
    In furious fight or turbid rout;
When thy semblance, looking dire,
    From the tough staff flutters free,
Then a kindling, troubled fire
    On every cheek around we see.
Strong, and steady, stubborn, ready,
    Is their rank where strife is hot;
Fear of foe they never know—
    They are rocks that tremble not;
Group'd together, fleeing never,
    Unyielding wood of oak are they,—
Their shout of triumph 's oft been heard
    O'er fields of death where foemen lay.

If violence should assail thee
    From strangers' bounds, and seek thy hurt;
If foemen should draw near thee,
    With ill will, and strife, and sturt,
Many an Islay hilt* then,
    With a strong smooth blade in it,

---

* Islay hilts, invented by a celebrated smith of the name of MacEachern, who lived in Islay, were famous all over the Highlands. "Blades with Islay heads," were considered the very finest and most efficient weapons.

Beneath thy silken stream would gleam
    To fight for thee and succour thee.
Thine are men who would not bend
    In showers that pierce the body through;
Nor yet be slow to rise and go
    Where heads were hack'd and fury grew;
When, over all the tumult spread,
    The thundering pipes were heard afar,
That might put spirit in the dead
    To rise for gallant deeds of war.

Clan-Donald's tree is all thine
    Its bough and branches ever held,
As true a wood as ever stood—
    Chieftain-like, unparallel'd;
When all its tribes came trooping round
    So·manly where the Lion's seen,
Then woe betide whoever tried
    To pluck his beard or rouse his spleen.
Their hands and heads you'd lop and prune
    With the glittering claymore's sweep.
Till on the grass their blood would splash,
    And run in little streams and creep;
Your stinging dark-blue blades would make
    The heads of Galls* to steam in gore;
And groaning hard and moaning,
    Resound the site of battle o'er.

Where in all this kingdom.
    Are men of deed your race excel?
When songs incite you to the fight,
    Your thousand virtues who can tell?

---

* *Gall*, though usually applied to the Lowlanders, here means any one unfriendly to the MacDonalds. There is an old song on the massacre of Glencoe, in which the Campbells, and all who had a hand in that bloody tragedy, are called *Galls*.

Your anvils strong and precious,
    Of true steel that weakens not,
Who always have been faithful,
    And word of truth have ne'er forgot;
Hounds of fight, like arrows' flight,
    Down with glistening swords you break,
Nor rest a moment till a breach
    Through and through your foes you make;
Trunks are cleft and steel is shaken,
    You feel a bloody, bloody thirst;
Battle raves and whistling glaives,
    And dreadful shout around you burst.

There are thousands now in Alba
    As stout as are in any land;
The grey Gaels from Scotia,*
    Who cheerful round your colours stand;
With love of hardy deeds and bold,
    They fasten round you steadily,
Where the Lion's furious hold,
    And his paws shine bloodily.
Bring with you then your well fed men—
    Your stately, stalwart heroes show—
Your dexterous, lively, active line,
    Who with a will to battle go;
You ne'er were seen where strife was keen,
    To blench or shun its reddest tide;
But foes have fled, where'er have been
    Their speckled banner fluttering wide!

---

* "Scotia," in this last stanza, occurs in the original, but is printed in italics. The Irish warriors who invaded Britain and fought with the Romans about the year 360, called themselves Scoti, a Gaelic word that means warriors. *Scoth* is an old Gaelic word signifying warrior. Caledonia is not a Gaelic name but a Pictish or Iberian one.

DUNCAN BAN MACINTYRE.

Duncan Ban Macintyre, the hunter Bard of Glenorchy, on whom his admiring countrymen have long agreed to confer the flattering title "of the Songs," was born on the 20th March, 1724, at Druimliaghart in Glenorchy, Argyllshire. His parents living on the outskirts of a large and thinly populated district had no opportunity of sending their son to the distant parish school: the only one, seemingly, which a wide extent of country offered in those days, for the acquisition, even of the common rudiments of education. So this future poet never learned either to read or to write. Yet, though thus destitute of the very elements of school learning—though he lived a simple life in a humble station, and never had the benefit of a large experience of society to furnish his mind with the materials of thought—though he never associated with learned men whose conversation might stimulate, direct, and cultivate his faculties, he has left behind him a name which is not likely soon to perish. He deserves to be remembered, not only on account of his really genuine gift of song, and of his fresh and truly beautiful poetry, but has also a claim on our remembrance, even on account of his wonderful memory. Wellnigh six thousand lines of his poetry have been published —all of which he must have composed, arranged, and carried about with him in his mind for years; and this too independent of what he knew of the popular poetry of his country, with which he was well acquainted, and of which he is said to have picked up, by ear, a large quantity. Along with this his poetry is thoroughly national. It is pervaded and enlivened by the very spirit of Highland scenery, and embalms though unconsciously, yet with good effect, the tone of that phase of life of which the Bard himself partook, and even for these reasons too he will have some hold on the consideration of posterity, and a hold which will not likely be, at least for a time, a decreasing one. Duncan Ban is said to have early manifested that strong passion for field sports which distinguished him to the very last. As a youth, in his lonely and wild but romantic habitation, with his strong natural tastes, his inquisitive and observant mind, and his musical and poetic temperament, he may be supposed to have passed his time and nursed his rising genius—having the appearance, to a casual observer, of such another roving young mountaineer as Captain Dalgetty describes in the grandson of Ranald Mac Eagh—"a smart and hopeful youth, whom I have noted to be never without a pebble in his plaid-nook to fling at whatever might come in his way, being a symbol that, like David who was accustomed to sling smooth stones taken from the brook—he may afterwards prove an adventurous warrior." By and by, the pebble in the plaid-nook would be exchanged for a fishing rod, and then a gun; for Duncan Ban became a noted marksman in his maturer years, and was so fond of his guns that he mentions them very frequently in his poetry, as if they were dear friends and companions, and composed a song expressly for each of the three principal weapons of this sort which he possessed during his life.

His first song was composed on a sword with which he was armed at the battle of Falkirk—where he served on the royalist side as substitute for a neighbouring gentleman. This sword the poet lost or threw away in the retreat. On his return home therefore, the gentleman to whom it belonged, and whose substitute he had been, refused to pay the sum for which he had engaged Duncan Ban to serve in his stead. Duncan consequently composed his Song on "the Battle of the Speckled Kirk"— as Falkirk is called in Gaelic, in which he good-humouredly satirised the gentlemen who had sent him to the war, and gave a woeful description of "the black sword that waked the turmoil," and whose loss, he says, made its owner "as fierce and furious as a grey brock in his den." The song immediately became popular and incensed his employer so much, that he suddenly fell upon the poor poet one day with his walking-stick, and striking him on the back, bade him "go and make a song about that." He was, however, afterwards compelled by the Earl of Breadalbane to pay the bard the sum of 300 merks Scots (£16 17s. 6d.) which was his legal due.

The Earl of Breadalbane was always a great patron of Duncan Ban's, and appointed him his forester and gamekeeper in "Corie Cheathach" and Ben Dorain—places which the Bard has celebrated in his two finest poems, so successfully that their names have now something of the same charm to a Gaelic ear as Loch-Katrine or the Banks of the Doon bear to that of the English reader. He for a short time afterwards served the Duke of Argyll in the same capacity of forester at Buachaill Eite.

Then he joined the Earl of Breadalbane's fencible Regiment, raised in 1793, and remained with it, holding the rank of sergeant until 1799, when it was disbanded. For some time after this he belonged to the city-guard of Edinburgh, so celebrated by Sir Walter Scott, and by Ferguson the poet. He remained in the city-guard until 1806, after which time, according to his biographers, he was "enabled to live in comparative comfort on his little savings, and the profit of the third edition of his poems, published in 1804." He died in Edinburgh, May, 1812, in his eighty-ninth year. He was buried in the Greyfriars churchyard, in that city, on the 19th of May, and over his remains a suitable monument has since been raised. A notice of his death appearing in one of the Edinburgh papers, but not till the following October.

About twenty-two years after the composition of his first song on the Battle of the Speckled Kirk, Duncan Ban became so famous as a poet, that his friends thought his verses worthy of a wider circulation than his singing or theirs could give them, and the son of a neighbouring clergyman, himself afterwards well known as Dr. Stewart of Luss, one of the translators of the Gaelic Bible, was at the trouble of taking them down to the poet's own dictation, with a view to their publication. They were accordingly printed in Edinburgh, and published in the year 1768, with the following title:—"Gaelic Songs, by Duncan MacIntyre." They were of course in one volume, not large, consisting of 162 pages, 12mo.

A second edition, with many additions, appeared in 1790, when the poet travelled over a good part of the Highlands, disposing of the issue. The third edition came out in 1804. There have been three editions since —making six in all.* But in the shape of extracts, the favourite poems like "The last Farewell to the Hills," &c., have appeared in many other books besides. There are Highlanders too who knew Duncan Ban, and have learnt to sing his Songs, who never read them at all.

With regard to the poet's personal appearance we know that he was called Bàn, on account of his fair hair; and his biographers tell us, that in his youth he was remarkably handsome. There are still living people who saw him, and have a distinct recollection of him as a fine and striking looking old man—venerable and patriarchal, with his silvery hair and his long pilgrim staff—a man to attract notice, and treated always with the greatest respect, wherever he was known. It is said he possessed a very easy and agreeable disposition; although, when greatly provoked, he could let his enemies feel the power of his satire, as may be seen from verses he composed on an impudent piper, named Uisdean, who lampooned him—he never failed in his attachment or his gratitude to his friends. "He was like the rest of the poets, very fond of company and a social glass; and was not only very pleasant over his bottle, but very circumspect."

* A seventh edition was published in 1871.

As a poet, his great characteristics are his clear and sure perception, his fine ear, his excellent judgment, and his command of his native language, which he invariably uses with admirable precision, purity, and effect. He sings always of things which he knew well—things which he had learned for himself—things which he was quite sure of—which were not the least obscure to him. He is always self-possessed and master of himself. His mind never drifts helmless before an overpowering emotion; yet his verse is essentially lyrical, even in description—and frequently expressive of deep and genuine feeling—of sweet and unchanging devotion. His style is clear and simple. His rhythm varied, free, and sonorous. In reading Duncan Ban one feels that he was a sweet-tempered, amiable, unaffected man. Perhaps it is partly owing to this, as well as to the fine faculty his poetry displays, that he is decidedly the best loved of the Highland Bards. But so excellent were his gifts that, notwithstanding his want of culture, no other of the Gaelic Poets is held in the same esteem, or placed on the same level with him, excepting Alexander MacDonald. These two are universally considered and spoken of as the chief singers among the mountain melodists. Sometimes the one is preferred, sometimes the other. Duncan Ban had less variety—less wild vigour than his predecessor—but he is clearer, smoother, more equable, more harmonious. Then something must be allowed for his untutored efforts,—for that ever blind "groping of the Cyclops"—that utter want of one limitless external aid, which claims for him so unique a place among his country's most distinguished Bards. If some consideration might be demanded for Burns, and justly too, (were it not for his mighty powers) on account of his imperfect training, and his want of leisure for mental labour, still more might be asked for this man; for Burns was learned compared to him, yet he too does not need it—a proof of the reality and purity of his master gift.

The pictures of the external things, animate and inanimate, with which he was acquainted, are not inferior for truth, vividness and beauty, to those of any descriptive poet. His address to his wife—*Màiri bhàn òg*—may be read beside the sweetest and most expressive of the Lowland lyrics—while it certainly breathes a refined courtesy and a purity of sentiment which these do not always possess, and which is not in any way insignificant in such a man, whether taken as an index of his moral nature, of his intellectual endowments, or of the kindness of nature in gifting him with such unaffected manliness and good taste. How much education and more favourable circumstances might have done for Duncan Ban MacIntyre as a poet, it will ever remain impossible to determine. As it is, his admirers need have no hesitation in claiming for him a higher and more noticeable place, than he now possesses, among the "tuneful dead, whose names are honoured by his nation."

INTRODUCTION TO BEN DORAIN.

IN the celebrated poem which Duncan Ban dedicates to the hill, Ben Dorain, he throws the whole soul of the hunter Bard, and true poetic son of nature into his description of the place and of its sprightly denizens. This poem, consisting of five hundred and fifty-five lines, is the longest of Duncan Ban's compositions. It is adapted to a pipe tune, into all the varieties of whose wild rhythm he moulds his language throughout with such spirit and success, that even considered as a piece of elaborate versification, carried out to such a length, and on so unique a plan, it is no small feat to have been achieved by such an author, and so circumstanced, that it was only by crooning it over in his memory he could give his diction the necessary finish.

The poem is divided into eight parts, corresponding to the variations of the pibroch, which, as Duncan Ban understood it, seems to have be made up of what he calls the "Urlar" and "Siubhal," played alternately—the first four times repeated, and the last three times—the whole ending with the "Crunluath," or quick motion. The following passage is entirely from the first of these heads —the "Urlar," which is the one indeed chiefly used by the poet—nearly the half of "Ben Dorian" being constructed altogether of this measure—and its principal peculiarity which consists of a regular and frequent occurrence of the broad sound of *o*, or *au*, to round every cadence being found throughout the poem. This was done to imitate a certain quality of the bag-pipe, which goes far to give its tones their own fierce and warlike character. The Gaelic language, in which the broad sound of *o* is very common, falls into this rhythm very easily, and with good effect. It is more of a novelty in English, and the reader will do well to bear its nature in mind, when reading the following extract from "Ben Dorain."

BEN DORAIN.

The honour o'er each hill
    Hath Ben Dorain ;
Scene, to me, the sweetest still
    That day dawns upon :
Its long moor's level way,
    And its nooks whence wild deer stray,
To the lustre on the brae
    Oft I've lauded them.

Dear to me its dusky boughs,
    In the wood where green grass grows,
And the stately herd repose,
    Or there wander slow;

But the troops with bellies white,
  When the chase comes into sight,
Then I love to watch their flight,
  Going nosily.

The stag is airy, brisk, and light,
  And no pomp has he;
Though his garb 's the fashion quite,
  Never haughty he:
Yet a mantle's round him spread,
  Not soon threadbare, then shed,
And its hue as wax is red—
  Fairly clothing him.

The delight I felt to rise
  At the morning's call!
And to see the troops I prize
  The hills thronging all:
Ten score with stately tread,
  And with light uplifted head,
Quite unpampered there that fed,
  Fond and fawning all.

Lightsomely there came
  From each clean and shapely frame,
Through their murmuring lips, a tame
  Chant, with drawling fall.
In the pool one rolled a low—
  With the hind one played the beau,
As she trotted to and fro,
  Looking saucily.

I would rather have the deer
  Gasping moaningly,
Than all Erin's songs to hear
  Sung melodiously;

For above the finest bass
   Hath the stag's sweet voice a grace,
As he bellows on the face
   Of Ben Dorain.

Loud and long he gives a roar
   From his very inmost core,
Which is heard behind, before,
   Far and fallingly;
But the hind of softer notes,
   With her calf that near her trots,
Match each other's tuneful throats,
   Crying longingly.

Her eye's soft and tender ray
   With no flaw in it,
O'er whose lid the brow is gray,
   Guides her wandering feet:
Very well she walks, and bold,
   Lively o'er the russet wold,
Tripping from her desert hold
   Most undauntingly.

Faultless is her pace,
   And her leap is full of grace—
Ha! the last when in the race
   Never saw I her:
When she takes yon startled stride,
   Nor once turns her head aside,
Aught to match her hasty pride
   Is not known to me.

But now she's on the heath,
   As she ought to be,
Where the tender grass she seeth,
   Growning dawtily;

The dry bent, the moor grass bare,
    With the sappy herbs are there,
That make fat, and full, and fair,
    Her plump quarters all.

And those little wells are nigh,
    Where the water-cresses lie,
Above wine she likes to try
    Their waves' solacing;
Of the rye-grass, twisted rows,
    On the rude hill side it grows,
Than of rarest festal shows
    Is she fonder far.

The choice increase of the earth
    Forms her joyous treat;
The primrose, St. John's wort,
    Tops of gowans sweet,
The new buds of the groves,
    The soft heath o'er which she roves,
Are the tit-bits that she loves,
    With good cause too.

For speckled, spotted, rare,
    Tall, and fine, and fair,
From such food before her there
    She grows sonsily;
And it is still the surest mean
    To cure the weak ones and the lean,
Who for any time have been
    Wasted, wan, and low.
Soon it would clothe their back
    With the garb which most they lack—
That rich fat, which they can pack
    Most commodiously.

She's a flighty young hind
   When leaves ward her,
Near her haunts where they bind
   The brae border:
Lightsome and urbane
   Is her gay heart, free of stain,
Tho' rash head and somewhat vain—
   Somewhat thoughtless.

Yet her form, so full of grace,
   She keeps hiding in a place,
Where the green glen shows no trace
   Of a falling off;
But she's so healthy, and so clean—
   So chaste where'er she's seen—
Should you kiss her lips, I ween
   'T would not cause you shame.

Greatly prized is she, I know,
   By the stag with crested brow,
Whose thundering hoofs around him throw
   Such a saucy sound;
When with him she meets the view
   Red and yellow in her hue,
And of virtues not a few
   That belong to her.
Of cold she is free of fear,
   And in speed without a peer,
And the primest ear to hear
   In all Europe's hers.

Oh! how sweetly they embrace,
   Young and fawning,
When they gather to their place
   In the gloaming;

There, till silent night is by,
    Never terror comes them nigh,
While beneath the bush they lie—
    Their known haunt of old.

Let the wild herd seek their bed,
    Let them slumber, free of dread,
Where yon mighty moor is spread,
    Broad and brawly;
Where, with joy, I've often spied
    The sun colour their red hide,
As they wandered in their pride
    O'er Ben Dorain.

INTRODUCTION TO "COIRE CHEATHAICH."

EQUALLY celebrated with Ben Dorain, and an equally good specimen of Duncan Ban's poetic powers, is the poem of "Coire Cheathaich," which now follows. These two poems divide the voices of Gaelic readers as to which of them is the abler and more finished.

"Coire Cheathaich," however, being divided into stanzas, almost every one of which contains a complete picture of its own, has the advantage of being better known perhaps in some of its parts than Ben Dorain, where the description is more extended. The verse that speaks of the salmon leaping over the whirling eddies, is the most famous thing of its kind in the Gaelic language.

There can hardly be any Highlander, with the slighest turn for poetry, who has not repeated it approvingly himself, or been called on by others sometimes to admire it. In about equal esteem, however, are those verses on the early morning and the singing of the birds; and they are even more musical with their fine metrical succession of soft vowel sounds. But the flowers, trees, streams, and living creatures, throughout his excellent poem, are all nearly equally good.

To point out everything in it that was highly thought of, would be in fact only to go over the whole of it. "Coire Cheathaich" is considered as fine a specimen of the harmony of which the Gaelic language is capable, as any other production of the Celtic muse. This translation is in the rhythm of the original, and verse for verse with it.

CORRY CEATHACH.*

My misty Corry! where hinds are roving;
   My lovely Corry! my charming dell!
So grand, so grassy, so richly scented,
   And gemm'd with wild flowers of sweetest smell.
Thy knolls and hillocks, in dark green clothing,
   Rise o'er the gay sward with gentle swell;
Where waves the cannach and grows the darnel,
   And troop the wild deer I loved so well.

A strong, well-woven and double mantle—
   A lasting garment and good for wear,
All rough with rich grass, whose verdant ringlets
   In each small dew-drop a burden bear—
Is round my Corry, my green-knolled Corry,
   Where reeds and rushes so thickly grow;
They'd yield a harvest, were reapers able
   Among their quagmires and bogs to go.

---

* C is always hard, and *th* frequently silent in Gaelic. *Ceathach* is therefore pronounced almost as if it were spelt, "Kayach." The name MacKeoch, comes from it, and means, "Son of the Mist."

'Tis a gay clothing, shows off the long plain,
  With pastoral smooth grass from side to side;
A painted garment, by rains well nurtured,
  As fair as can be by man descried.
On this side Paris I do not fancy
  A brighter raiment hath e'er been seen;
Oh may it fade not! and then what fortune
  To haunt, at all hours, its varied green.

About Ruadh-Aisridh long locks are hanging—
  Close, crisp, and clustering, and crested high;
In every moist spot their tops are waving,
  As this or that way the breeze goes by;
There the straight rye-grass, the twisted hemlock,
  The sappy moor-grass that ne'er gets dry,
And the strong bent grow, and close set groundsel,
  Beside the dark wood where heroes lie.

The mountain ruin, where lived MacBhaidi,
  Is now a desert that howls alone;
Yet near its white stones is often nurtured
  The brown ox, shapely and fully grown;
The cows with calves there that wander houseless,
  Grand-group'd on hill-tops, are often seen;
Their calves so peaceful, in light and darkness,
  Frequent in numbers the south Clach-Fionn.

The garlic chooses the nooks and bendings
  Of steps that climb up the mountain-head;
While the kind sun-slopes are spotted rarely
  With countless berries—round, ripe or, red:
The dandelion and penny-royal,
  And cannach smooth-white, there wave or rest,
As from its broad base, they deck thy mountain,
  Unto its lofty and haughty crest.

The tallest crag there is richly coated
  With softest mosses above—below;

Unsullied, stainless, whene'er they 'er needed,
   O'er things unsightly these sweetly grow :
While in the hollows, beneath the sharp peaks,
   Where shaggy verdure is thickliest spread,
Beside the primrose, right often peeping,
   The feeble daisy lifts up its head.

A frowning eye-brow of verdant cresses.
   Round all the fountains and wells is seen ;
And bunchy sorrel conceals the deep roots
   Of those great rough stones the spring that screen :
With plunge and gurgle, and dancing motion,
   In heartless boiling these quit the ground ;
And each dear streamlet leaps, laughs, and lingers,
   And runs and loiters in circles round.

The salmon leaving the wild-waved ocean,
   Within the rough dell his white breast shows ;
There darts rejoicing, and snaps* the small flies,—
   So truly steers he his crooked nose :
On fierce whirled eddies his pompous leaping
   Displays his splendid and blue-gray mail,
His silver spangles, his fins, his speckles,
   His outstretched, wing-like, transparent tail.

The Corry Ceathach is sweet and joyous,
   A royal site for the hunter's pride ;
There the dark lead-shot his blazing powder
   Sows thickly over the deer's dun side ;

   * *Kep*, is the word used here in the original. It is a Gaelic word, but adopted by the Scotch, and used by Burns : as for instance in the "Lament for Captain Matthew Henderson,"

    "Ilk cowslip cup shall *kep* a tear."

The word means primarily, to prevent something from going farther. Then, to stop anything which is thrown or coming towards you by making a snatch at it, is to *kep* it. It is probably the root of the English word, *keep*.

And there his needy and light-foot gazehound—
  With bloody fierceness, without a fear—
Runs madly, leaping with hardy spirit,
  Pursuing boldly his red career.

Within thy lone brakes there never fail'd yet
  The fawn, the red stag, the hornless doe;
So 'twas our glory in sunny morning
  Through deer-trod dingles a-hunting go:
Nor would the wild heath e'er leave us lying
  Before the rain-storm exposed and bare.
No! In the forest were low-browed grottoes,
  With well-fenced couches to stretch us there.

Then when the morning's white calm would wake us,
  Beneath the steep cliff 'twould charm my ear
To list the moor hen grown hoarse with croaking,
  Or courtly red-cock bend murmuring near;
The lively wren to his own small trump play'd,
  And flung his steam off so brisk and boon;
The starling bustled beside the red-breast,
  Who lilted gaily a warbling tune.

All the hill-songsters, in flocking numbers
  From leafy branches, there poured their praise;
First came the gay lark, that noted lyrist,
  And shrilly chanted its cheeriest lays;
The merle and cuckoo, on tall thin tree-tops,
  Gave out their music with might and main,
When up this sound rose so light and lovely,
  The glen was breathing a choral strain.

Then every corry within the mountain
  Sent forth the live things within its bound;
First, treading proudly, the antler'd red deer
  Stepp'd, snorting loudly and looking round;

Throughout the wild fen he dash'd in rapture,
  Or near the brown hind more gently play'd—
His charming princess, so strong, so stately,
  So spare, so active, so fine, so staid!
In shy recesses the yellow doe crept
  Beneath the light twigs, and cropp'd them bare;
While o'er his proud couch the lordly buck stood,
  And poked and stamp'd it with gloomy stare:
The little kidling of speckled, smooth side,
  Of placid nostril and noble head,
Found sleeping snugly in some lone hollow,
  Among the rushes a cosy bed.
How many a light foot, when autumn ripen'd,
  Tripp'd gaily over that hill's brown side,
And sought and shared all the store it offered
  With manly kindness and gentle pride!
In a soft round nest they got the honey
  Of the small spotted and brindled bee,
That labours, flying from flower to flower,
  With lonely murmur and peaceful glee.
There nuts well-season'd—no scanty harvest
  Of wither'd kernels—were growing seen
In great abundance; thin skinn'd, smooth cluster'd,
  They'd suck'd the life-juice from branches green,
Where purl'd the streamlet throughout the sweet strath,
  And rowans ripen'd their berries red,
And many a sapling, in graceful mantle,
  Kept waving gently in new-clad head.
From far, surrounding the lonely desert,
  Lay moor and grey glen where small knolls stood,
With shaggy tufts and with warm soft shelter—
  Choice spots for wild birds to rear their brood:
Thence from soft couches in May's sweet morning
  Rose up the dun doe and stag of ten;
While glanced the red light upon the tall sides
  Of the rough Corry—the Misty Glen!

E

INTRODUCTION TO "MAIRI BHAN OG."

DUNCAN BAN was still a young man when, according to his own account, at "the board of the change-house" he first saw "*Màiri Bhàn òg*," the Bonny Jean of Gaelic poetry, whose name has been sung in some of the finest and tenderest, manliest and sincerest of Highland songs. Duncan Ban at the time of his meeting with her was somewhat poorer than she was. The father of *Màiri Bhàn* had been a baron bailiff—a small freeholder, or sort of under-factor in the neighbourhood, and she, as the poet tells us, had some cows and calves of her own for her dowry. He, however, fell in love with her at once, and for three months suffered a death-pang; for he was afraid she would despise him on account of his want of wealth. He attempts to excuse his poverty in the first song he addresses to her, saying that twelve things had kept him poor; and of these he enumerates ten, viz., drink, the feast, and weddings, music, manners, purchases, gay meetings, wooers' gifts, and thoughtlessness and youth. But *Màiri Bhàn* had too kind a heart, too fine a nature, and too delicate a perception to think little of her admirer because he was not rich. The poet got no reason to despair, and he soon recovered, under her gentle treatment, from his three months' pain.

Duncan Ban represents his young heroine as somewhat tall and round, and graceful; with a profusion of curly fair hair, a pure complexion, white teeth, fine eyebrows that knew not a frown, and a mouth from which, of all others, the mountain lays had the sweetest sound. She had a good temper, a lively disposition, a light foot, and a happy heart. So gay was she, she made her love's heart dance with rapture when she was playful. So winning a way was hers, she could, when she pleased, draw from him his dearest secrets; "There was not a thing worth the telling but she could soon wile me to say." She was gentle, humane, almsgiving, liberal—she was like the surpassing bough in the forest that is covered with blossoms—like the fresh sea-trout just landed from the river, and yet lying on the green bank, splendid, and dazzling, and white. She was the star of the morning, whose beauty delighted every bosom. But that which delighted him most was that firmness in good which was hers. Yet was she very accomplished and very useful—the best of dancers to the pipe or fiddle, the cheeriest of companions, the most attractive of speakers. On summer evenings she could milk the cows at the fold by the bend of the river, while the calves around her played; or in winter, with her well-formed and lady-like hand, sew her bands, and her plain seams—yes, and the rarest embroidery, in the lighted room that shone like day. This is the portrait, drawn by a loving hand of the most famous of Highland humble maidens. Duncan Ban thought he had secured an inestimable prize, far more than he deserved, when he got for his own this peerless milker of the cows, this "prettiest low-born lass" that trode the Argyllshire heather.

Màiri Bhàn is the heroine of three of Duncan Ban's published Songs. One of these, "A song to his Spouse newly wedded," here given, is considered, on account of its united purity and passion, its grace, delicacy and good feeling, to be the finest love song in the Gaelic language. Not but there is at least another, namely, MacDonald's "Address to Morag," which is held to be quite as good, taken merely as an intellectual display, or a vehicle of passion of a certain kind. The stanzas in the present poem, beginning, "I went to the wood," &c., and, "I cast out my net," &c., have been very generally admired, but not less commendable is the concluding verse, "I'd plough or drive in spring-time for thee," &c. The verses that follow from "Thy manners were womanly ever," give a very fine picture of truly amiable feminine characteristics. It is very pleasant to hear the poet tell his young wife,—

> "On the good thou has done, I'm persuaded
> Thy spirit for ever shall feed."

And also, notwithstanding all her beauty, with which she delights every bosom,—

> "What makes me rate thee the highest
> Is that firmness in good which is thine."

Take notice too, how respectful he is with the amiable young milkmaid,—

> "When I took her apart for a moment,
> To speak of my love and my pride,
> My ear caught the fluttering tumult
> Of my heart beating fast on my side."

Then there is something very manly and sensible, surely, as well as affectionate, in his assuring *Màiri Bhàn*,—

> "Ne'er shall the hearth's harsh wrangling tease thee,
> Nor make thy clear temper its prey."

While the deep feeling and delicate pathos of this truly tender exclamation cannot be overlooked,—

> "Oh! could I but take thee and hide thee
> In a place well secured from decay."

This is indeed a poem which is altogether very creditable to its author, and pleasant to comment upon, in evidence of the goodness of both his head and his heart.

A SONG TO HIS SPOUSE, NEWLY WEDDED.

Màiri Bhàn òg,* thou girl ever thought of,
  Still where I am may thou be,
Since the clerk-given right, so long wish'd for,
  I've got, dear wife! over thee.

---

* "*Màiri Bhàn òg*" means, Fair Young Mary, "The *ai* in *Màiri* is pronounced like the *a* in father."

With cov'nants and bands, strong and lasting,
    A knot now ties thee to me;
That thou art mine, with thy friends all consenting,
    Fills me with health and with glee.

When sick in our courtship's beginning,
    To me none in kindness came near;
'T was then, at the board of the ale-house,
    I marked the sweet girl now so dear:
I drew to her side, and she promised
    My life with her love to cheer;
Oh! the joy when I won her, and with her,
    A part of the old baron's gear.

Monday morning—long though the journey
    I travelled to meet with my bride;
I ran like the wind to be bound in
    The knot that will ne'er be untied:
I took her apart for a moment,
    To speak of my love and my pride;
And my ear caught the fluttering tumult
    Of my heart beating fast on my side.

For Cupid had shot a whole bundle
    Of sharp-winged darts in my breast,
That dried up my pulses, and downward
    My strength like a burden press'd:
Then I told the sweet cause of my anguish,
    How no Leech could give me rest;
But my wounds, with her virtues, she cured them,
    As myself she gently caress'd.

Then kiss'd I the round and soft maiden
    Who'd grown up so mild and so sweet—
So comely so tall, and so curly,
    So womanly, graceful, and neat:

In many a way am I favour'd,
   Such a love as hers to meet ;
When her vows and herself she gives me,
   A cheaply bought bargain I greet.

I went to the wood with its saplings,
   And glorious it looked all around ;
But my eye caught a spray, all surpassing
   High in the dusky shade found ;
It was quite covered over with blossoms—
   I bent it down to the ground,
And cut it—a sad sight for many ;
   But my fate with it was bound.

I cast out my net in true waters,*
   And strained hard to draw it to land,
And, lo ! I had caught a bright sea-trout,
   That lay like a swan on the strand :
Pleased was my soul with the fortune
   That came with such joy to my hand .
My spouse ! thou 'rt the star of the morning !
   Blest be thy slumbers and bland !

Thy manners were womanly ever,
   Gentle in word and in deed ;

---

* Water that flows from a spring is called, "true water" in Gaelic. It shows the originality of Duncan Ban's mind thus to have drawn his similes from his own occupations, chosen them so well, and used them so happily. A sea-trout, just fresh from the ocean, is always pure and bright looking. Any person who has had the good fortune to see one caught at the mouth of the sea, as the darkness came on, will no doubt remember how it flashed with a silvery lustre among the other fishes, almost indeed "like the star of the morning." I once saw one caught accidentally in this way, by some working people who were, with their nets, dragging a little port near a river for saithe. Whenever the net touched the shore, the stranger that was entangled in it, leaping and glittering so lively and bright, attracted every eye, and when landed it really did lie "like a swan on the strand." Something of this sort must have been in Duncan Ban's mind. He had cast

So genial, so kind, and so glowing—
　Free of grudging, and closeness, and greed;
Almsgiving, liberal, pitying,
　Humane with all that had need;
On the good thou has done, I'm persuaded,
　Thy spirit for ever shall feed.

When I studied to form thy acquaintance,
　With words that were courteous and gay,
Thy breath smelt as sweet as the apples,
　Golden and ripe on the spray:
There was not a thing worth the telling
　That thou couldst not wile me to say;
And shouldst thou now leave me, the linen
　And grave soon would hide me away

Thy talk and thy singing are pleasant,
　Thy nature is charming always—
Mirthful, noble, and free from
　A shade of reproach or disgrace.
For three months I suffered a death-pang;
　But once thou hadst heard of my case,
A treasure of solace thou gav'st me,
　Of sorrow it left not a trace.

Since last year I've risen in value,
　With the calves thou broughtest and kine;
Now a choice sheaf of wheat, ripe and rustling,
　With the best of corn is mine:
But what makes me rate thee the highest,
　Is that firmness in good which is thine;

his net into the waters, and instead of landing an ordinary fish like the others, lo! his was a bright sea-trout, that lay like a swan among the rest. So also with the preceding verse, he had not merely got a green bough like others, but one that was "quite covered over with blossoms," beautiful and blooming with sweet hopes. The imagery is particularly fresh and charming in both verses.

Yet thy beauties delight every bosom,
  So sweetly and softly they shine.

Thy fair hair, close set and excelling,
  Rolls in curls and wavelets free;
Thy features are mild, modest, womanly,
  Fine eyebrows, where frowns never be.
A winning blue eye, full, smooth-lidded;
  No fault in thy face I see;
Thy teeth are strong, white as ivory;
  Thy still mouth speaks modestly.

Thy breast's like the fresh and smooth pebble
  That lies on the shore day and night;
Thy body so slender and stately,
  Like cannach is pure and white.
Soft and thin is thy palm, fine thy fingers,
  The lady's warm hand, shoulders bright;
Thy foot in its shoe is close-fitting;
  Graceful thy step is and light.

The lone shieling glen canst thou traverse,
  Where the wandering cattle stray;
At the bend of the river to milk them,
  While the calves around thee play;
Nor less is thy worth near the candle,
  In the room that shines like day;
Sewing thy bands and plain seams,
  Or working embroidery gay.

Mild art thou, wife, come from Mam-Charry,
  Thy love steals my senses away;
For a heart such as thine is, Oh! surely
  Small was the price I'd to pay!
The blood of great nobles and famous
  Rolls in thy blue pulses' play—
The blood of the King and Mac-Cailean,
  And him who in Sleat held the sway

Oh! could I but take thee and hide thee
  In a place well secured from decay;
For now, should death leave me without thee,
  I'd love not another for aye;
But ne'er shall the hearth's harsh wrangling tease thee,
  Nor make thy clear temper its prey
Thou shall hear but the choice of clear measures
  My mouth can sing or can say.

I'd plough or drive in the spring-time for thee,
  When the young horse in harness is dress'd,
Or seek on the shore with the fishers
  Whate'er to the hook wileth best;
I'd kill for thee swans, seals, and wild geese,
  And birds on the bough that rest;
Nor e'er shall thou want while a forest,
  Lies near with one antler's crest.

On occasion of some visit to Edinburgh, Duncan Ban composed a song in praise of Dunedin, in which he chronicles minutely everything he thought worth noticing in the city; but, as will be seen, he regards all the novelties he speaks of with that clear intelligence and steadfast heart, neither attracted or repelled by the mere strangeness of the scenes and habits he refers to, which indicate of themselves no small amount of talent. The song on Edinburgh is as follows:—

THE PRAISE OF DUNEDIN.

'Tis a great town Dunedin,
  It charmed me to be there;
A broad and hospitable place,
  And pleasant everywhere:

With a garrison—a battery—
  A rampart tight and good—
A castle—and great houses
  Where camps right often stood.

A royal camp stood often here;
  And beautiful 't would be,
With troops of horsemen plentiful,
  To guard it faithfully;
And everyone so disciplined
  In every art of war—
Before you got a rank like theirs
  You might search near and far.

Here's many a gallant gentleman
  Who is polished and well-bred,
Wears powder plaster'd on his hair
  To the crown of his head;
With folds and plaits, and many curls,
  Well-woven, over-spread;
And, on the top, a bunch like silk
  When the card has smooth'd its thread!

There's many a noble lady
  A poor man here may meet,
In gown of silk and satin
  That sweeps along the street;
And every pretty thing wears stays,
  To keep her straight and spare;
And beauty spots on her fair face,
  To make her still more rare.

Each one, as well becomes her,
  Polite among the rest;
And proud, and rich, and ribbony,
  And round and gaily dress'd :

The clothes on the young maidens
    Just showing to your eye
A strong and pointed well-made shoe—
    I thought its heels too high.

When I went to the Abbey
    It was a noble sight
To see the kings in order,
    From King Fergus, as was right;
But now, since they are gone from us.
    Our Alba wants the Crown—
No wonder, then, her once gay Court
    Is like a desert grown.

There is a lantern made of glass,
    With a candle in each place,
That yields a light to every eye
    Around a litle space.
Nor less a cause of pleasure
    Are the instruments they play,
That give a sweeter music
    Than the cuckoo does in May.

A stately sound the coaches make,
    With their trotting and their whirr;
The hard-hoof'd, smooth-pac'd horses
    They always keep a stir:
They frisk and raise their heads on high,
    In their spirited career;
Not such our heather pastures,
    Nor the wild moorlands rear.

In the close of the Parliament,
    There the same horse is shown,
Still standing where he used to stand,
    On the bare way of stone;

They've bridled him and saddled him,
　　And set the King* thereon,
Whose was the right of all these realms,
　　Though they banish'd far his son.

The great House of the Parliament
　　Is worthy a good view;
There reasonable gentlemen
　　Deliver judgments true:
They have a power given them,
　　Will last them many a day—
To hang the faulty up on high,
　　And let the good away.

And here a Healing-house I see,
　　Where the best Leeches go;
And cure each kind of suffering
　　That limb and body know:
The man who is in want of health,
　　Whom Leeches long attend,
Here is the place for him to come,
　　And keep him from his end.

Dunedin is a bonny place
　　In far more ways than one—
A town that must not yield to it
　　In this whole realm is none.
So many gentlemen are there,
　　Of tribute-raising line—
Men who may daily quench their thirst
　　With the good Spanish wine.

---

* The Statue of King Charles the Second, in the Parliament Square, is here referred to, although Duncan Ban speaks of it as if it were that of King James the Second.

Though great and long the distance
    From Glasgow unto Perth,
Yet am I sure, although I saw
    Each mansion there of worth,
I could see none more charming
    Than the Abbey or the Bank ;
Or houses rich and large, whose guests
    Might be of kingly rank.

FROM THE "SONG OF GLENORCHY,"

The Bard's birth-place, and where there is now an appropriate monument erected to his memory. Contributions to the fund for raising this well deserved monument, came from all parts of the world.

    CLACHAN-an-Diseirt,*
        How pleasant to be there,
    Sitting in its wondrous church,
        Its pew so richly fair ;
    And listening to his mellow voice,
        Whose council none should spurn,
    The Bible tale rehearsing,
        That yields the great return.

    That Glen is dry and balmy,
        All good things there are grown ;

---

* The derivation of this name is interesting. "Clachan" means, in the first place, a village where there is a place of worship. Clachan-an-diseirt is resolved then into "Clachan an Dé 's àirde," *i.e.* The worshipping place of the highest God. This name, like Dundee, had its origin probably in early Pagan times.

In little level inches,*
   Where the seed-corn is sown;
And where the ripening crop gets white,
   As curds upon the whey,
Productive, sappy, wholesome,
   In regular array.

In winter was it cheerful,
   Such sports in weddings gave,
When all, without a heavy thought,
   Heard the smooth pibrochs rave;
While fiddlers on the lively strings,
   The dance-tunes played so well;
And damsels lent their voices,
   The cheerful sound to swell.

The spring-water salmon there
   Winds all the streamlets through;
Hill-birds are there in numbers,
   And thousand black-cocks too.
The small doe paws beside her kid,
   And strong bucks not a few,
In that Glen's wild forest scenes,
   The gallant youths pursue.

. . . . . .

Then when we all drew homeward
   It was our pleasant way,
To gather to the tavern
   For dance and song and play.
Cordial one to another,
   The hides for pay were near;
So when they cried "Another stoup,"
   No hunter felt a fear.

---

* Inches—in Gaelic, Innis—sometimes an Island—sometimes choice pasture land, such especially as the green round flats on the banks of a river.

Duncan Ban was the author of several convivial songs, which are very popular. The one which follows is certainly not the longest of the most elaborate of these, but it contains at least some relics of old manners which may make it interesting. Whatever opinion may be entertained of the dram in the morning there can be no doubt that there is a most estimable cordiality—a cheerful look of dear and genuine, though old-fashioned kindness, about the hospitable lady in the second verse of this song, who leaves her room in the early morning, and meets her guests with the big bottle in her hand, filled to the brim with Usquebay,

> " And as we drink to one another,
> You are welcome,' doth she say."

A RHYME TO THIRST.

Woeful after health is sorrow;
  Thirst is after drink as sore;
Sad to sit the board surrounding
  When the stoup is filled no more.
I like to see our cordial gentry,
  With their store of wealth alway;
Who can drink whene'er they're thirsty,
  And off-hand the women pay.

A dram is pleasant in the morning,
  When it comes at peep of day;
As the lady leaves her chamber,
  To spread pleasure on her way.
The big bottle in her hand,
  Full to the brim of Usquebay,
And as we drink to one another,
  "You are welcome," doth she say.

'Tis the right fashion in the tavern,
  With great might it fills the breast
He who does not like the brandy,
  Abuses us because we taste.
But the boon companion says thus,
  " Fill again the cup I pray—
Much the jovial drink upbraids me,
  But my thirst will not away."

INTRODUCTION TO
"LAST FAREWELL TO THE HILLS."

DUNCAN BAN visited the Highlands after an absence of many years, and spent a whole autumn day in wandering, with melancholy pleasure, over Ben Dorain, whose beauties and delights he had, years before, sung and celebrated so joyously in his longest poem. It was one of the favourite haunts of his youth, and vigorous manhood. Near it he was born ; on it he had a thousand times hunted the deer, feeding his thoughts meanwhile with music taken from the bards of other days, or drawn from the sweet, unpretending fountain of his own inspiration. Then his heart was full of life, his mind and body overflowing with energy. Then the fresh breath of young vitality played about his nostrils like a mellow breeze of summer, singing down the rude, rough gorge, and waving the green heather, and then the wild hill and its environs were oft times trod by gallant, friendly youths, and sometimes cheered by the sweet lilt of kind, warm-hearted women. But now the whole was changed. The poet himself was getting old. He could run, and leap, and press the heady chase no more. The mirthful shieling had vanished, and the song of the women was terribly and solemnly silent. The friends of his youth, with whom he had trod the wide stretching moor so often—

where were those friends he loved? Alas! even the hill itself was changed. Its proud sights were gone—its grandly sweeping troops of wild deer, its graceful does, its innocent and lovely fawns. Its sweetest music, the brave crowing of its red-cock and its black-cock was nowhere to be heard. The very heather had disappeared, and sheep, sheep everywhere, were all that could be seen. "Oh! dear," said the poet, "when I looked round and perceived this I could not feel gay. Since the hill itself has changed, surely the world has deceived me." Such is the spirit of the song composed by Duncan Ban on occasion of his last visit to Ben Dorain, as he looked in the multitude of his tender thoughts on the well-known scenes whose every step was alive to him with the stirring sentiment—the moving memory of other years. "Sweet, though mournful to the soul, is the memory of the years that are past;" and Duncan Ban, touched by that sacred sorrow, so often the inspiration of his most celebrated poetic countryman, and breathing this most natural of human plaints, "Ah! for the change 'twixt now and then!" embodied the elevating emotion that filled him, in melodious verse. This song of his is interesting, not merely on account of its delicate, intellectual pensiveness, its true love and devotion, and its pure sentiments; not merely on account of the originally humble condition of its author, whose total want of education did not prevent his feelings and reflections from being attractive, nor his expression of them from being eloquent and delicate. It is interesting even on account of the great age of the fine old man at the date of its composition, 19th September, 1802. Duncan Ban was then seventy-eight years old. Not many poets have lived to that age, very few of them have used their strength, and fed their lamp so well, as to compose some of their best poetry so late in life. There is a sadness even in the title of this ballad of fading years, "The last Farewell to the Hills." The poet had made up his mind to look on the dear scene no more.

Why, or by whom this day is so carefully noted, does not appear; but this is the only one of Duncan Ban's compositions which is so accurately dated.

THE LAST FAREWELL TO THE HILLS.

Ben Dorain I saw yesterday,
   And trod its gorges grey,
Amid its well-known dells and glens,
   No strangers did I stray;
And think how joyful 'twas of yore,
   To seek that mountain high,
As the sun shone o'er the morning hoar,
   And the deer were belling by.

How charming was their lordly herd,
   When loud they rushed away,
While fawn and doe they scarcely stirred,
   Where by the fount they lay;
Then did the roe-buck bellow round,
   The black-cock, red-cock crow,
I think, than these, no sweeter sound
   Can morning ever know.

How cheerfully I rose and went
   The rugged brakes to roam,
I sought them early, but unspent,
   Though late I wandered home;
For the breath of those great mountains,
   Was health and strength to me,
And a fresh draught from the fountains,
   Like a new life would be.

And once I stayed a little while,
   In a gay shieling near,

With sport, and mirth, and laugh, and smile,
    And woman's kindness dear :
Alas, 'twas not in nature's power,
    That such blythe joy should last,—
Too swiftly came the parting hour,—
    I sighed and onward pass'd.

And now old age has struck me sore,
    With its long lingering blight,
My teeth are fresh and sound no more ;
    Ah! me, my fading sight.
I could not now give eager heed,
    If the chase should cheer the day ;
Whatever now should be my need
    I could not haste away.

Yet though my hair be hoary white,
    And my beard thinner grown,
Than when upon the proud stag's flight
    My greyhounds fast have flown,
I ween the chase still charms my heart,
    Though if it swept yon heath,
I could not do my wonted part,
    With this remnant of my breath.

Ill could I drive its headlong pride
    As once I used to do,
By glen, and dell, and mountain side,
    Rough stream, and mosses through.
Ill could I join a social throng,
    And share their autumn cheer,
Ill could I sing a pleasant song
    At the falling of the year.

My days were in their spring-time then,
    And follies kept me poor ;
Though nought, save luck, renews to men
    Their good, or keeps secure.

In that belief content I live,
    Though far from rich I be,
For George's daughter* still will give,
    I hope, my bread to me.

And yesterday I trod yon moor—
    How many a thought it moved!
The friends I walked with there of old—
    Where were those friends I loved!
I looked and looked, and sheep, sheep still
    Were all that I could see:
A change had struck the very hill—
    O world! deceiving me.

As I turned round from side to side,
    Oh dear! I felt not gay;
The heather's bloom, the greenwood's pride,
    The old men were away:
There was not left one antlered stag,
    There was not left a roe;
No bird to fill the hunter's bag—
    Such old things—all must go.

Then wild heath forest, fare-you-well,
    Ye wonderful bright hills;
Farewell sweet spring and grassy dell—
    Farewell the running rills,—
Farewell vast deserts, mountains grand,
    With peaks the clouds that sever;
Scenes of past pleasures pure and bland—
    Farewell, farewell for ever!

---

* "George's daughter" was the musket which he carried in King George's name, as a member of the city-guard. The gun which he used among the hills he called, "Nic Coiseam," or "Coiseam's daughter." He composed a characteristic song to both these weapons.

DUGALD BUCHANAN.

DUGALD BUCHANAN, a man of somewhat remarkable character, one of the earliest, and still the most esteemed of the Gaelic writers of Sacred Poetry, was born in Strathtyre, in the parish of Balquhidder, Perthshire, in in the year, 1716. We are told by himself that both his parents were religious, but especially his mother, who taught him to pray as soon as he could speak; and strove earnestly to engraft on his young mind those strict principles of doctrinal piety by which her own life was actuated. But she died when he was only six years of age, and for twenty years after he underwent a severe moral discipline, in vain attempts to get rid of religious convictions altogether, or in equally useless endeavours to reconcile his heart to the stern form in which the Christian faith seems to have been presented to him. Of this momentous period of his life he has left a long and elaborate account, written in English, in a good style—sometimes with considerable force, and displaying occasional marks of his imaginative talent. From it we learn that when still quite young he learned to curse and swear, that he became very loose and immoral in his habits, and associated much with bad company; that on these accounts he suffered frequently and severely from the reproaches of conscience, and a remorseful sense of guilt, until finally, and by slow degrees, he attained unto the repose of steadfast principle and devout faith. The book closes with a dedication of himself to God, which the author solemnly signs. Its concluding words are as follows:—" Now, Lord, let the dedication of myself to thee, and my accepting of thee as my God in Christ, and my being the subject of thy spiritual work, be not like the day that is past and cannot be recalled again,—let it be ratified in heaven and I will sign it upon earth.

DUGALD BUCHANAN."

Buchanan's parents, who were in pretty easy circumstances, appear to have given their children as fair an amount of education as the Highlands could afford in their day: Dugald, particularly, was so well grounded that at the age of twelve years he was considered qualified to look after the education of a young family who lived at some distance from his father's farm of Ardoch. In his Memoir he adverts to this circumstance as follows:—
" When about twelve years of age I was called to a family for the purpose of teaching the children to read; for at that time I was sufficiently qualified to read the Bible. This family, into which I came, was singular for every species of wickedness; each one of its members exceeding the other in cursing, swearing, and other vices, with the exception of the mistress who, I believe, feared the Lord. She was like Lot in Sodom. I was scarcely a month in this family when I learned to speak the language of Ashdod; yea, in a short time I exceeded every one of themselves—so much so that I could not speak without uttering oaths and imprecations, and my conscience being lulled asleep, I sinned without restraint, except occasionally when I would think of death."

After leaving this situation, Buchanan attended school at his native village for two years, and was then removed to Stirling for other two years, and afterwards sent to Edinburgh for six months, that he might enjoy the benefit of the superior means of education these places possessed. His father, at this time, is said to have intended him for a profession, but changed his mind in consequence of his son's loose and reckless habits, and unsettled principles. He urged on him therefore to make choice of some trade, which Buchanan at last did—binding himself apprentice for three years to a relative of his own,—a house-carpenter at Kippen. He quarrelled with his master, however, before his term was out, and leaving him, went to Dumbarton, where he engaged with some other person in the same trade. He does not seem to have remained very long here either, for in his twenty-sixth year we find him settled in his native village of Ardoch, in possession of a mill which formerly belonged to his father, and following the occupation of a miller. In this situation he does not appear to have been very successful, as he is next found, not many years after, in charge of a small school in a remote village in Perthshire. Out of this obscurity, however, he began to be generally known and respected, as the author of some excellent religious poetry, and as a man of exemplary character, and interest was made for him with "The Society for Propagating Christian Knowledge in Scotland," who at once appointed him as one of their teachers.

In 1755 he was appointed Schoolmaster and Catechist at Kinloch Rannoch, and he laboured there faithfully until his death, thirteen years after. Kinloch Rannoch formed part of an immense parish in those days. The minister, or his assistant, was only able to visit it once in the three weeks, so the Sundays, according to Buchanan's biographer, were spent "in vain and sinful amusements." As he could not by any means induce them to come to join with him in worship, he at last followed the people to their own gatherings, and reasoned with them there with such power and effect, that he gradually brought them to a more sober and devout frame of mind, and they attended readily on his ministrations. He preached with such fervour and eloquence, that by and bye crowds from all parts came to hear him, until his school-room was found much too small to hold the numbers that were attracted to his meetings. Then he used to adjourn with them to a rising ground on the banks of the river Tummel, where, in the open air, his hearers mingled their praises with the sound of the murmuring waters.

Soon his fame as a preacher became so great, and his usefulness so evident, that a request was made to the Presbytery of Dunkeld, to give him a regular licence as a preacher of the Church of Scotland; but there were technical difficulties in the way of meeting this wish, and so the matter dropt. Nor was the modest poet himself at all disconcerted at this issue to the well-meant kindness of his friends.

Buchanan was in Edinburgh in 1766, superintending the printing of the Gaelic New Testament. While in that city he took the opportunity offered him of increasing his knowledge and cultivating his mind, by attending the classes for Natural Philosophy, Anatomy, and Astronomy, at the University.

In 1768 he died of fever, in the fifty-second year of his age. In May of that year he returned home from a long journey, to find his family suffering from this disorder, which soon seized upon himself. All his children, his two servants, and himself, were ill at the same time. His wife then about to be confined, could get no one to assist her in attending on them; so great was the dread of infection entertained by their neighbours. In his delirium Buchanan frequently sang psalms, and spoke of the Lamb in the midst of the throne. On the second of June he died.

In Reid's "Bibliotheca Scoto-Celtica," it is asserted, that the poet's whole family, six in number, was carried off by the same fever, and at the same time as their father. But this is a mistake. Buchanan left two sons and two daughters behind him—one of the latter was alive in 1836.

In person Buchanan was considerably above the middle size, and of a dark complexion. His face is said to have been very expressive of kindness and benevolence, especially on a near view. Among his familiar acquaintance he was cheerful and sociable; his company being much sought after on account of his stock of pleasant anecdotes, and generally intelligent conversation. His usual dress was a blue bonnet and a black suit, over which he often wore a blue great-coat. He was so highly respected that great numbers gathered to attend his funeral, many of them from a far distance. The people of Kinloch Rannoch, fondly attached to him, wished to have him buried among themselves, but that his kindred—equally attached to his memory—would not permit; and so they carried his remains to his native place. A plain stone with a neat inscription, marks the spot where his ashes rest, in the burial ground of the Buchanans, at Little Lenny, near Callander. In 1883 a monument was erected to his memory at Strathtyre.

His "Spiritual Songs," of which there are only eight in all, were first collected and published in 1767. His "Memoir of himself" was first printed in 1853. How or where it was preserved so long does not appear; but its genuineness is not doubted. It has been translated into Gaelic, and is now, in its original shape, out of print. His poetry is extremely popular, and has gone through nearly twenty editions. No other book that has appeared in Gaelic has been so extensively circulated. This is undoubtedly due, in some measure to its religious character; it being a work which can be conscientiously and profitably read on the working man's "Great Leisure Day." It is also partly owing to its being very widely distributed through means of the "Colporteurs" that travel over the Highlands. Something too may be allowed for its price, which is at present only threepence, and a good deal still left for its own merits, which are truly great.

Buchanan has been called the Cowper of the Highlands, but his poetry bears little resemblance to Cowper's. It is much more like Blair's, the author of "The Grave." Once or twice he is indebted to Dr. Watts for his subject, and partly too for his manner of dealing with it, as in the hymn entitled, "The Hero;" not that there is discernible here or anywhere else in his writings such a thing as servile imitation. But he is the only one of the Highland poets whose works display any trace of their author's English reading. He was, however, the one who, if not the most learned in some points, was at least the best informed, probably of them all.

There is a letter of Buchanan's extant, a somewhat remarkable production, published originally in a volume of "Consolatory Letters, addressed to bereaved mourners," collected and edited by Dr. Erskine, one of the ministers of Edinburgh in the last century. In this letter we find Milton quoted, a work of Dr. Watts referred to, and the following passage which contains, either a striking, undesigned coincidence with part of Constance's lamentation for Arthur in "King John," or manifests some sort of acquaintance with Shakespeare. The letter is addressed to friends of Buchanan's who had lately lost one of their children, and the poet writes thus:—"Our memories, treacherous enough on other occasions, here are over-faithful, and cruelly muster up in a long succession all the amiable qualities of our departed friends, and thus tear open our wounds to bleed afresh. Imagination is set to work, and *stuffs up their empty garments in their former shape*, when we miss them at bed or table." In like manner, but in no better terms, Constance says, almost in the same words however,

"Grief stuffs out his vacant garments with his form."

Dugald Buchanan's "Spiritual Songs" exhibit, on the whole, great vigour of thought and expression, and bear the stamp of a solid understanding, and of an imagination capable of lofty excitement. Perhaps the best and most characteristic of his productions is the poem of "The Skull," from which an extract is here given:—

THE SKULL.

The grave was new-made,
And a skull had been laid,
Close to its brink on the ground,
  I stooped where it lay,
  And my tears welled away
As I raised it, and turned it around.

No beauty was there,
No knowledge, no care
Of the men that passed it by—
  Its jaws both were bare,
  And no tongue now could e'er
In its empty mouth sing melody.

Yet this cheek once was red,
And thick locks clothed this head,
And this ear once could list to my song;
  And these nostrils could smell,
  That damp earth soon and well,
Now so weak where they all were so strong.

There no lustrous orb glows,
And no lids ope or close;
There's no sight the known pathway to trace;
  But the gross worms instead
  Have for long made their bed,
And dug holes in the eyes' wonted place.

Aye, such looks will not show,
What thou wast long ago;
Whether King's skull or Duke's I now hold:
  Alexander the Great
  Thus owns no more state
Than his slave on the dunghill cold.

Come thou grave-digger near,—
  Come and tell in my ear
Whose it is I have got in my hand;
  Till I question the head
  Of the life it once led,
Though little 'twill heed my demand.

Wert thou once some young maid
  In beauty arrayed,
And virtuous and pure in thy ways,—
  With thy charms fairly set,
  To ensnare like a net,
The hearts of the young with their grace?

And now those bright charms,
  That woke love's sweet alarms,
Are thus loathsome to every one.
  Out, out on the grave.
  That spoiled thee so bare
Of that beauty such triumphs that won.

. . . . .

Or wert thou the Leech,
  Who thy patients could teach
Every ache, every pain to allay—
  Boasting elate,
  Thy specific so great,
That could snatch from Death's hand his prey?

Alas! and that power
  Was lost in the hour
When relief thy own sickness did crave—
  And then all thy skill,
  In the bolus and pill,
Could not keep thee a day from thy grave.

Or in tavern rout,
Didst thou revel and shout,
With the mirth which the dram-drinking bred?
And never a thought
Of God's providence sought,
If the barm raised it not in thy head?

No music was there,
But to curse and to swear,
As you tried whose fist was the best;
Till, as senseless and coarse
As a cow or a horse,
You lay dizzy and spewed in your rest.

. . . . .

Or some great man and grand,
Do I hold in my hand—
Lord of acres, fertile and wide,
Who kindness would show
To the mean man and low,
And the poor from his plenty supplied?

Or didst thou, with hard mind,
Thy weak tenantry grind,
And thin their worn hair 'neath thy sway—
With thy law's cruel mock,
Distraining their stock,
Though their poverty moaned for delay?

Letting them stand,
With bonnet in hand,
When they dared in thy presence appear:
And making so light
Of their locks thin and white,
And the wind that blew aches in their ear.

Now the poor drudge,
Free of rent and of judge,
Unrespecting lies down by thy side:
　Great praise be to Death,
　Who so soon stopt thy breath,
Nor 'neath the sod suffered thy pride.

. . . . .

Or once in this head
Was godly faith fed—
Didst thou walk in the way of the wise;
　Then, though thou liest there,
　So naked and bare,
Without nose or tongue or eyes.

Be bold,—do not grieve,
For yet thou shalt leave
At the sound of the trumpet blast,
　This baseness behind,
　With the earth-worm that's blind,
When the grave and its power is past.

. . . . .

The opening stanzas of Buchanan's Spiritual Song, called "Winter," are as follows. After giving a description of the season, the poet moralizes over it, and applies it according to his manner:—

The Summer now leaves us,
And near Winter grieves us—
Vegetation's true foe;
　For our havoc who's braced,
When for spoil thus he rises,
All grace he despises,
Free of softness and pity,
　Full of plunder and waste.

His dark wings overspreading,
And the solar rays shading,
From their nest he calls forth
   His chill ravaging brood;
Snow pure white, and flying,
Or in drifts and heaps lying,
And hailstones like shot,
   And the north's stormy mood.

Once he breathes in his power,
Then its soul leaves the flower;
His lips clip like scissors
   The garden's pride bare;
Woods and groves he assails them—
Of their gay garb unveils them,
And the streamlets he chokes
   While his dark flags they wear.

His breast's frozen whistle
Calls the wild winds to bristle—
Tha barm-swollen ocean
   That rolls rough and high:
And he curdles the sleet-shower
The hill-tops that flits o'er,
And clean scours the stars,
   Till they dazzle the eye.

FROM THE DAY OF JUDGMENT.

Oh! ye who did the world so prize,
   Come now and see its doleful case;
When, like a man that struggling dies,
   It sinks in death's most fell embrace.

Its cold, clear veins that knew no rest,
   But coursed the glen with playful pride,

Now shrink within its burning breast,
    And boiling, thread the mountain side.

How the world quakes! Lo! the great stones
    And rocks that fall from off the hill;
Oh! hear those heavy, deadly groans
    That through its bursting bosom thrill.

There the blue curtain from the sun,
    That, cloak-like, round the globe was spread,
In fierce fire shrivels up, undone,
    Like a thin leaf on embers red.

And dense clouds choke the air throughout,
    With dark smoke-heaps about it wound,
For which the flames, far-flashing, spout
    In curls that wreath and twirl around.

And over all the earth there rise
    Dread and loud-sounding thunder peals,
Whose lightning, with the glorious skies,
    Like sparks with the dry heather deals.

But more—to swell the tumult yet—
    From all their arts the strong winds stray,
Like angels for destruction met,
    And haste this wasting work each way!

"The Day of Judgment," consisting of one hundred and twenty-seven verses, in the measure given above, is the longest of Buchanan's poems. From what an early period that theme occupied his mind will appear from the following extract from his "Memoirs:"—"Then the Lord began to visit me with terrible visions—dreams in the night—which greatly frightened me. I always dreamed that the day of judgment was come, that Christ appeared in the clouds to judge the world; that all the people were gathered together before His throne; that He seperated them into two companies, the one on His right hand, the other on His left; and that I saw myself, along with others, sentenced to everlasting burnings. I always saw myself entering into the flames, and so would instantly awake in great fear and trembling. These dreams continued for about two years, so frequent that scarcely a month passed by in which I had not some such dream, and subsequently became so very frequent that I did not regard them. At last, however, they ceased, and I was no more troubled with them. This was about the ninth year of my age."

It is told of Buchanan that when in Edinburgh superintending the printing of the Gaelic translation of the New Testament, he became acquainted with several of the distinguished men of that city,—amongst others with David Hume, who asked the poet to his house. When Buchanan called he found the philosopher for a moment engaged, so he sat down, and while waiting for his host took up a book and began to read. The book was a volume of Shakespeare, and the place where Buchanan read was in "The Tempest." When Hume entered he asked his visitor what he had been reading, no doubt feeling curious to know what choice of book such a man would make, or what opinion he would form of an English classic. Buchanan told him, and pointed to those celebrated lines:—

> "And, like the baseless fabric of this vision,
> The cloud-capp'd towers, the gorgeous palaces,
> The solemn temples, the great globe itself,—
> Yea, all which it inherit shall dissolve;
> And, like this insubstantial pageant faded,
> Leave not a rack behind."

Hume asked him if he thought he had ever read anything so sublime before? Buchanan declared he had, and while admiring these lines he professed there was a book in his house which contained a somewhat similar passage, but even more sublime, " and this is it," he said. We have been told that he was a man on whom anything great or touching made a visible impression, causing him often even to shed tears; so, he no doubt, repeated very effectively those solemn verses:—" And I saw a great white throne, and him that sat on it, from whose face the earth and the heaven fled away; and there was found no place for them. And I saw the dead, small and great, stand before God; and the books were opened: and another book was opened, which is the book of life: And the dead were judged out of those things which were written in the books, according to their works. And the sea gave up the dead which were in it: and death and hell delivered up the dead which were in them; and they were judged every man according to their works." Rev. xx. 11-13. Hume said, "That is the Bible, sir. Yes, it is very sublime; but it never somehow struck me so forcibly before."

Buchanan, in his " Memoir," tells us of his lying awake a whole night in great terror during a storm of thunder, lightning, and hail, expecting every moment that the heavens were to open and the Judge to appear. He refers very frequently throughout the book to the same subject, so much so indeed as to show clearly that it was from first to last his great point of contact with the invisible world.

[In the life of the Rev. Alexander Duff, D.D., LL.D., the prince of Indian Missionaries, it is stated that "one of his constant schoolmasters out of school was the Gaelic poet, Dugald Buchanan, Catechist in the neighbouring Rannoch a century before, who has been well described as a sort of Highland repetition of John Bunyan in his spiritual experiences. The fire, the glow, of the missionary's genius was Celtic by nature, and by training. The fuel that kept the fire from smouldering away in a passive pensiveness was the prophetic denunciation, varied only by the subtle irony, of poems like "Latha 'Bhreitheanais"—*The Day of Judgement*, and "An Claigeann"—*The Skull*. The boy's great and fearful delight was to hear the Gaelic lamentations and poems of Buchanan, which have attained a popularity second only to the misty visions of Ossian read or rehearsed by his father and others who had committed them to memory."]

ROB DONN.

Robert MacKay, the Sutherlandshire Bard, commonly called, "Rob Donn, from the colour of his hair which was brown, was born in the parish of Durness, Sutherlandshire, in the year 1714. He very early showed his poetical talents,—some verses which he is said to have composed between his third and sixth year being still preserved. At the latter age he had the good fortune to attract, by his ability, the notice of a gentleman who took him into his own house, and kept him in his employment until the period of the bard's marriage. Shortly after this he was entrusted with the charge of his Chief's (Lord Reay) cattle, at that time an office, though a humble one, of considerable responsibility and trust. This office he held for the rest of his life, with the exception of two or three years, during which he was a soldier in the first regiment of Sutherland Highlanders, and another much shorter time while a misunderstanding of some sort caused a slight estrangement between him and his patron.

Rob Donn died in 1778, being then sixty four years old. He was greatly regretted over the whole country, where his fame is still most warmly cherished. No other of the Highland bards has had such justice done him after death as Rob Donn. A Doctor of Divinity collected, arranged, and edited his poetry, and wrote the Bard's biography. A monument was raised to his memory, and inscriptions composed for it in Gaelic, Greek, and Latin,* by a learned clergyman of the Church of

---

* The Gaelic epitaph has been translated into English by Professor Blackie of Edinburgh.

Scotland. And finally, Sir Walter Scott* himself reviewed, in "The Quarterly," Dr. Mackay's edition of Rob Donn's works, and gave his opinion that this illiterate herdsman was entitled to a place among the true sons of song. Rob Donn was certainly a very shrewd, clear-sighted mortal, with a certain musical turn in his mind, and with no contemptible powers of satire. That he was a poet no one can doubt who knows his wit, his point, and his sharpness. But even the verdict of Sir Walter cannot blind us to the fact, that Rob was not a man of lofty character, that he was somewhat wanting perhaps in deep feeling, and that, consequently, he had no very high powers of imagination. Very few, if any, of his own countrymen will be inclined to place him on the same pedestal with MacDonald or MacIntyre, but all are ready to acknowledge in him a sensible, intelligent, and remarkable man, with a really refreshing and influential gift of song.

The following pithy little poem entitled, " The Greedy Man and the World complaining against one another," may pass for a specimen of his satires. The Greedy Man opens the dialogue thus :—

GREEDY MAN.

Grudging art thou, O World ! and always art so,
Parting with those who have no wish to part so ;
The man whose greedy passions tie a string to thee,
Falls on his back with nothing when he pulls it free.

---

* Dr. MacKintosh MacKay's visit to Sir Walter Scott, at Abbotsford, in May, 1831, was the occasion of introducing to the notice of Lockhart the poems of Rob Donn, and this led to the well known review in the *Quarterly* of July, 1831. This review has often been ascribed to Scott, but was really written by Lockhart.

THE WORLD.

'Tis you, ye fickle men! who always start so;
Ill do ye keep by me who would not part so,
My sod supports you underneath, as you see;
But away you flit at once—and well may you be!

GREEDY MAN.

Oh! if thou wouldst keep me, I'd be thine indeed,
Since beneath the sun lies all the good I heed:
How canst thou let me go, perhaps to endless pain,
When of heaven than of thee I am far less fain?

THE WORLD.

Nay; but thou shouldst set thy wishes much more truly
Where lasting pleasure in return comes duly.
Although the boor I nourish for a season,
To keep him long I've neither might nor reason.

Rob Donn composed a great many songs; some of these are not considered of a very high quality, and some of them are not of a very pure character. One which took its rise on the poet's being forsaken by his sweetheart is the best of the number. Rob Donn, following his vocation in connection with his master's cattle, was absent on a certain occasion for more than a year from his native district. On his return he found his faithless mistress engaged to a fair-haired Lowland carpenter. The song is descriptive of his feelings on making this melancholy discovery. But Rob appears to have had so buoyant a temperament that he could not help being a little smart, even in his grief. He was the author of the music as well as the words of the song. Its title is this:—

THE SHIELING SONG.

Oh! sad is the shieling,
   And gone are its joys!
All harsh and unfeeling
   To me now its noise,
Since Anna—who warbled
   As sweet as the merle—
Forsook me—my honey-mouth'd,
   Merry-lipped girl!
      Heich! how I sigh;
      While the hour
    Lazily, lonelily,
      Sadly, goes by!

Last week, as I wander'd
   Up past the old trees,
I mourn'd, while I ponder'd,
   What changes one sees!
Just then the fair stranger
   Walk'd by with my dear—
Dreaming, unthinking,
   I had wander'd too near,
      Till, "Heich!" then I cried,—
      When I saw
    The girl, with her lover, draw
      Close to my side—

"Anna, the yellow-hair'd,
   Dost thou not see
How thy love unimpair'd
   Wearieth me?
'Twas as strong in my absence,
   When banish'd from thee—
As heart-stirring, powerful,
   Deep as you see—

>   Heich ! it is now,
>   At this time,
>   When up like a leafy bough,
>   High doth it climb."

Then, haughtily speaking,
    She airily said,
" 'Tis in vain for you seeking
    To hold up your head :
There were six wooers sought me
    While you were away ;
And the absentee surely
    Deserved less then they.
        Ha ! ha ! ha !
           Are you ill ?
        But if Love seeks to kill you—bah !
           Small is his skill ! "

Ach ! ach ! Now I'm trying
    My loss to forget—
With sorrow and sighing,
    With anger and fret.
But still that sweet image
    Steals over my heart ;
And still I deem fondly
    Hope need not depart.
        Heich ! and I say
           That our love,
        Firm as a tower gray,
           Nought can remove.

So Fancy beguiles me,
    And fills me with glee,
But the carpenter wiles thee,
    False speaker ! from me.
Yet from Love's first affection
    I never get free ;

> But the dear known direction
>   My thoughts ever flee.
>   Heich! when we stray'd
>   Far away,
>   Where soft shone the summer day
>   Through the green shade.

The airy, haughty, heartless coquette of this little ballad is sketched with considerable spirit. "Ha! ha! ha! Are you ill?" is a touch of Nature. One sees the poor disconsolate bard standing bewildered before her without a word in his head—so utterly cast down is he at the ill-placed mirth and cruel triumph of his fair-haired beauty. He has contrived, however, to make the lady show a little pique too,—"If love seeks to kill you—bah! small is his skill!"—as if to console himself with the idea that his old favourite was not so utterly destitute of feeling, nor her old love, after all, so easily cast off without leaving a trace behind.

It would not perhaps be altogether unsatisfactory to know that "Anna, the yellow-hair'd," met with some little bit of a disappointment herself in the end, in spite of her vaunted powers of attracting six lovers in one year, —and such is said to have been the case. A Gaelic note to this song declares that she married the fair-haired carpenter, but led an unhappy life with him, and never quite recovered her old spirits after the memorable parting at the shieling, recorded above.

The date of the following song is 1784. On the day when the news of the death of Henry Pelham, the prime minister, reached Durness, Rob Donn sallied forth among the neighbouring mountains in search of deer. After wandering about the whole day he found himself towards evening in a very remote glen, far from any human habitation, except one where lay a solitary old man suffering fearfully from asthma. The gloom of night, the melancholy and desolate scenery, the lonely hut, and the poor old man, whose every gasp seemed to be his last, powerfully affected the mind of the poet, as he sat by the fire he had made, and thought and listened sadly, until blending the news of the morning so interesting to the whole country, with the scene before him, about which nobody cared, he began to chant to himself as follows :—He spoke to Hugh as if he were already dead; but just as he was closing the song, and going over the concluding verse for the last time, and styling the old man the meanest of mortals, he glanced up and saw that the miserable subject of his elegy—indignant at the turn the verses took—had risen from his pallet, armed himself with a stick, and was about to let it descend with all the force he could muster on the singer's head. Rob had only time to avoid the blow, and experienced some difficulty afterwards in pacifying the querulous sufferer, and leading him back to bed. The bard's friends are said to have sometimes laughed at this incident, but he himself always looked grave when it was mentioned, and seldom could be brought to speak of it at all.

THE DEATH-SONG OF HUGH.

DEATH! how oft we're reminded
    To cry out for aid!
When the small fall before thee—
    The great low are laid;
Since autumn closed o'er us
    The hint you renew,
With this stride from the court
    To that death-couch with Hugh.

Oh! if we believed thee
   Not blind should we go,
When there's none of mankind
   You disdain to lay low;
High and mean dost thou take them—
   That byeword is true—
Yonder's Pelham the high one,
   And here lies poor Hugh.

You come in the one way—
   Great griefs then arise;
You come in the other,
   And nobody sighs;
Yet who can repose him
   Where you ne'er pursue,
In a golden mean careless
   'Twixt Pelham and Hugh.

They drop all around,
   As if struck down with ball;
The report is our warning,
   And loud is its call:
Thou, the least among many,
   Hast thou heard of poor Hugh?
Thou, our chief man, forget not
   Pelham, grander than you!

Oh! should we not tremble all—
   Brethren and friends,
When we're thus like the candle
   That's burnt at both ends?
Where in all this wide world
   Was one meaner than Hugh?
And the court the great Pelham
   But one higher knew.

WILLIAM ROSS.

WILLIAM Ross, a sweet lyric poet, who has been very incorrectly styled, the Burns of the Highlands, but who might, without impropriety, be called the Gaelic Michael Bruce, was born at Broadford, parish of Strath, Isle of Skye, in the year 1762. His parents were able to give him a good education, and young Ross, at a very early age, distinguished himself highly by his proficiency at the parish school of Forres, which he attended.

His father having become a packman, and travelling in pursuit of his calling over most of the Western Isles, William, while still a youth, accompanied his father in order that he might study all the dialects of the Gaelic language at the fountain-head, and make himself thoroughly acquainted with them all. He was so successful in this endeavour that he was reputed among the first Gaelic scholars of his day. He is also said to have known Latin and Greek well. He sang pleasantly, though his voice was not strong, and he played on the violin, flute, and several other instruments with considerable skill.

He became parish school master at Gairloch, Ross-shire, and was very successful as a teacher. He showed a great deal of kindness, which attracted and attached his pupils, and possessed a pleasant humour with which he used to amuse them and lighten the weary drudgery of their tasks He held this situation, however, but a short time. Asthma and consumption closed his life in 1790, when he was only in his twenty-eighth year.

William Ross is a graceful poet, perhaps the most polished of any of the Highland minstrels; although he is certainly inferior to more than one of them in point of strength and energy. He is tender, and easy, and plaintive; never aiming at great things, nor reaching lofty heights. In his system of versification he is generally even more elaborate, and always quite as successful as any of his compeers. In his descriptions of nature he is very sweet and pretty; but throughout all his poetry there appears that soft shade, along with that lack of vehemence and vigour, so observable in most of those poets who die young.

William Ross is said to have been disappointed in love, and to have suffered such grief in consequence that it shortened his life. After having been sometime confined to bed, he rose one fine evening in May, and strolling out, full of melancholy reflections, sat beneath a tree on which a cuckoo soon settled, and began to shout over his head. The beauty of the evening, the stillness of the scene, and the sweet voice of the spring-bird, together with his own sad condition, filled the heart of the poet and melted it, until it flowed spontaneously in the following strain. The poem is called, "The Cuckoo on the tree." In it its author probably bade farewell both to love and poetry. He speaks of the loss of his mistress, and of his own approaching death, with sweet and tender pathos—in diction that possesses his customary finish, and in a style that is pervaded by his usual elegance and grace. The beginning of the fifth stanza, with its pastoral beauty, reminds one of Solomon's song—especially the fourth line:—

> The curl of her hair was so graceful and fair,
>   Its lid for her eye a sweet warden;
> Her cheeks they are bright, and her breast limy white,
>   And her breath like the breeze o'er a garden.

But altogether indeed the poem has no little beauty. It might be compared, or rather perhaps contrasted with Keats' pathetic and imaginative "Ode to the Nightingale," as at least the circumstances of the two poets, if not their sentiments or their genius, were somewhat similar, in the composition of poems which may, not inaptly, be styled the elegy of each young and plaintive minstrel by himself.

THE CUCKOO ON THE TREE.

SMALL bird on that tree, hast thou pity for me,
   Out through this mild misty gloaming?
Would I were now 'neath the dusk of the bough,
   All alone with my true love roaming:
I would raise up a bield her fair form to shield,
   From the chill moory tempest blowing;
And rest by her side in my fondness and pride,
   And kiss her young lips, sweet and glowing.

I slept late and dreamed, but 'twas no lie that gleamed
   On my mind—Oh! so sad and despairing—
When a husband I spied with his beautiful bride
   Affection's pure transports sharing:
How my old love returned and cold reason it spurned,
   Till I moaned and wept, wildly crying;
Every pulse, every vein, boiling—bounding amain—
   With the blood from my heart quickly flying!

Yes,—I'm pledged to her still in spite of my will;
   Alas! and I'm wounded badly;
But a look's all I lack of her face to bring back
   The health I have lost so sadly:
Then I'd rise without fail, and her would I hail,
   Light with joy and not thus, sorrow laden;
She's my own tender dove—my delight and my love—
   The sun over every maiden.

Yet nought to me but a sting all her bright beauties bring—
    I droop with decay, and I languish :
There's a pain at my heart like a pitiless dart,
    And I waste all away with anguish.
She has stolen the hue on my young cheeks that grew,
    And much she has caused my sorrow ;
Unless now she renew with her kindness that hue,
    Death will soon bid me, "Good morrow !"

The curl of her hair was so graceful and fair,
    Its lid for her eye a sweet warden ;
Her cheek it was bright, and her breast limy white,
    And her breath like the breeze o'er a garden.
Till they lay down my head in its stone-guarded bed
    The force of these charms I feel daily,
While I think of the mirth in the woods that had birth ;
    When she laughed and sported gaily.

Her mouth was so sweet, and her teeth white and neat ;
    Her eyes like the sloeberry shining :
How well will she wear, with her matronly air,
    The kerchief where nobles are dining !
Oh ! if she could feel the like ardour and zeal
    Which so long in my breast have been glowing ;
And if she were mine, with the blessing divine,
    I might turn from the way I am going.

Softly, some day, will they make in the clay
    My bed, since her coldness so tries me ;
I've wanted her long, and my love has been strong,
    And the greenwood bough still denies me.
If she were thus low, with what haste should I go
    To ask how the maiden was faring :
Now short the delay till a mournful array
    The brink of my grave will be bearing !

MARY MACLEOD.

MARY MACLEOD, authoress of the following poem, is the first, in point of time, of the Modern Gaelic Bards. Before her day all that exists of Gaelic poetry is fugitive, and of uncertain authorship, or is Ossianic; that is attributed to Ossian directly, or known, or supposed to be by some noted and professed bard of the middle ages, whose name is still attached to one song, or perhaps two —mostly in the ancient style, and on some Fingalian subject, but who has left behind him no body of poetry, and set no stamp of his own character and manner on the language of his race. Since her day, while the nameless popular poetry has all along been vigorously flourishing, there has also been a succession of bards who cultivated their gifts assiduously and successfully, and whose works, still extant, are classed under their name, and bear the mark of their peculiar faculty. These have carried Gaelic Poetry to as high an excellence as it is likely ever to reach. The Golden Age of the Highland Muses was in the middle of last century, when MacDonald, Duncan Ban, Buchanan, Rob Donn, and others were all living and composing together. The Mountain Melodies have since been on the decline.

The earliest of this modern school of Gaelic poets was Mary MacLeod, better known among her own countrymen as, "*Màiri nighean Alastair Ruaidh,*" (Mary the daughter of red-haired Alexander). She was born in Harris, in the far away Hebrides, in 1569, and died at Dunvegan, Isle of Skye, in 1674, at the great age of one hundred and five years. She never learned either to read or to write, yet her poetry is pure and chaste in its diction, melodious, though complicated, in its metre, clear and graceful, and frequently pathetic.

The song here given was composed by Mary MacLeod, on her being banished from Dunvegan, for some real or imaginary offence, by the arbitrary young Chief, whose praises she sings with such delight and enthusiasm,—as sitting by the sea-side in Mull, her heart is oppressed by the thought of her absence from her beloved Skye, and from his gracious presence, who was to her its hero and its sun. It is satisfactory to know that the young gentleman of whom poor Mary has given so flattering a portrait —probably his only remaining title to consideration— relented sufficiently at the sound of his own praises, or in respect for the genius of his clanswoman, that he gave her permission to return forthwith to his dominions, and he even sent a boat to bring her back. He is said to have been particularly good to the affectionate poetess ever after.

MACLEOD'S DITTY.

Alone on the hill-top,
  Sadly and silently,
Downward on Islay
  And over the sea—
I look and I wonder
  How time hath deceived me:
A stranger in Muile*
  Who ne'er thought to be.

Ne'er thought it, my island!
  Where rests the deep dark shade
Thy grand mossy mountains
  For ages have made—
God bless thee, and prosper!
  Thy chief of the sharp blade,
All over these islands,
  His fame never fade!

* Mull.

Never fade it, Sir Norman!
  For well 'tis the right
Of thy name to win credit
  In council or fight;
By wisdom, by shrewdness,
  By spirit, by might,
By manliness, courage,
  By daring, by sleight.

In council or fight, thy kindred
  Know these should be thine—
Branch of Lochlin's wide-ruling
  And king-bearing line!
And in Erin they know it—
  Far over the brine:
No earl would in Albin
  Thy friendship decline.

Yes! the nobles of Erin
  Thy titles well know,
To the honour and friendship
  Of high and of low.
Born the deed-marks to follow,
  Thy father did show,—
That friend of the noble—
  That manliest foe.

That friend of the noble—
  From him art thou heir
To virtues which Albin
  Was proud to declare:
Crown'd the best of her chieftains
  Long, long may'st thou wear
The blossoms paternal
  His broad branches bare!

O banner'd Clan Ruari!
   Whose loss is my woe,
Of this chief who survives
   May I ne'er hear he's low;
But, darling of mortals!
   From him though I go,
Long the shapeliest, comliest
   Form may he show!

The shapeliest, comliest
   Faultless in bearing—
Cheerful, cordial, and kind,
   The red and white wearing,
Well looks the blue-eyed chief;
   Blue, bright, and daring,
His eye o'er his red cheek shines,
   Blue, bright, calmly daring.

His red cheek shines,
   Like hip on the brier-tree,
'Neath the choicest of curly hair
   Waving and free.
A warm hearth, a drinking cup,
   Meat shall he see,
And a choice of good armour
   Whoe'er visits thee.

Drinking-horns, trenchers bright,
   And arms old and new;
Long, narrow-bladed swords,
   Cold, clear, and blue—
These are seen in thy mansion,
   With rifles and carbines, too;
And hempen-strung long-bows,
   Of hard, healthy yew.

Long-bows and cross-bows,
    With strings that well wear;
Arrows, with polish'd heads,
    In quivers full and fair,
From the eagle's wing feather'd,
    With silk fine and rare;
And guns dear to purchase—
    Long slender—are there.

My heart's with thee, hero!
    May Mary's son keep
My stripling who loves
    The lone forest to sweep;
Rejoicing to feel there
    The solitude deep
Of the long moor and valley,
    And rough mountain steep.

The mountain steep searching
    And rough rocky chains;
The old dogs he caresses,
    The young dogs he restrains:
Then, soon from my chieftain's spear
    The life-blood rains
Of the red-hided deer or doe
    And the green heather stains.

Fall the red stag, the white-bellied doe;
    Then stand on the heather,
Thy gentle companions,
    Well arm'd altogether,
Well taught on the hunter's craft,
    Well skill'd in the weather;
They know the rough sea as well
    As the green heather!

MACGREGOR'S LULLABY.

"On the sixteenth of June, 1552," says the curate of Fortingall, "Duncan MacGregor and his sons, Gregor and Malcolm Roy, were beheaded by Colin Campbell of Glenurchy, Campbell of Glenlyon, and Menzies of Rannoch."* The authoress of the following ballad was a daughter of Colin Campbell of Glenurchy, and the wife of Gregor MacGregor, whose death she so feelingly laments. The Black Duncan mentioned was her brother. He was called "Donnachadh dubh a' Churraichd," or Black Duncan of the Cowl, from some peculiar head-dress he was in the habit of wearing, and in which it is said he is represented in his picture, still preserved at Taymouth Castle. This chief, the seventh laird of Glenurchy, was a man of some mark in his day. He played his part in the fierce politics of the time, and managed his own estate, as is seen from contemporary records, in a very businesslike and careful manner. Like his unfortunate sister, however, he had also something of a finer turn. "Black Duncan," says Professor Innes, "had a taste for books—read history and romance—and is not quite free from a suspicion of having dabbled in verse himself." Although his sister does not spare him in her denunciation of her kindred, he must have been quite scatheless of causing her sufferings, for he appears to have been only seven years old when Gregor MacGregor was executed. Duncan Laideus, *alias* MacGregor, father of this Gregor, has had his name, some time or other, put at the head of an interesting old Scottish Poem, from which Professor Innes gives some very pleasing extracts. It is called "Duncan Laideus, *alias* MacGregor's Testament," and is "found written on the blank leaves at the end of one of the copies of the romance of Alexander," a favourite book with "Black Duncan of the Cowl."

*Sketches of early Scottish History, page 255, &c.

GREGOR MACGREGOR'S LAMENT.

Early on a Lammas morning,
  With my husband was I gay;
But my heart got sorely wounded
  Ere the middle of the day.
    Ochan, ochan, ochan uiri,
      Though I cry, my child, with thee—
    Ochan, ochan, ochan uiri,
      Now he hears not thee nor me!

Malison on judge and kindred,
  They have wrought me mickle woe;
With deceit they came about us,—
  Through deceit they laid him low.
        Ochan, ochan, &c.

Had they met but twelve MacGregors,
  With my Gregor at their head;
Now my child had not been orphaned,
  Nor these bitter tears been shed.
        Ochan, ochan, &c.

On an oaken block they laid him,
  And they spilt his blood around;
I'd have drunk it in a goblet
  Largely, ere it reached the ground.
        Ochan, ochan, &c.

Would my father then had sickened—
  Colin, with the plague been ill;
Though Rory's daughter, in her anguish,
  Smote her palms and cried her fill.
        Ochan, ochan, &c.

I could Colin shut in prison,
    And Black Duncan put in ward,—
Every Campbell now in Bealach,
    Bind with handcuffs, close and hard.
            Ochan, ochan, &c.

When I reached the plain of Bealach,
    I got there, nor rest, nor calm;
But my hair I tore in pieces,—
    Wore the skin from off each palm!
            Ochan, ochan, &c.

Oh! could I fly up with the skylark
    Had I Gregor's strength in hand;
The highest stone that's in yon castle
    Should lie lowest on the land.
            Ochan, ochan, &c.

Would I saw Finlarig blazing,
    And the smoke of Bealach smelled,
So that fair, soft-handed Gregor
    In these arms once more I held.
            Ochan, ochan, &c.

While the rest have all got lovers
    Now a lover have I none;
My fair blossom, fresh and fragrant,
    Withers on the ground alone.
            Ochan, ochan, &c.

While all other wives the night-time
    Pass in slumber's balmy bands,
I, upon my bedside weary,
    Never cease to wring my hands.
            Ochan, ochan, &c.

Far, far better be with Gregor
  Where the heather's in its prime,
Than with mean and Lowland barons
  In a house of stone and lime.
            Ochan, ochan, &c.

Greatly better be with Gregor
  Where the herds stray o'er the vale,
Than with little Lowland barons
  Drinking of their wine and ale.
            Ochan, ochan, &c.

Greatly better be with Gregor
  In a mantle rude and torn,
Than with little Lowland barons
  Where fine silk and lace are worn.
            Ochan, ochan, &c.

Though it rained and roared together,
  All throughout the stormy day,
Gregor, in a crag, could find me
  A kind shelter where to stay.
            Ochan, ochan, &c.

Bahu, bahu, little nursling—
  Oh! so tender now and weak;
I fear the day will never brighten
  When revenge for him you'll seek.
      Ochan, ochan, ochan uiri,
        Though I cry, my child, with thee—
      Ochan, ochan, ochan uiri,
        Yet he hears not thee nor me!

The terrible persecution which the MacGregors were subjected to—the cruel sufferings which for many years they had to struggle against, when their whole tribe was outlawed, their lands confiscated, and their name proscribed—Sir Walter Scott has made familiar to many who would perhaps have never heard but for him of the valorous endurance of the "clan that was nameless by day." That the great novelist has done justice to the indomitable energy, the terrible prowess, the courage, and the wild heroic fidelity of this much-wronged sept, there is no one can venture to dispute. But certain warm-hearted Highlanders—who feel peculiarly interested in all the brave men who spoke the mother tongue of the Gael in other days—assert that the poet, to say the least of it, has fixed too exclusively on the fiercer and more savage attributes of the banished clan. It may be Sir Walter really did exaggerate, for artistic purposes, those harsher traits of character which must have in some degree existed among the MacGregors when subjected to such vile treatment as theirs was—unless they were actually something more than mortal; or it may perhaps as likely be that the kindly partiality of the modern Celts has closed their eyes, when they think so, on some of the ruder doings of the outlawed and exasperated mountaineers. At any rate, there seems to be some force in the reasoning which the novelist has put into the mouth of Ranald MacEagh in Argyll's dungeon, when he says, "I am a man like my forefathers; while wrapped in the mantle of peace we were lambs; it was rent from us, and ye now call us wolves. Give us the huts ye have burned, our children whom ye have murdered, our widows whom ye have starved; collect from the gibbet and the pole the mangled carcasses and whitened skulls of our kinsmen; bid them live and bless us, and we will be your vassals and brothers; till then let death and blood and mutual wrong draw a dark veil of division between us." There is here a natural eloquence and logic of facts which cannot fail to find an echo in the most peaceful heart amongst us. If the Children of the Mist did not feel such sentiments, at least they are amazingly like the sentiments by which we can most readily suppose we would be actuated in their circumstances. But, however that may be, certainly the following song does not breathe the fiery energy of Ranald's hostility ; nor is it at all tinged with the vindictive spirit which scandalized Captain Dalgetty in the parting injunctions of the old cateran to his grandson, Kenneth of the Mist:—

There is sorrow, and sorrow, and sorrow now fills me—
   Poor pitiful sorrow no man can redress ;
It is sorrow, and sighing, and sadness that thrills me—
   Oh ! terrible sadness I cannot repress.

MacGregor has perish'd—MacGregor, pine-banner'd—
   MacGregor, beloved in Glenlyon the green—
MacGregor, the brave, by whose foes ever honour'd
   The threatening roar of our pibroch hath been.

His badge was the pine—known the steep hill ascending—
   His arrow were wing'd from the true bird's *brown side;
'T was a joy for a prince when the hero was sending
   The smooth polish'd shafts from the bow of his pride.

By that strong arm well aim'd, son of Murdoch the fearless—
   Swift, silent, and deadly they darted from thee ;
Then, if wrong e'er was done us, MacGregor the peerless
   Soon our foes saw thy standard, and trembled to see !

But now when they hurt us, we bear uncomplaining—
   MacGregor and all that would help us are gone ;
And the thoughts of our sad hearts with them are remaining
   In the chapel that stands near the valley alone.

   * The true bird (*am fior eun*) is a poetic name for the eagle. The common name is *Fiolair*, a word rather difficult to pronounce with a right accent.

My kinsmen, co-nurtured! O you that could right me!
    It grieves and it wounds me the blank you have made
Your death and your absence for ever affright me,
    And the dark narrow bed where your heads low are laid!

Now in shirts of pale linen so lonely you're lying,
    No bands and no silks and no tartans you wear;
Ourselves sew'd your white robes, with sorrow and sighing;
    No gentle dames wrought with us—wept with us, there.

Now this counsel of me, who your safety am seeking,
    Take you for your guidance, young clansmen of mine;
When you go to the inn where the strangers sit speaking,
    More than one draught, for your life's sake, decline.

Take the dish which they offer; be cautious and wary—
    There is no man you meet with but may be a foe;
While you drink, remain standing, and then do not tarry,
    But turn round and haste ye—delay not, but go.

For summer take spring-time—for autumn take winter—
    And away and away to wild solitudes hie;
Where the heat and the cold the crag shiver and splinter,
    And see you sleep lightly wherever you lie.

The squirrel is rare, but the hunters deceive him,
    And draw him away from his nest in the tree;
And the falcon is noble, but men will not leave him
    His daring, his speed, and the blue heavens free.

"More than one draught, for your life's sake, decline."
At this place Mrs. Grant makes the following remark:—
"The single draught in this verse is particularly expressive
of the constant apprehensions which haunt the mind of
him who knows that this life is haunted with malicious
diligence. The ancients tell of dogs on the borders of the

Nile who always drank running, for fear of the crocodile. This is one of the liveliest images of habitual terror." There are other parts of the song equally expressive.

There is another song of the Children of the Mist, which is called, "Cruachan a' Cheathaich;" or the Braes of the Mist. It is in print, and well known; but I translate from a copy taken down from the singing of an Islayman, who is a smith, and well acquainted with the traditional poetry and legends of the Highlands. Neither this man nor the transcriber knew that the song had ever been published. Each thought he was doing his best to save an ancient fragment that was just about to perish. This again serves to show the care with which Tradition watches over the few prized treasures which the tyrant, Time, leaves with it. The ballad is sung to a wild and melancholy pibroch tune, to which the translation has been adapted. The story connected with it is interesting. In the last line of the poem the singer speaks of her father, but the tradition says it was her husband and two sons, whom she had concealed in her house when some of the bitter enemies of the MacGregors were observed approaching. They were already close at hand There was no time for escape. The woman concealed her friends in a bed, and then sitting down at the fire or at the door proceeded to sing this song. She represents herself waiting in solitude for her persecuted kindred; and saying, since they had not then returned, they must either yet be at Lochfyne—as when she last heard of them—or far away in the glens of the Mist, hunting and fishing; and consequently, as it was now so late, obliged to pass the night in a poor hut, where she had left some tokens of her presence, and it is to be inferred some rude preparations for their reception. She then concludes, praying for their safety, and expressing her own sadness on account of their many dangers; some of which she enumerates with the minuteness of intimate acquaintance. In such circumstances, the prayer must have come emphatically from the singer's heart. It was answered to her wish on that occasion at least. The people outside listened as the woman sung, and, believing what she said, passed on without disturbing her. A very good subject surely for a picture this woman would make, singing so at her fireside, in the hearing of her friends and her enemies—her heart's most precious wishes depending on the effect produced by her ballad.

The song represents her sitting on the highway—her most cruel foes not unobserved, though unnoticed by her; her dearest friends in the power of those foes if they only knew it; and she—with the twilight, and the dim, misty mountains looking down on her—their deliverer, if she could sing her lyric in the right character to the end. Seldom, indeed, has song or ballad been composed or chanted in circumstances of such intense excitement.

―――

THE BRAES OF THE "CEATHACH."

I sit here alone, by the plain of the highway,
For my poor hunted kin, watching mist, watching by-way;
I've yet got no sign that they're near to my dwelling;
At Lochfyne they were last seen—if true be that telling—

Drinking wine with the nobles, the street proudly stepping
With Gregor Og Rua—that hard hand behind weapon—
And Gregor Mor Maimach, my household commanding,
Son of him of Strath-Startail, round whose hearth, often standing—

I've heard the bard harping, and oft seen them playing
With the dice, and with chess, and the fiddle's mirth
    swaying.
In the Glen of the Mist is the stag from you flying?
On the moor are you leaving the bonny bird lying?

For the raven a prey do her bloody plumes quiver?
Or draw you its dark blue flock from the bends of the
    river?
You must pass this lone night in a hut low and narrow,
Where the dagger I left, and the belt and the arrow.

May the King of the Universe save you for ever
From the flash and the bullet, and the store of the quiver;
From the keen-pointed knife, with the life-blood oft
    streaming;
From the edge of the sharp claymore, terribly gleaming.

In Briagh-Bhaile, on Sunday, they won without fighting,
But since then no smile my sad face has been lighting;
Small wonder I say so—greater shame 't would be rather
Not to say so with grief—when they call thee my father

From internal evidence, this song may be pronounced at least two hundred years old. It forms a fit companion for MacGregor o' Ruara," and the preceding " Lullaby, —all belonging to the same clan and the same era, and having been produced under somewhat similar circumstances.

FUGITIVE SONGS.

MANY of the most popular of Gaelic love songs are by unknown authors, or, as is the case also in Lowland Scotch, by authors who composed one song and no more. Their distinguishing characteristics are simplicity, tenderness, and expressive sincerity. There is a great deal of music generally in their language and rhythm, and such a correspondence with the tune to which they are sung, as if they were the twin births of the one passionate experience. This is also the case with their Lowland kindred, which have very much the same rural grace and freshness, which we discover in the Highland lyrics. In them music and poetry are truly wedded, till they become of one sound and nature, and are helps meet for one another. Especially is this the case with the chorus and with one or two verses of the lyric—such as we may suppose might be struck off in the first heat of emotion. Sometimes, for a few lines, it would almost appear as if it were difficult to say where the music begins, or the words end—they blend and fit so curiously together. This, I suppose, must be partly attributed to the nature of the Gaelic language, which, without being particularly soft, is very flexible, and full of vowel sounds. But it must also be attributed, in a certain degree, to the musical genius of the people, which I look upon as decidedly evident, and one of their prominent characteristics; though, of course, existing as yet in some districts, in a very uncultured state.

The Highland melodies are often of the most touching beauty—sometimes wildly melancholy, sometimes exuberantly gay. They remind one more than anything else of what Mr. Carlyle says so happily of Burns' songs, when he calls them "fitful gushes; warblings not of the voice only, but of the whole mind." Springing full-formed and at once out of some real emotion, the few sweet notes that form their music might pass for the plaintive or cheerful tones of some singing creatures who had been gifted indeed with melody, but denied the use of articulate language to express their overmastering feelings; and who were therefore fain to utter them as the birds do—yet with all the difference of a profound and intelligent consciousness. These little gushes of melody have passed down from age to age, exciting or soothing kindred feelings with those that were their own origin—like pure fresh fountains that look so clear and sweet, they at once excite a wish to taste them in those who at the moment need them not, and help to quench the longing thirst of those who actually do. There is little or no art manifest in the arrangement or finish of these airs; they are consequently to be regarded rather as germs of sweet music than as perfect melodies.

OCH! MAR THA MI.*

THE following Islay song, known as, "Och mar tha mi," I give verse for verse with the original, and in its rather peculiar metre, exactly as it was sung to me by a lady well acquainted with, and much interested in Highland popular poetry. It must be noted that words of two syllables are in Gaelic invariably accented on the first;

* The *th* being silent in Gaelic, and the *i* sounded as in all other languages except English, these words are pronounced, "*ha mi!*" This is an exclamation of grief, and means literally, "Och! how am I!" or, rendered more freely, "Alas! what a state am I in!"

the second syllable becoming frequently little more than a mere breathing. There are also far fewer monosyllables in Gaelic than in English. This will serve to account for Gaelic verses ending as they often do—not with a long syllable as in English, but with a word of a long and short syllable, as in this song—what the ancients called a trochee.

It is very difficult to give verses constructed on this principle a metrical sound in English at all; but, to adapt words to a great number of the Highland melodies, such a form is absolutely necessary. Every one who has heard Gaelic songs sung by those who give them the raciest intonation, must have observed how prone they were to dwell on the second last syllable of each line, and drop the last almost inaudibly. That is the right style for singing, "Och! mar tha mi"—the air of which is very pretty.

Och! mar tha mi! here so lonely,
    Despair has seized me, and keeps his hold:
Oh, were I near thee, in Islay, only
    Before thou'st taken that man for gold!

This doleful morning, how sad my waking!
    My eyes with tear-drops fast running over,
For old love leaving and old vows breaking—
    Thy banns are call'd with that other lover.

When sleeping sweetly the rest are lying,
    Wild dreams of anguish my mind is weaving.
I'm like the swan that drops wounded—dying;
    My love exhausts me with bitter grieving.

Alas! thy kind eye, so brightly shining;
    Thy neck so comely, like cannach blowing;

Those ebon eyebrows thy forehead lining;
   Thy cheeks like berries on rowans glowing.

Though all earth's maidens my heart were seeking,
   I'll love no more from this doleful morning.
Thou spirit thrilling! thou sweetly-speaking!
   Since thou has left me, and without warning.

Since thou has left me, and without warning,
   Alas! and taken a man for gold!
Had I been by thee, false wisdom scorning,
   Thyself, my dear one! thou hadst not sold.

Thy love could raise me from wasting fever,
   And fill my pulses with health abounding—
Like the strong salmon that leaves the river,
   And leaps, rejoicing, where waves are sounding.

Och! mar tha mi! here so lonely
   Despair has seized me, and keeps his hold.
Oh, were I near thee, in Islay, only,
   Before thou'st taken that man for gold!

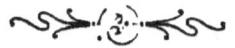

THE "GILLE DUBH, CIAR DUBH."*

The following song is sung to a beautiful and winning air, which, like many other Highland airs, only requires the delicate touch of some true genius to become a melody as deep, as noble and expressive as any of those national lyric gems we are so fond and so proud of. I don't know whether it spoils the sentiment, or gives another interest rather, to be told that one who sung so sweetly and loved so well did marry her " Gille dubh, ciar dubh " in the end.

> Once o'er the wide moor wending,
> Or round the green hill bending,
> Gay words and wild notes blending
>   Spread far my good cheer :
> For then my heart, light-leaping,
> In waking, in sleeping,
> Had no dubh, ciar dubh keeping
>   Its joys far from here.
>
> And now that, together,
>   Dubh ciar dubh, dubh ciar dubh,
> We faced the rude weather
>   On hills bleak and blue !
> Some peaceful spot near me
> I'd choose, and there cheer me ;
> No grey-beard to fear me,
>   And thou in my view.

---

* Pronounced " Gille doo, keear doo." " Gille " means a young man ; and " dubh, ciar dubh," dark, dusky dark.

Thy health-draught, if drinking,
  My gille dubh ciar dubh,
Mud-pools, to my thinking,
  Like sweet wine would be;
Yet though I've no dower,
If some had the power,
They'd take thy wild flower,
  From thee, love! from thee.

My bonny dubh, ciar dubh!
Let sharp tongues assail thee,
One heart will not fail thee
  That knows to be true.
Dubh ciar dubh! dubh ciar dubh!
Though poor, poor thou be,
No rich old man can please me
  Like thee, love, like thee!

My gille dubh! kind one!
I never will leave thee;—
I'd choose thee, believe me,
  Amid thousands five:
Should they stand on the heather,
All ranged there together,
Like thee should I find none
  With whom I could live.

In sadness oft sleeping,
I wake up, half weeping,
Such wild dreams, come creeping
  Over me, dear!
I've heard the old folks say
That grief makes the hair gray;
Then, gille dubh! this love may
  Make mine so, I fear.

HOOG ORIN, O!

THE following song is the wild wail of an unhappy woman, whose friends had forced her to marry against her inclination; or who had allowed herself to be more influenced by false sense and worldly policy, than she found afterwards consistent with the tranquility of a powerfully sensitive heart. It tells of that intensest misery, which is perhaps felt among us more frequently than it is spoken; and which oftener, it may be, than either, lurks darkly, like an inexorable Fate, where it is never acknowledged, even in the shape of a distinct feeling, by the dull and dreary heart that counts for years the heavy hours with sad and listless beatings. All marriages of interest, by whomsoever planned, cannot turn out well. Some of the parties in them have surely reason to sing, with this miserable Highland woman:—

> I am married,
> > Hoog Orin, O!
> Married! worried!
> > Hoog Orin, O!
> They took me from my own lover—
> Gave me to the western drover.
> > Where I hated
> > I am mated.
> > > Hoog Orin, O!
> > Wife ill-fated.
> I am married—I am worried,
> > Hoog Orin, O!
> Mated! married! wearied! worried!
> > Hoog Orin, O!

They gave me to the clumsy drover—
Like my father, not my lover.
I am dreary
  In his dwelling!
    Hoog Orin, O!

I am weary
  Of the knelling
Of my heavy heart!
    Hoog Orin, O!
Of the tears for ever swelling
  From this heavy heart—
Sadly swelling, faintly knelling—
  O my soul! depart—
Leave this strife
With weary life!
    Hoog Orin, O!
  Ill fated wife.
I am married—I am worried,
    Hoog Orin, O!
I am mated where I hated,
    Hoog Orin, O!
Mated! married! wearied! worried!
    Hoog Orin, O!

Equally unhappy with the ill-fated wife of "Hoog Orin, O!" was the unmarried heroine of the next song. Her lover was long absent. She watched for him, but he came not. Hope deferred made her heart "Sick! sick! sick!"—forcing the sad conviction on her that she was wilfully neglected; and she became "a-weary, a-weary," and even thought he "wished her dead."

  Sick! sick! sick!
    Oh, the pain! oh, the gloom!
  He has no wish to save me
    From the cold tomb.

Love! love! love!
  The fair cheek, the dark hair,
The promise forgotten;
  'T will go with me there.

False! false! false!
  Oh, youth is false for ever;
He loves far more than living me—
  The lifeless heather.

The hunting field,
  The greenwood tree,
The trout, the running deer, he loves
  Far more than me.

He loves—loves—loves
  To stalk the frighten'd doe;
He never heeds the pain he gives,
  His skill to show.

Oh, the dark blue eye—
  A flower wet with dew;
Oh, the fair false face—
  Too sweet to view!

Fare-thee-well—well—well
  Though thou'st forsaken me;
May every good thing follow—
  Follow—follow thee!

A very sensible literary lady, commenting on the conduct of Mariana in "The Moated Grange," who was "a-weary, a-weary," and wished that she was dead, said that it would have been better for Mariana to have minded her household duties, and given over singing. And so, perhaps, it would; and better for our unfortunate Highland singers, too. It is easy, however, for the kettle on the hob to tell the kettle on the fire not to boil. When their souls were pierced through with bitter sorrows, and their poor hearts were full and overflowing, how were those tuneful females to accommodate themselves to the sedate proprieties of their cool and undisturbed sisters, whose feelings had perhaps never in their life given them much trouble in the grand concern of looking after themselves? Nothing more, perhaps, remained for the tender lyrists than to speak or die; or, it may be, speak and die. Their language betrays no guilt, at least. If anything was wrong in them, it was merely an excess of feeling—neither a great nor a common fault. Whatever cool-headed ladies may think of these poor sufferers,—of our sex, at all events, it may be said, that those of us who do not value a true and unaffected sensibility more than any amount of practical good sense in a woman—who do not intuitively prefer a Mary to a Martha, in fact—will possess but little sensibility, or sense either, themselves. The title of the next song is,—

A MAIDEN'S LAMENT.

My heart is broken! broken!
   What was bright in it is bleak:
Its joys are gone, and gone away,
   This many and many a week.
They are gone away with him
   Who was fairest of us all—
Fairest whitest, whiter
   Than the snow-flakes as they fall!

He was manly; he was nobly brave;
   He was first in every need.

I loved him, and I loved him not
  In word, but all in deed.
Too well, too well I loved him:
  For now I can but mourn—
I mourn and waste my heart away,
  And pine till he return.

My heart is like a lump of lead—
  I walk, but feel a stone;
I eat not, drink not with the youths;
  I always feel alone.
My soul is black with sorrow;
  Why should I lay it bare,
Or tell 'tis he who left last week
  That causes all this care?

When he rein'd up a prancing steed,
  How waved his curly hair!
How confident he look'd and proud!
  How manly was his air!
Not like a boy or woman
  Did he discourse with men—
His words were choice and pretty,
  As if written with a pen.

He was to me a gem—a gem
  Like the bud a brier wears;
He was as choice as is the tree
  Bent with the fruit it bears.
And I was willing secretly
  To wed—wed him alone:
He should have laid me, ere he left,
  Beneath the cold grave-stone!

Ah me! 'tis little wonder
  I grieve that he's away,
When I think how we two loved and lived,
  For many and many a day,
The sweet, sweet love we cherish'd—
  The wandering alone—
Oh, the change, if he has cross'd the sea!
  Oh, my weary, weary moan!

THE BOATMAN.

THE number of boatmen, fishers, and half-sailors in the Western islands, is out of all proportion to the rest of the inhabitants; especially on the margin of the thousand creeks and inlets and arms of the sea that calmly nestle in the land. When night is falling on the long and winding loch that leads to a murmuring fishing village, the heavy sound of oars is heard incessantly along the silent shores; or in the summer twilight, when the wind is favourable, many and many sailing-boats may be seen gliding silently, as ghosts, over the smooth, hill-sheltered floor of the fresh western sea-way. Then the far-carried sound of voices comes to the wanderer on the bank, and reminds him, as he looks into the dim gloaming whence they issue, of the mysterious paths that are on the great ocean. Sometimes wild storms overtake the fisher, and anxious hearts wait for him at his home. Sometimes a fierce mountain squall leaps like a wild beast upon him, as he passes by in his careless security, and drives him far away from his warm and blazing hearth; or, as I have known more than once to happen, overturns his frail bark, and sinks him in the hissing, tumbling waters.

Where the fishers have large boats they go a great
distance, and remain for weeks away. Very frequently
they take a voyage or two abroad, and all of them are at
least half, and many of them thorough-bred, sailors. The
fishing population and the agricultural population differ
a good deal in their dress, and a little even in their
appearance; of course their associations are dissimilar.
The fishermen are a very much respected class, however;
and no doubt they think a good deal of themselves. It is
of one of them the following very popular song treats.
This " Man of the Boat " had gone over the sea, and was
like never to return. He had left some one behind him,
who mourned his absence greatly.

How often hunting the highest hill-top,
    I scan the ocean thy sail to see :
Wilt come to-night, love? Wilt come to-morrow?
    Or ever come, love! to comfort me?

My soul is weary; my heart is breaking;
    With frequent tear-drops mine eyes o'erflow.
Wilt come to-night, love? May I expect thee?
    Or, sighing sorely, the door put to?

I question fondly thy friends, and ask them,
    Where last they saw thee? where thou art now?
But each one, jeering, some answer gives me,
    That sends me homeward with burning brow.

They call thee fickle, they call thee false one,
    And seek to change me; but all in vain.
No; thou'rt my dream yet throughout the dark night
    And every morn yet I watch the main.

Dost thou remember the promise made me—
    The tartan plaidie—the silken gown—

The ring of gold with thy hair and portrait?
　That gown and ring I will never own.

For not a hamlet—too well I know it—
　Where you go wandering, or stay a while,
But all its old folk you win with talking,
　And charm its maidens with song and smile.

And yet I dare not deny I love thee;
　And not a month,—oh, nor yet a year,
But thee for ever,—since first in childhood
　I stroll'd beside thee, and thought thee dear.

My friends they warn me, and oft advise me,
　To let thy false vows forgotten be:
As vain their counsel, as if they order'd
　Yon little streamlet roll back the sea.

So here I wander, a tearful mourner—
　A stricken cygnet, with music-moan,
That sings her dirge-note by grassy fountain,
　When, all forsaken, she dies alone!

MONALTRI

WENT to the moor to hunt, and falling over a rock was killed. The following verses, as if by a flash of lightning in a dark night, gives us a vivid glimpse of the confusion and grief which attended the accident. The lines are very slight and sketchy; but they serve their end better, perhaps, than many more elaborate things. They remind us a little of "Bonnie George Campbell." It treats of a similar misfortune; is equally rapid in its narration, and catches as successfully the right tone in which to deal with its kindred sorrow. If it falls short, in some other respects, of the rare masterpiece it resembles, that need not surprise us, for "Bonnie George Campbell" carries as much of a sad tale and a wild lamenting, in a very small compass, as probably any song in the English language.

> There's a sound on the hill,
>   Not of joy but of ailing;
> Dark-hair'd women mourn—
>   Beat their hands, with loud wailing.
>
> They cry out, Ochon!
>   For the young Monaltri,
> Who went to the hill;
>   But home came not he.
>
> Without snood, without plaid
>   Katrina's gone roaming.
> O Katrina, my dear!
>   Homeward be coming.
>
> Och! hear, on the castle
>   Yon pretty bird singing,
> "Snoodless and plaidless,
>   Her hands she is ringing!"

"MALI BHEAG OG!"

There is a much-admired production of the Celtic muse that goes by the name of "Mali bheag òg," which may be rendered "Young little May." Who the author of it was, I don't think has been well ascertained. Its story is nearly the same as that of the ballad of "Kirkconnel Lea," and resembles in some respects the Laureate's "Oriana." The slaying of young and lovely women accidentally, forms the theme of several of Ossian's episodes; one of which, at least that of "Fainasollis and Mayro Borb, the King of Sorcha's Son," or "Stormy Borbar," as MacPherson calls him—has all the appearance of considerable antiquity, as may be plainly enough seen from a version of it published in Appendix XV. to the Highland Society's Report on the Poems of Ossian. Indeed, this most heart-rending misfortune is one which we might expect sometimes to hear of in a state of society where the red genius of war appeared armed and openly at the board, the hearth, the trysting tree, the hunting field, as well as in his own more legitimate scenes, where the softer sex might escape meeting with his valourship. What can we conceive more natural than wrath driving fiery and inflamed spirits, with the tools of death always at their command, into instant and ill-placed strife; and women, as they would be sure to do, shrieking, and throwing themselves before the weapons? More than one strong man must, in past days, have felt his angry soul frozen into dispair from hot fury in a moment, when he saw the tender breast his hand had blindly wounded, sobbing out its life-blood; and the poor pale face he liked the most to look upon turned forgivingly upon him, in the last gleam of life's reflection, full of love and pity that were inextinguishable by death.

The hero of this melancholy Gaelic song we have now to do with met his mistress, clandestinely, on a Sunday evening, in a lonely glen near her father's house. Her kinsmen waylaid him; and, furious at his attempt to carry off their relative, attacked him with their swords in her presence. She rushed between her friend and her angry brethern, and was killed by a chance blow of her lover's hand. He was immediately taken prisoner, confined, and condemned to death. The night before his execution he sang as follows:—

  Canst thou feel for a captive's sigh,
    Young little May!
  Condemn'd by thy friends to die,
    Young little May!
  Though thy soft eye of heaven's blue,
  Thy lip of the honey dew,
  Never more can bless my view,
    Young little May!

  Oh, the sad tryst—that fatal day!
    My own little May!
  Its blood will not wash away,
    Poor little May!
  Why, before thy sweet, startled face,
  Just touch'd by thy meek embrace,
  Did our fell foes beset my trace,
    Dear little May!

  'T was for thee that I trembled then,
    Kind little May!
  Though surrounded by cruel men,
    Sweet little May!
  But oh, that some hostile blade,
  This hand on the ground had laid
  Ere that wound in thy side it made,
    Brave little May!

Then didst thou lie so low,
    Pale little May!
Wild flower, that so sweet did grow,
    Loved little May!
Like glimpse of the sunny glow,
In mild morning rising low,
Such brightness thy face did show,
    Lost little May!

Oh, the deep love I give thee,
    My own little May!
Oh, could it not save thee,
    My choice little May!
How thy hair like the sunbeam,
Thy cheek like my heart's stream,
Rejoiced my last flattering dream,
    Dear little May!

Through the world I could roam away,
    Loved little May!
To meet thee some distant day,
    Dear little May!
I could run, I could leap then
As the deer of the mountain glen
Bounds through the flashing fen,
    Choice little May!

Curs'd be thy kinsmen's spite,
    Sweet little May!
That forbade me thy love—thy sight,
    Dear little May!
But were their love as mine is, dear!
Oh! ne'er had I languish'd here,
Wringing this bitter tear,
    Bright little May!

Yet now were I safe from death,
    Dear little May!
Cumbrous would be my breath!
    Sweet little May!
Much better to die, and go
Where no blood—where no blood can flow,
O my God! than thus wail thee low,—
    Dead little May!

"BREIGEIN BINNEACH."

I GIVE this song, as it was sung to me by a lady who was a good deal amused with it, though ashamed of remembering such nonsense so well. It belongs to a class of songs of which there are a considerable number in the Highlands, though they seldom find their way into printed collections. It would seem that both the genius and the taste of the people lead more to melancholy than to mirth in their compositions. At the same time, when they happen to be cheerful, their efforts are not less effective, while their grave faces still keep masking the quaint humour and cordial mirthfulness which their words embody. The verses, though only a mere sketch, serve to explain her situation. The hero of the ballad she calls "Breigein Binneach"—words which may be translated "The lilting little liar." It is a foolishly ambitious and absurdly deceived woman who sings.

    I went away with Breigein Binneach
        And MacGregor Clairy.
    He told me of his splendid house,
        His kitchen, and his dairy;

But not a house or hall saw I,
  Save, on the hillside airy,
A littly bothy where he lived
  With his sister Mary!

He has got but one dun cow,
  Though he bragg'd so rarely—
It hardly gives enough of milk
  For himself and Mary :
In my father's barn at home
  I could lie as fairly
As in this bothy by the hill,
  Which is so damp and airy.

I would leave it fast enough,
  If my sire forgave me ;
I would work, and work enough—
  Do anything to save me
From the Breigein Binneach's tongue
  And his sister Mary's ;
I'd thrash, or plough, or keep the cows,
  Or cart, or keep the dairy.

MAIRI LAGHACH.

This song was composed by the late Mr. John MacDonald, Crobeg, Lewis. He was not one of the noted bards, and is not the author of any other song that has become well known. He left in MS. a few paraphrases in verse of several passages of Scripture. His grand-daughter, Miss Maggie MacDonald, Carloway, Lewis, inherited his fine poetical genius. The present, able, and cultured, Free Church Minister, Rev. W. J. MacDonald, M.A., Kirkcaldy, is a grandson of the poet. The song is very popular, and very few song collections are without it. Several English translations of it have already appeared in print.

    Young wert thou and I, Mary,
      In yon lone Glensmole,
    When Venus' little urchin
      Pierced me to the soul;
    And we drew together
      With an ardent zeal—
    I think such love no other two
      Have felt, or e'er can feel.

    Oft wert thou and I, Mary,
      In the desert wild,
    And ne'er with thought of evil
      Were our hearts defiled;
    Since each for each we cherished
      Affection good and true,
    And bright, as were the beams that shone
      The high green branches through.

    Though Albion all were mine, Mary,—
      Its silver and its gold—
    How could I contented be
      Should that love grow cold?
    I'd rather hold thy hand
      With love's own right, by far,
    Than own the jewelled stores of wealth
      In Europe's bounds that are.

    How thy curly locks, Mary,
      Round thy small ears stray!

O'er every other hair, by right,
    They bear the prize away :
Thy neck is like the sea-gull
    Sailing o'er the sea ;
With thy fine eyebrows, Mary,
    Dark frowns can ne'er agree.

Above a king's our state, Mary—
    That happy pride of ours,
When 'neath the budding leaves we sat
    On tender grass and flowers ;
The desert with its scented air,
    Our very hearts to feed,
Where the sweet streams roll'd past us
    To nourish every seed.

There never was an instrument
    Beneath the sun could play,
A music half so sweet as ours,
    When thus we'd steal away —
The lark above the little pool,
    The thrush on every spray,
The cuckoo with its "goog-go,"
    In fragrant morn of May.

THE LOVE THAT WILL NOT FADE.

(An gaol nach fàilnich.)

The love that will not fade,
    The love that will not fade,
For thee—for thee my fair-haired maid—
I feel the love that will not fade,
    The love that will not fade.

Thy golden hair—thy sunny hair—
  It seems to me the day beams there;
And in thy face that is so fair,
Where ne'er I saw black passion's shade,
  O never passion's shade.

Thine eye is blue—thine eye is bright—
  And shining with celestial light;
To watch thy smile was my delight,
O'er all thy face it sweetly played,
  From thy red lips it played.

Beautiful—O beautiful!—
The kind, good thoughts within thee rule,
  O beautiful and beautiful;
To see thy soul with meekness swayed,
My fair, my good, my Highland maid—
  Thy soul with meekness swayed.

The love that will not fade
  I give to thee my fair-haired maid;
O in the grave let me be laid
Before I lose thee—lowly laid—
And in my winding sheet arrayed,
  In winding sheet arrayed.

These Fugitive Songs were composed mostly by men and women who knew nothing of any other literature than such as happened to be contained in their own language. They formed the heart-treasure of men and women who were generally no better instructed than the authors of them. They come, for the most part, directly from the mint of nature, and have, many of them, a freshness and simplicity about them—an artless confession of sentiment, which appear in every case to have been actually experienced; and simple as they are, there is a certain charm pervades them, not always found in more elaborate and ambitious compositions.

ANCIENT GAELIC BARDS.

OSSIANIC POETRY.

How MacPherson's Ossian took its present form,—whether it grew gradually in the lapse of ages into its present size and dignity, or was moulded by some single mind—MacPherson's own or another's—rolling together all it could collect of the ancient remains, and welding them by additions of its own, where these were considered necessary, in the heroic dimensions and shape in which it now appears,—this is a question which has long been agitated, but yet is not likely to be soon, if ever, finally and authoritatively, settled. As the controversy, however, has all along raged round the English Ossian, it can easily be imagined that some new light may yet be added to it, by a diligent and efficient examination of the Gaelic, which has scarcely, hitherto, been touched. The grand question now, and the key to the whole mystery—if there is any key to it—is, who wrote the Gaelic Ossian? MacPherson is declared by all who knew him to have been unfit for the task. He is said not to have been a very accomplished Gaelic scholar. He required the help of a friend in writing down the poems recited to him in his journey throughout the Highlands and Islands. He consulted his friends with regard to obscure words and difficult phrases in his manuscripts. He has slurred over some words, and mistranslated others; and finally, there is a well known story told of him and a witty Highland bard, named MacCodrum, which proves that MacPherson did not always use the most correct Gaelic idiom, even in ordinary conversation. But the writer of the Gaelic Ossian had need, not merely to have been a fine poet, but so complete a master of the language which he used, that he could compose it in a style which defies detection—supposing it to be modern,—and all this too, not as a person would now do it, with his work before him, but altogether without a model. The style, besides, of the Ossianic poetry, is totally distinct from that of all other Gaelic compositions, and notably original: the ring of it is recognisable in a moment. Who then wrote it? Is it to be supposed that MacPherson, while reaping all the honours and profits accruing from his connection with the most famous work of the age, got a good easy Highlander, qualified as a poet and scholar for the undertaking, to compose in secret—in obscurity and in neglect—a Gaelic Ossian from the English, and that this Highlander could have done his work, without giving a hint to any one of what he was about, and even without being apparently suspected, by any inquisitive acquaintance, of being a little busier than usual? Is this credible? To my mind it certainly is not. But then again it may be said that MacPherson, by diligent study, at last fitted himself for the work; for the Gaelic Ossian did not appear until after his death. But on the other hand, we have to remember that the seventh book of Temora was published in Gaelic, along with the first English edition, and that MacPherson positively declares, that "a copy of the originals of the former collection lay for many months in the bookseller's hands, for the inspection of the curious."

Let it be added to this, that the Rev. John Farquharson, a Jesuit missionary, before the middle of last century,— that is about twenty years before the publication of MacPherson's Ossian— made a collection of Gaelic poems about Strathglass. This interesting MS. was afterwards unfortunately destroyed—torn up by the students of the

Scots College of Douay, who did not understand Gaelic and did not know its value, and used by them as long as it lasted, in lighting their winter fires. The Rev. James MacGilvray, who was at the Douay College, from the year 1763 to 1773, "during which time Mr. Farquharson was Prefect of Studies there, states that this MS. was a large folio, about three inches thick, entirely in Mr. Farquharson's own handwriting, and written pretty close, so that it must have contained a good deal." "Mr. MacGilvray could not say positively how Mr. Farquharson had collected the poems—that many of them certainly must have been obtained from hearing them recited; and he had a sort of remembrance that Mr. Farquharson frequently mentioned his having got a great many of them from Mrs. Fraser, and indeed it must have been so, as she first gave him a relish for Gaelic poetry, by the fine pieces with which she made him acquainted."

Mr. MacGilvray farther observes, "that in the year 1765, or 1766, Mr. Farquharson first saw MacPherson's translation of Ossian. It was sent to him by Mr. Glendoning of Parton. That he remembers perfectly well his receiving it, although he did not recollect the exact time; but Mr. Farquharson said when he had read it, that he had all the translated poems in his collection. That Mr. MacGilvray had, an hundred times, seen him turn over his folio when he read the translation, and comparing it with the Erse [Gaelic], and he could positively say that he saw him in this manner go through the whole poem of Fingal and Temora."

Perhaps, however, we need not conclude from this that Mr. Farquharson had " the whole poems of Fingal and Temora" in the very form in which they are given by MacPherson. From all that appears, they may have existed in his MS., partly as ballads, and partly as detached and polished poems, like Dr. Smith's "Old Lays." It is entirely credible that Mr. Farquharson making his collection before the rebellion of 1745, and assisted by Mrs. Fraser, whose first acquaintance with Gaelic poetry would date considerably farther back, might have obtained such a quantity of Ossianic poetry of all ages, that he could, very modestly, say he had in his MS. "the whole poems of Fingal and Temora," and prove this too by turning up any striking passage in either. We know that Dr. Donald Smith, using only the MS. collections in the possession of the Highland Society, put together out of their contents, as many as *eight hundred and ten lines*,—rather more than a fourth of the epic poem of Fingal given in MacPherson's Ossian. Now Mr. Farquharson enjoyed many advantages in making his collection over MacPherson. He preceded MacPherson by twenty years at least, and gathered his poems before the Highlands had suffered those rude changes, and great transition from one form of life into another, consequent on the rebellion: so he may have made a much more extensive collection than MacPherson's. We must, however, bear in mind that Mr. Farquharson made no objection whatever to Mr. MacPherson's Ossian, except that it did not equal the original in his hands.

"Mr. MacGilvray did not remember to have ever heard Mr. Farquharson tax Mr. MacPherson's translation with deviating essentially from the sense of the original, which he could not have failed to have done had he found reason for it; for he very frequently complained that it did not come up to the strength of the original; and to convince his friends of this, he used to repeat the Erse [Gaelic] expressions, and to translate them literally, comparing them with MacPherson's This difference, however, he seemed to ascribe rather to the nature of the two languages, than to any inaccuracy or infidelity in the translator."

To this remarkable and most explicit statement no more need be added than that MacPherson was seen, and even assisted, by various people while at his work.

Amongst these was Professor Adam Ferguson, himself a Highlander, and acquainted with the Gaelic language. He examined some of MacPherson's MSS. "much stained with smoke, and daubed with Scots snuff," and compared with the translations, the latter appearing exact and faithful, wherever so compared.

From these considerations it may be seen, that there is something yet unexplained about the Gaelic Ossian, and that they are therefore overhasty who ascribe it without reserve to MacPherson; although I allow that it is extremely probable that he had a hand in making, at least part of it up into its present form. I consider it, however, likely that MacPherson had, quite as frequently, to supply blanks caused by his rejection of such passages as did not come up to his standard, or did not suit his peculiar views, as by actual want of material. This may be easily seen from the other collections which contain things,—such as the adventures of Diarmad, of which he takes no notice. But it is also obvious, especially from Dr. Smith's "Old Lays," that there was a great quantity of floating poetry, very readily accessible in his day throughout the Highlands, as fine and tender, and polished, and elevated, as anything in his Ossian, which he seems somehow never to have come across.

Dr. MacIntyre of Glenorchy, charged MacPherson with being the author of the greater part of Fingal. "You are much mistaken," said MacPherson, "I had occasion to do less of that than you imagine." Mr. MacPherson was not the man to underrate his own abilities, or understate his own performances. To be "much mistaken" in considering such a man the author of "the greater part of Fingal," is to be almost altogether wrong in calling him its sole author.

In short, when we consider that the finest parts of MacPherson's Ossian are incontestibly proved to have been popular poetry long anterior to his appearing, I think we should throw all prejudice aside and affirm, that whoever composed the poems attributed to Ossian, James MacPherson was not the man; and whatever merit may belong to him as a translator, or whatever claim he may have to be considered their compiler in their present form, he has no legitimate title to be called their author. They are substantially older than he, probably by many centuries, and the case, as it rests at present regarding them, may be thus unhesitatingly stated:—MacPherson was not the first to polish the poems of Ossian, even admitting that he did so; neither was his the earliest, nor the ablest, nor the finest Highland mind that was kindled, since the end of the sixteenth century, into a glow of poetic fervour by the hero-lighted fire and hoary inspiration of the blind old bard of Cona.

In giving translations of poetry that comes under the general head of Ossianic, I may state once for all, that I will make use of no part of it which is not proved, by unimpeachable testimony, to be older than MacPherson. I do no say that it is by Ossian; for I believe, that not only has Ossianic poetry been handed down from the earliest ages, by tradition, in Scotland, but that Ossianic poetry has been composed throughout the Highlands, in every age, for six hundred years at least, down even to our own times; but it shall, in every case, be genuine popular Highland song.

Before giving any specimens of Ancient Gaelic Poetry, it will only be proper to say a few words of him who is the primal source, of all such poetry—in fact the patriarch of all Highland bards. The conception of his character entertained in the Highlands is in itself a poem, and I think one of the most touching and telling things in literature. Ossian, "the sweet voice of Cona," is the descendant of a race of heroes. Trenmore, in remote antiquity, was the great founder of the family. The name of this mighty shade, derived from his surpassing prowess, was still familiar in men's mouths when Ossian himself was an aged man. Trathal, his son, also a celebrated champion and ruler, succeeded him, leading the Fingalians, in their own poetic phrase, east and west with joy, and winning for himself, on account of his military glory and uniform success, the appropriate soubriquet, "of the routs." After him came his immortal grandson, Fingal, Cumhal's son, of the victories, conqueror in a hundred fights, the hero of a thousand lays, and the father of the bard and warrior to whom he owes his fame. Ossian was himself a hero, and his son, Oscar, the pride and hope of Selma, after being distinguished in many battles—after having met and vanquished the tyrants of the world on the banks of the Carron, was treacherously slain, while still a youth, and his grey stone raised on the field of his fame. One by one the other heroes followed, the great Cuchullin, the beautiful and brown-haired Diarmad, the stout and valiant Gaul, the son of Morni, the rash Conan, the hardy Ryno, and the swift and gallant Cailta. Fingal himself, somehow and somewhere, departed to the fathers, and the bard was left alone, with the silent mountains peopled by dim shades above him, and the rough streams that roared beneath him, and the winds that breathed around him, charged in their rising and their falling, with the memory of what had been, and never more could be. At last much of this too was gone. As age increased and solitude became deeper, the eyesight of the poet failed. He became blind, but was not even then utterly without consolation; for Malvina, the white-armed daughter of his ancient comrade, Toscar, who was to have married his son, and who still sometimes dreamed of the fallen young hero, and mingled her tears with those of his fond old father, as they mourned his untimely fate, she ministered to the sightless bard. Often too, as he basked in the bright sunshine, or meditated in the calm evening, or sat silent in the still soft moonlight, sweet, though mournful to his soul, came back the energetic years that had elapsed. Then all their vanished life—their aspiration and their power—murmured round him, like the muffled voice of the far-distant waves, when they spread moaning gently through the deep inland calm. Then the spirits of the mighty moved past him on their clouds—the harp-strings vibrating and sounding as in their sad and awful majesty they swept voicelessly ; but the soul of the poet recognised the dear familiar ancestral shades, and his mind's eye opening, kindled and flashed on the ever-memorable deeds of old, while his rising voice recited them, and sighed over them the heartfelt lamentation,—" last of my race !"

This is the picture given of the great Celtic Bard, Ossian, the son of Fingal, the assumed author of a vast quantity of Gaelic poetry, who lived, let us say, in the fourth century of the Christian era. It is a most poetic picture, and is, in its most essential features, so old, that this phrase, " Ossian after the Féinne," has passed long ago into a proverb.

It is quite unnecessary to enter into the question, how much of this picture is fact, and how much of it is fancy. All we need ask is, does the picture, in any respect, resemble the author or originator of the Gaelic Ossianic poetry? And for my part, I answer at once, that I think it does. It would be casting all tradition, unique, and uniform, and consistent as it is, most unwarrantably behind us, to say it does not. But when I assert that this picture does resemble the originator of the Gaelic Ossian, I would be understood as meaning only, either that such a man as the one described gave, at least the key-note to which is set all the succeeding poetry which is called Ossianic, or, at any rate, that this picture given, was the conception and work of him who first set the fashion in which the Ossianic muse has ever since been habited. I think it, however, right to say, that the last supposition appears to me much less probable than the first, seeing that the æsthetic sense of a primeval people, or what we might perhaps venture to call, their poetic etiquette, is of too frank a nature either to admit of or to admire, an undisguised personation of a fictitious character. People like to see and to embody in their pristine poetry, not merely truth but fact, that is to say, not merely a lasting agreement with the principles of thought, feeling, and action, which are always in nature; but even some actual manifestation of these, or some actual antagonism to these—something in fine, which they doubt not has been—so then, I think, we may safely conclude, that he, who long ages past, first originated the Ossianic poetry, was, with reverence let it be spoken, Ossian, the son of Fingal—last of all his race. That he was a great poet, cannot be questioned—he whose name and whose influence has survived so long, and spread so wide—who has been imitated so often, and who first touched that tender note which, in so many an exquisite fragment, still reaches our hearts so truly.

The first poem which I give, although not in this finer style, still displays no small skill in the poetic art. It is quite original, and a very pretty and fresh idea lies at its root. With wonderfully delicate touches a variety of personages are presented to us, and their distinct characters most artfully revealed. Altogether it is a pleasant little story, and most gracefully told. I give it in the metre to which we are most familiar in our Lowland ballads, although that changes slightly the measure of the original. All other necessary explanations I hope it will give for itself—

THE SWEETEST SOUND.

Once, when the kingly feast was spread,
　On Albin's golden slope,
The bards they sang of bliss and woe,
　Despair, and love, and hope.

And, heroes as they drained the bowl,
    With joy or sadness heard;
For those good harpers, as they pleased,
    Men's rising feelings stirred.

Lord of the feast there Fingal sat—
    His fair hair touched with grey—
Near his first son, the warrior bard,
    Strong as the noon of day.

The good MacLuy there conversed
    With Oscar, young and bright,
And bald-head Conan, rash and bold,
    Who never shunned the fight.

And Diarmad there sat, beautiful,
    And rolled his eye of blue,
When Fingal spoke, and all the board
    His regal question knew.

"Come, tell me now, my chieftains good,
    At Fingal's feast who be,
What sounds are they that form for each
    The sweetest harmony?

"What are the notes that charm you most,
    And send your cares to flight—
What sound most charms your inmost core,
    And thrills you with delight?"

Then Conan—the rash Conan spoke—
    Of all that company
The first to speak, the first to fight
    The last to think was he.

"The rattling dice I love the most,
    When the play is running high;

And my coming chances strain my ear,
    And almost blind my eye."

"When heroes rush together,
    When battle wakes around
With clash and clang and crushing blows
    I hear my sweetest sound."

So Oscar spoke.—Thus Diarmad said,
    "When in my secret ear
Sweet woman whispers love for me,
    My best loved sound I hear."

"When first I catch my good hounds' cry,
    Where the proud stag stamps the ground,
And stands at bay," MacLuy said,
    "I hear my sweetest sound."

Then Fingal said, "My music is
    The banner's fluttering fold
When winds blow free, and the brave I see
    Beneath its streaming gold."

Alas! alas! my sweetest sound
    Was once in Fingal's hall;
To hear bards sing, and heroes speak,
    And now they've perished all!

As these men spoke so admirably in character, we may think that they all answered well; except perhaps the rash and impulsive Conan. He is always prompt, testy, and foolhardy and never appears possessed of much judgment. Diarmad is gay and gallant, as might be expected in the lovely hero, of whom the prose tales say, he had an irresistible beauty-spot on his forehead, on which, whoever looked, loved him. Another ballad appropriately represents the last words of Diarmad to have been, "Farewell to courtship forever!" He, therefore, gives his opinion quite in keeping with his peculiar character. Oscar, the brave son of Ossian, speaks like a hero of the order of Achilles,—young, ardent, and aspiring; he utters his sentiments with the same rapid and impetuous energy with which he entered the field of battle. MacLuy again speaks as became a true hunter of deer and a fearless warrior, as he undoubtedly must have been; while Fingal himself is quite majestic, like the great ruler and shepherd of the people, as he always seems. Ossian himself appears in the last verse, looking back from his after solitude on that pleasant, well-remembered scene.

There is another little poem in which Ossian records his own tastes in sweet and chaste strains, and much more comprehensive than that of any of the hearers who spoke above. Having altered the rhythm I may have, consequently, slightly affected the expression of the original in what follows:—

Sweet is man's voice in solitudes, and sweet
The voice of birds amid the woods of spring—
Sweet is the sound when rock and water meet,
Where Bun-da-treor hears the surges sing:
Sweet are the light winds softly murmuring:
Sweet are the lonely heron's notes, and sweet
The cuckoo's, with the aged thoughts they bring:
Sweet the warm sun which whistling blackbirds greet—
The sun that brightly shines on Cona's rocky steep.

Sweet is the eagle, with her far-heard cry,
Sailing above great Morven's mighty sea,
When sleeps the noonday in the deep-blue sky,
And o'er the pool the hern bends silently:

Sweet is the lark that sings from heaven on high;
And one thing more is sweet,—Fingal's my sire!
Seven valiant bands he leadeth far and nigh:
When for the chase his hounds are all on fire,
Sweet is their deep-mouth'd bay—sweet as the bardic choir.

I am sure the reader will agree with me in thinking that our great and venerable bard had a very fine taste, and has here made a very beautiful selection—a choice bouquet—of what is still sweet and pleasant in the sights and sounds of our beloved Highlands. From the last lines of this little poem, as well as from the spirit that pervades it throughout, we may fancy that it was composed when the bard was still young—when his heroic career was opening out, and all nature lay bright and beautiful before him. Here every object is bright and happy; but more frequently, in the Ossianic poetry, it is no gay and glad eye that looks on nature: on the contrary we feel, as we listen to him, what a deep melancholy fills the heart of the singer.

The next specimen I give shows the same capacity with the first one, of perceiving at a glance and making instantly available, the most striking and pictorial treatment of which a subject is susceptible. This power must obviously be of the same use to a poet as that quickness of eye, which at once detects the main point of attack or defence in a position, is to a General; for in like manner it enables the poet so to arrange his conceptions, and so to lead them up to one apprehension, that they, most completely and effectually, take possession of the imagination. This power is displayed to good purpose in the following ballad. The Fingalian heroes are marshalled here in quite an imposing array. The original will be found in "MacCallum's Collection of the Poems of Ossian, Orrann, Ulinn, and other Bards who flourished in the same age". The collection was made orally, about the beginning of this century. There is a poem which in part closely resembles it in the Dean of Lismore's book; but the present version treats its subject in a far more picturesque and dramatic manner. I have not thought it necessary to enter into all the minutiæ of the slaughter, as it is given in the original. Oscar, for instance, is represented killing seven troops with his own hand, and the nine sons of red-haired Manus besides. Cailta and Gaul do execution in a like proportion; and the Féinne themselves suffer an immense loss.

THE BANNERS OF THE FEINNE.

On a hill stood the King of the North, and looked
    To the sea, where his proud ships rode;
Then he looked to the shore, where his camp strech'd along,
    And the heroes of Lochlin abode.

Then he turn'd to the land; and there, far away,
    A terrible hero came,
And above him a banner of Albin's gold
    Floated, and shone like a flame.

" Bard of sweet songs," said the King of the North,
    " What banner is this I see?
And the champion tall at the head of yon host,
    Is he of the sons of Victory?"

" That," said the bard, " is Diarmad MacDoon,
    His is the banner you see;
When the hosts of the Féinn' to the battle go forth,
    The first in the fight is he."

" But, bard of the songs, there's another now,
    And it is red as blood—
A mighty hero's at its head,
    High waves it o'er a multitude ?"

" That," said the bard, " is the banner of Raine,
    A manly chief and a good;
Heads are oft cleft 'neath its folds in twain,
    An ankles are bathed in blood."

" Again, what banner is this I see,
    Thou bard of beautiful song,
Dreadful the chief by its side appears,
    And heroes around it throng?"

" That is the banner of Gaul the Great;
    Yon yellow silken shred
Is the first to advance and the last to retire;
    From its shelter none ever has fled."

" There is another, thou tuneful bard,
    And a mighty man at its head,
It waves o'er a host—has it ever waved
    O'er a field of the conquer'd dead?"

" The dark and dread banner of Cailt'," said the bard,
    " Comes fluttering now to your sight;
Fame hath it won where the hosts have been great,
    And bloody the terrible fight."

" There is one other yet, bard of song and of tale!
    Yonder it waves o'er a host,
Like a bird in the air, o'er the roar of the surge,
    As it breaks on a storm-travers'd coast:"

"That is the besom of Peril, you see,
    The standard of Oscar," he said;
"First in renown in the conflict of chiefs,
    Still flutters yon banner of dread."

We rear'd up the Sunbeam—the standard of Finn;
    Fair gleam'd that banner on high,
With its sprangles of gold from the fields of its fame,
    As it greeted the morning sky.

There were nine chains of gold tied the flag to the staff,
    There were nine times nine chiefs for each chain;
Sad to the foe was that banner of light—
    They strove 'gainst its heroes in vain.

Then Finn spoke aloud, "Bend your heads, O my chiefs
    And redeem your pledge to me;
Show to Lochlin the hardy deeds he will find
    On our hills that look down on the sea."

We rush'd to the fray like a torrent,
    Down the mountain that rolls in spray;
And the fire from the strokes of our heavy swords,
    In columns of sparks broke away.

Many a shoulder, and head was gash'd
    Ere they turned from us in our ire,
And we heard the wild shrieks of our foes, as they fled,
    Like the snake when the heather's on fire.

That was the victory won by our king;
    And I, though now aged and grey—
Many a warrior fell by my hand
    On that dire and terrible day.

With respect to the age of this ballad, it would be needless to make any conjecture. It may belong to the time of the Vikings, and therefore be subsequent to the eighth century; or it may be even older in its first form, as there is said to have been a lively intercourse between Scotland and Scandinavia at a much earlier period. The following sentences, in reference to this subject, I quote from the work of a very intelligent foreigner:—"They— that is, the Songs of Ossian—have quite a peculiar interest for the Scandinavian North, from the striking agreement both in tone and spirit which they present to several of the Sagas and Edda. These last, again, afford a strong proof of the genuineness of those attributed to Ossian, since the songs of Sagas and Edda, at the time MacPherson published his 'Ossian,' were either not at all or but very imperfectly known even in Scandinavia itself, not to speak of other countries. The real age of Ossian's songs is very uncertain, and very difficult to discover; but this much is clear, that they indicate a lively intercourse between Alba (Scotland) and Lochlin (Scandinavia) long before the times of the Vikings, and previously to all historical accounts of connections between those countries." *

OSSIAN AND EVIR-ALIN.

A POET'S WOOING LONG AGO.

"Suiridh Oisein," or Ossian's wooing, is one of those old and popular bits of Highland poetry which, after having been sung for many generations, or many centuries perhaps, in ten thousand huts and houses, are still well

* "Warsae's Account of the Danes and Norwegians in England, Scotland, and Ireland." The Norwegians in Scotland. Section 9.

remembered and repeated by people who never read them in a book. It, and the "Lay of Diarmad," and the "Death of Oscar," and the "Banners of the Fingalians," and also the "Address to the Sun," are, to this day, found among old people who learned them from their fathers, who had again got them from theirs, and so on. The legitimate traditionary lineage of every one of these pieces can even yet be traced back with ease for more than a hundred years, in a good number of Highland cottages, where heroic poetry is never seen in print.

In the middle of last century, and before MacPherson published his far-famed work, "Ossian and Evir-Alin" was one of the most popular of Gaelic Ballads, as may be seen by a reference to the correspondence printed by the Highland Society in their report on Ossian. It is also found in all the collections of Gaelic poetry. The different versions of it all agree in their essential features. The age of the ballad it would not be easy to determine. It is probably one of the oldest of all the Ossianic fragments:—

Who is this friend that would soothe my grief?
    Who comes my age to cheer?
I know that light step and that gentle approach—
    It is thou, my daughter dear!

Daughter! a time was when I, now so weak,
    Could speed in the wild roe's flight:
When I, now so blind, could the beacon descry
    Far of in the dim dark night.

The time has been when, with sounding step,
    Away with the chieftains I'd wend;
Though this night thou must see me so lonely and sad,
    Without father, son, or friend.

My son! O my hero! how mournful the tale
  Which Cona's slow wave tells of thee!
And Fingal and Fillan are all pass'd away—
  Not one of the leaders I see.

Alas! and my sight too has faded,
  Nought around I descry, or above;
Gone is the hue of my youth—all is gone;
  But the grave cannot alter my love.

White-handed maiden! this night though you see me
  Old and forlorn in this place,
Renown'd have I been as a hero
  In my youth, with the bloom on my face.

On that day when soft-hair'd Evir-Alin,
  White-arm'd maiden follow'd me,
Daughter of Branno of the silver beakers,
  Of many loved, herself of love still free.

Sons of kings and sons of nobles,
  She refused them great or small;
Cormac woo'd her, gloomy chieftain,
  But him she hated worst of all.

Her I resolved to win, for I loved her
  With pure heart and steadfast truth;
And with twelve of Fingal's chiefs I went;
  We strode in the strength of youth.

We came to the dark lake of Lego;
  There a noble chief came to meet
And conduct us with honour to Branno—
  With honour and welcomings sweet.

Me he saluted—the twelve youths he hail'd;
  We sat with Branno at the feast;

But ere the evening pass'd away,
    Ere yet the mirth had ceased.

Branno inquired, "What is your purpose?
    What would you have of me?"
And Cailta said, "We seek thy daughter,
    Her would we have of thee."

Then Branno said, "But which of you would have her?"
    "Fingal's son." said Cailta: "this is he."
"Mighty hero of the wide ship-havens,
    Happy is the maid gets thee."

"So high the place, O Ossian!
    Do men's tongues to thee assign,
If I twelve daughters had" said Branno,
    "The best of them should be thine."

Then they open'd the choice and spare chamber,
    That was shielded with down from the cold;
The posts of its door were of polish'd bone,
    And the leaves were of good yellow gold.

Soon as generous Evir-Alin
    Saw Ossian, Fingal's son,
The love of her youth, by the hero—
    By me, young maid, was won.

Then we left the dark lake of Lego,
    And homeward took our way:
But Cormac, fierce Cormac, waylaid us,
    Intent on the furious fray.

Eight heroes Cormac had with him,
    And their men behind them stood;
The hillside flamed with their armour,
    Their spears were raised like a wood.

Eight heroes, with Cormac the stately,
  Of the Firbolgs, the best at need;
MacColla and Durra of wounds, and Tago,
  And Toscar's son good to lead;

Fresdal, the dangerous son of the king,
  And Dairo joyful and bland;
With Dail in straits hardy and good,
  He had Cormac's flag in his hand.

Eight came with Ossian the lofty,
  All equal to shield him in war;
Mulla and Skeno's son the generous,
  True Skellachie, known near and far.

Fillan and Cairdal the rash were there,
  And the black son of Revi, fierce and wight;
And Toscar, placed on the western flank,
  March'd with my standard to fight.

Toscar and Dail met face to face;
  Fierce was their strife and long,
Like the winds that rush forth on the ocean
  When the waves are heavy and strong.

Toscar remember'd his little knife,
  'T was a weapon he loved to hold;
Nine wounds he gave to Dail, and then
  The foe before us we roll'd.

But Cormac fiercely roused them, and look'd
  Like the hammer a strong hand wields
While he shouted and roar'd, and rush'd through the fight,
  And struck on our helmets and shields.

Five times he dash'd on my buckler;
  Five times I hurled him back,

Ere I struck him down on the green-sward,-
   Cormac in battle not slack.

I swept the head from his shoulders,
   And held it up in my hand;
His troops they fled, and we came with joy
   To Fingal's mountain land.

Whoe'er had told me on that day,
   I should be thus weak to-night,
Firm must his heart have been, and strong
   His arm in the desperate fight.

THE DEATH OF OSCAR.

I NOW proceed to give a poem on the death of Oscar, one of the most popular and touching themes of the Gaelic muse. Oscar was the Achilles of the Fingalians, and Ossian was both his Homer and his father. No wonder, then, his death affords a favourite and pathetic subject both for the oldest ballads and their most modern imitations. The "Lay of Oscar" is still repeated. There is a version of it in the third volume of J. F. Campbell's "Popular Tales," got within the last five or six years in the Hebrides. It is in all the collections. If we take MacCallum's and Mr. Campbell's versions to begin with, we are carried on very well to near the end of the story; then, by filling in a little from Allan MacRorie's and Fergus the poet's accounts, as they are found in the Dean of Lismore's book, we see our subject a good deal clearer; and, finally, we can end the sorrowful recital as we began. We thus get this old and manly popular song in the most complete state possible for us nowadays :—

The feast was over; and the last day dawn'd
Which Oscar was to spend in Cairbar's hall;
The parting cup was quaff'd, the heroes stood
Arm'd and prepared to go, when Cairbar said,
With his great voice, " Brown Oscar, come from Alba ;
Let us exchange our spear shafts ere we part !"

" Why so exchange," said Oscar, speaking calmly ;
" Thou red-hair'd Cairbar of the port of ships ?
Why so exchange, and the feast hardly o'er ?
Thou knowest, in the day of war and conflict,
My spear is always ready for thine aid."

" Not much for me," said Cairbar—the rude Cairbar ;
" Not much for me, were cess and tribute paid me
By every warrior in your sea-beat isles;
Not much for me ; whate'er I need to get
From thee, from thine, whene'er my wish I tell."

" There's neither gold nor precious substance, Cairbar,
That might be ask'd for by a manly king,
Without dishonour to himself or us,
But thou or he should have whene'er 't was ask'd :
But this exchange of shafts without the heads,
It were unjust to ask us such a thing.
Cairbar ! thou hadst not dared have spoken thus,
Hadst thou not known that Fingal is not by."

" Though Fingal and thy father both were here,
As good as the best day they wore a sword,
I'd ask of them whate'er I ask of thee ;
And what I ask of them or thee, I'll have."

" If Fingal and my father both were here,
As good as the best day they wore a sword,
By thine own might thou couldst not then retain
The breadth of thy two soles on land of Erin."

"I make a vow," quoth Cairbar, " deer to drive
From side to side of Albin's sea-girt hills,
And spoil to carry from its plains to Erin."

"I make a vow, a vow 'gainst that," quoth Oscar;
" When thou has come to Albin for thy sport,
I with this spear will drive thee back to Erin."

Then Cairbar roar'd—" I make a vow ere that,
A lasting vow, that I will plant my spear
Beneath thy breast, in thy fair body, Oscar!"

" A vow! a vow!" cried Oscar, in his wrath;
" I make a vow that I will plant my spear,
Ere that shall happen, in thy forehead, Cairbar."

Cold fear and rage, by turns, the warriors shook,
When these fierce words they heard between the chiefs,
When Cairbar's lowering brow they saw, and mark'd
How rose the wrath of Oscar. 'T was then a bard,
With softest touch upon the harp, wail'd forth
The sounds that prelude a great hero's death.

Then Oscar seized with furious rage his arms,
And look'd around him where his followers stood;
Few were the chiefs of Alba that were there,
And Cairbar's host was great; but Oscar's friends
Were train'd to arms, and were full heroes all,
And so they gather'd undismay'd around him.

Then waged the strife. We heard the shouts afar,
And all the din of deadly, furious battle;
And up we rose, and hasten'd to the scene.
Each, as he reach'd it, joined the wide-spread fight;
And thus the bitter struggle lasted long;
And thus did many of our heroes fall.

But who could stay his hand or still his heart,
And Oscar's friends oppress'd, and Oscar's sword,
By numbers wearied, failing in its power?

We saw him struggling on the woful field;
We saw him rushing, in the tides of war,
Like a hawk darting on a flight of birds,
Or like the quick spray-spattering cataract.
He strove, like a great strong branch with the wind,
Like an old green tree with the woodman's strokes.
His course was the roll of the furious surge
In winter's storm, on the roar of the shore.

And, one by one, as we came, we engaged;
But the long-lasting fight spread far and near,
Till the Sunbeam of battle rose, at last,
Finn's standard, with the heroes by its side;
Then slowly backward bore the treacherous foe,
Foot after foot, until they fled away—
Scatter'd like sheep, and falling like brown leaves.
The wild pursuit roll'd by, and we were left
Alone—in silence—on the dreadful field!

I bent o'er Oscar, when the fight was done,
As he lay bleeding on the mournful plain.
He was my son; yet was I not alone
In mourning for my dearest on that day.
Cailta bent over seven of his brave sons;
And every living man amongst the Féinn',
Amid the grevious slaughter found a friend,
And wept beside the dying or the dead.
Some of the wounded lay and languish'd low,
Unconscious how their life had drain'd away;
Some moan'd, some writhed with pain, and could not speak.

But some were calm and knew their friends, and gave
Them a kind greeting from their couch of clay;

But many, many heroes there were dead.
Oh, 't was a grief, an everlasting grief—
A woe to be forgotten never, never!
To look upon that field—the swords, the shields,
That there lay masterless; the broken spears,
The bloody garments, and the coats of mail,
Borne by brave chiefs unto their last of fields,
From Albin's hills, from homes of Innisgail.
We ne'er had met so dire a day before—
So bloody, so destructive, full of woe—
So joyless and so sad a victory.

Among a thousand warriors stretch'd and dead
I found my son, my darling, living yet;
Resting his head on his left arm he lay,
His broken shield beside him, and his sword
Grasp'd in his terrible and strong right hand,
His blood, his priceless blood, on every side
Flow'd, through his harness, soak'd into the ground,
Unstanch'd and stanchless, from a mortal wound,

I dropp'd my spear upon the earth, and bent
Above him as he lay, and thought—O friend!
How lonely I should be for evermore!
It was a grievous thought. Oscar turned round,
And forth he stretch'd his hand one other time
To greet me—one long last time ere he died;
Kindly he look'd, and wished me to draw near.
I seized his hand and knelt upon the ground,
And gave a great and bitter cry of grief.
Then, my dear son, whose life was ebbing fast,
Said, "Joy, dear father, that thou art escaped!"
And I, I could not speak: but Cailta said—
The noble Cailta come to see my son—
" How dost thou feel thyself, dear friend?" he said.

"As thou wouldst have me—dying on the field.
Red Cairbar's venom'd spear hath pierced my side;
Mine on the forehead struck him," Oscar said,
"A blow no Leech can heal." Then Cailta probed
The wound red Cairbar's murderous shaft had made,
And gave a shriek, and fainting fell on earth.
When he found out how deadly was the hurt.

"Dear Oscar, we must part," at length he cried;
"Thou and the Féinne must part; thy fights are o'er."
My son replied not, but he press'd my hand,
Then we upraised him softly on our spears,
And to a fair green knoll we bore him silently,
While from the slain they gather'd round and round.
No man his son, his friend, his brother mourn'd,
But all stood near us, and with heavy sighs
They watch'd the hero as he slowly died,
And no one spoke as hour by hour went by.

"'T was now the evening, and the autumn sun
Shone bright and yellow on the fatal field,
When from afar Finn's standard we descried,
Returning from his triumph and pursuit.
Gladly we met it, and saluted Finn,
But no salute return'd he as he strode
In his dark grief to where his grandson lay.
When Oscar saw the King above him bend,
And look with anguish on his dying face,
He slowly spoke, and said, "I have my wish
Thus dying in thy presence, noble Finn!
Unconquer'd and with honour, mourn'd by thee."

Then Finn, the first of heroes, cried with grief,—
"Sad is my heart, good son of my good son!
To see thee die before me. Now I'm weak.
A heavy curse is on me to my grief;

It follow'd me from east and west, till here,
On this sad plain, it struck this fatal blow.
Farewell to fame and battle; and farewell
The victor's spoils, the triumphs and the joys
Which in this body I have ever had;
Farewell the feast; farewell the concourse sweet
By Cona's stream, in Selma's banner'd hall."
When Oscar heard the great king's wailing cry,
He groan'd, and stretch'd his hands, and raised his head,
And, looking round on all of us, he sigh'd,
And said, "Farewell! I shall return no more."
Then he sunk back; and so my hero died;
And Finn turn'd round, and strode a space away,
And sobb'd and wept. He never wept before
In sight of man—save when Bran died—till now.
And all the people gave three dismal shrieks,
And wail'd and wept until the night return'd.

Then Finn came back; and, standing near my side,
He bent again o'er Oscar, while he said:—
"The mournful howling of the dogs distress me—
The groaning of the heroes old and grey—
The people's wailing, and their blank despair.
O son! that I had fallen in thy stead,
In the dire battle with thy treacherous foes,
And thou hadst lived to be a chief and leader,
And bring the Fenians east and west with joy!
O Oscar! thou wilt never rise again!
O'er thee my old heart, like an elk, is leaping!*
Thou wilt return, thou wilt return no more!
'T was rightly said, 'I shall return no more!'"

---

* "Like an elk, is leaping;" or, "like a blackbird, flutters." The former, however, is at once the most literal, and, I think, the most expressive. We speak ourselves of the heart "bounding."

"The Death of Oscar" was MacPherson's first open attempt at Gaelic translation. We have this on the authority of Home,* the author of "Douglas." Some of the incidents referred to remind one of a little of Roncesvalles, and the death of Roland.

THE LAY OF DIARMAD; OR, FINGAL'S REVENGE.

The "Lay of Diarmad" is probably one of the oldest, and has, from time immemorial, been one of the most popular of the Ossianic poems. It is still repeated in the Highlands. Versions of it can be got, even at this day, from men who learned it, not out of old books, but as it was committed to their congenial care by that old traditionary tutor, who is now about to perish, with the last lingering remnant of his scholars, out of sheer decrepitude and vast old age. By calling the "Lay of Diarmad" an Ossianic poem, no more can be meant than

* The Rev. John Home, was the successor of the Rev. Robert Blair,—author of the "Grave"—at Athelstaneford in East Lothian. Home wrote a few tragedies, one of which was designated "Douglas", the plot of which is taken from the beautiful old ballad of "Gil Morice". "Douglas" was performed in Edinburgh and in London with great applause. The Author was present in the Edinburgh theatre at the first representation. In consequence of this violation of clerical propriety, he was compelled to resign his living in 1757. David Hume on hearing Dr. Carlyle of Inveresk preach in Mr. Home's Church, said to him, "What did you mean by treating John's congregation to-day with one of Cicero's academics? I did not think such heathen immorality would have passed in East Lothian." For his literary works, the Prince of Wales, after his accession to the throne, granted Home a pension of £300 a year. Home died September 5th, 1808, in his 86th year.

that it belongs to the Ossianic era; for it scarcely possesses the character of the poems of Ossian, and hardly harmonises with the sentiment which pervades them, or with the manners which their blind old bard has painted. This is especially evident in the conduct of Finn; also, in the absence of all the other heroes, so far as appears, from the great hunting. Not one of them, as will be seen, is mentioned by name. Gràinne lives in tradition as the faithless wife of Fingal—the Guinevere of ancient Gaelic song; but she does not appear, I think, in any of the finer heroic poems. This "Lay of Diarmad" is, however, as I have said, extremely popular; and the "Hunting of the Great Wild Boar" is one of the least likely of any of the Fingalian legends to be soon forgotten. There are good reasons why it should continue to be remembered. The boar's head is the crest of the Argyll branch of the Campbells, and all that great clan trace their origin back to the Sir Lancelot of the Féinne—Diarmad, the son of Duibhne—who slew the Wild Boar. There is a sept of the Campbells still called, "Clann Diarmaid." This was probably the name of the whole clan at one time. From a letter, written by Mr. Pope,[*] minister of Reay, in Caithness, to the Rev. Alex. Nicholson, minister of Thurso, 15th November, 1763, and published in Appendix, No. III., to the Highland Society's Report on the Ossianic poems, we learn that an old man of the name of Campbell, in that part of the country, could never be prevailed upon to sing the "Song of Diarmad" without first taking off his

---

[*] The Rev. Alexander Pope, minister of Reay, Caithness-shire, was the author of a Description of the Shires of Caithness and Sutherland. He also wrote a Description of the Dune of Dornedilla. In the summer of 1732 this Reverend equestrian rode on his pony from Caithness to Twickenham in England, in order to visit his famous literary namesake, Alexander Pope, the poet, who presented his clerical friend with a beautiful copy of the Odyssey, and a handsome snuff-box.

bonnet in honour of the ancestral shade. Mr. Pope's simplicity, and his manner of telling a story in his rather peculiar English, are both so charming that it would be almost inexcusable not to give his own words. It is a pity he did not write more letters about the eccentricities of his parishioners. A collection of them, if they resembled this one, would have made a very entertaining volume. Mr. Pope writes as follows:—" There is an old fellow in this parish who, very gravely, takes off his bonnet as often as he sings 'Duan Dearmot.' I was extremely fond to try if the case was so, and, getting him to my house, gave him a bottle of ale, and begged the favour of him to sing 'Duan Dearmot.' After some nicety, he told me that to oblige his parish minister he would do so; but, to my surprise, he took of his bonnet. I caused him to stop and put on his bonnet. He made some excuses. However, as soon as he began, he took off his bonnet. I rose and put it on. He took it off. I put it on. At last he was like to swear most horribly, he would sing none unless I allowed him to be uncovered. I gave him his freedom, and so he sung with great spirit. I then asked him the reason. He told me it was out of regard to the memory of that hero. I asked him if he thought that the spirit of that hero was present? He said not; but he thought it well became them who descended from him to honour his memory." This shows the fast hold which the notion of a descent from the Fenian hero took of the popular mind. Although Diarmad makes no great figure in MacPherson's "Ossian," he is a very conspicuous actor in the prose legends and other traditions of the Highlands. This poem— sometimes called Duan or Heroic Song, sometimes Laoidh (with the *dh* silent) or Lay, sometimes Bàs Dhiarmaid, or the Death of Diarmad—is in many of the collections of Gaelic poems. That of MacCallum has been principally but not wholly followed in this translation:—

THE LAY OF DIARMAD.

Hearken a little, I sing you a song
   Of the great and good who are gone—
Of Gràinne, and Finn the triumphant,
   And the woful fate of MacDoon.

Sweet is Glen-Shee, and the valley beside it,
   With the voice of elk and deer;
And pleasant its stream tinged so often,
   With blood from the Fenian spear.

Fairest of hill is Ben-Goolbain,
   Where the fawn and the doe wont to be;
And the hounds bay loudly together,
   When they drive the wild deer o'er the lea.

"O Diarmad! my own one!" said Gràinne,
   "Let the dogs drive the chase o'er the lea;
Come not thou near the proud son of Cumhal,
   Who is wroth with my hero for me."

"In spite of his anger," said Diarmad;
   "In spite of his wrath and pride,
I will go to the chase now as fearless
   As ever I trode by thy side."

With the bay of the dogs, and the shout of the heroes,
   In the calm of the morning air,
They roused the great Boar from his slumber,
   And watch'd every pass from his lair.

Up he rose in his wrath when he heard them,
   And rush'd round the glen where he stay'd;
He turn'd east, he turn'd west, ere he darted,
   Foaming with rage, from the shade.

From the shade of the rock down he rattled
    Past the hounds and huntsmen shear;
His huge bristles pointed like javelins,
    And his tusks like the point of a spear.

Then slipp'd they the dogs, and they drove him
    Down Lodram's mossy side;
Long strove they to tear him, but could not
    While the hunters cheerily cried.

"Son of Doon, dost thou wish to win honour?"
    Said Finn in his wrath and pride;
"Slay that boar by thyself, thou gay victor,
    Which the heroes so long has defied."

Diarmad's tough spear was soon chew'd into splinters,
    Like reeds on Lego that grow;
But the boar fell beneath his hard sword-blade,
    Victorious o'er many a foe.

Then Finn he lay down on the green sward,
    And moodily turn'd from the sight;
He grieved that the son of Doon had escaped
    Without wound, from the furious fight.

"O Diarmad! measure the boar," he said,
    "With thy bare feet, for great is his size,"
He measured the boar with the bristles,
    Sixteen good feet where he lies.

"O Diarmad! measure him back again;
    He is not so much," Finn cries.
He measures him back and a poisonous bristle
    Pierces his foot as he tries.

"O Fingal!" said Diarmad, "vouchsafe me
    One draught from thy life-giving shell,

For my strength and my vigour forsake me:—
    With one draught, O my king! make me well."

"Shall I bring thee a draught, thou fair hero!
    From the lake, with my life-giving shell,
When the ill in one hour thou has done me
    Outweighs all the good thou canst tell?"

"Eastward and westward I've served thee,
    And ne'er did thee ill, till the day,
When Gràinne, with love-witching magic,
    Drew me her captive away.

"Remember the smithy of Luno,
    How I in that fray help'd thee well,
When that sword was first won thou now wearest."
    "Thou shalt yet get no drink from my shell."

"Remember the conflict with Draidgal,
    And the strokes on thy shield that fell;—
'Twas I who then succour'd and saved thee."
    "Thou shalt yet get no drink from my shell."

"Then, thou'st forgotten the battle of Conhail,
    And the fate which that day had assign'd,
With the army of Bairbar before thee,
    Had not I and the Féinn' been behind.

"Alas! that I saw thee, Ben-Goolbain!
    Alas! that I faced thee to-day,
With the strength of my youth streaming from me—
    With my life-blood ebbing away!

"Hill of my love, O Ben Goolbain!
    Where the deer and the roe wont to be;

Farewell! thou wilt never come to me,
    Nor e'er shall my steps reach to thee.

"Farewell! now to courtship for ever!
    O king, what a sorrowful sight,
For the maids of the Féinn' thus to see me!
    Sad will their dreams be this night."

"Alas! that," said Finn, "for a women,
    I've slain my own sister's son—
For an ill woman slain him! Too noble
    To be slain for the lovliest one.

"Yesterday, green wert thou, Goolbain!
    To-day art thou bloody and red.
Hill of our sorrows, Ben-Goolbain!
    Beneath thy grey stones is his bed.

"Beneath thy grey stones, O Ben-Goolbain!
    The brown-hair'd chief is laid;
His blue eyes are sleeping for ever
    Under thy green grassy shade.

"Sad stood the heroes beside thee,
    O youth of the noble race!
And dim grew the eyes of each maiden
    When the mould went over thy face.

"And now, like the tree, I stand lonely—
    Wither'd, and wasted, and sear;
With the rude howling tempest to tear me,
    Where the shade of no green bough is near."

OSSIAN'S ADDRESS TO THE RISING SUN.

The poem which, on every account, ought to be first, as being the most ambitious in its nature, and certainly not the least successful in its mode of dealing with its theme, which comes under this head, is "Ossian's Address to the Rising Sun." This poem is found in English in MacPherson's Carthon. The version from which MacPherson translated was imperfect, like that in Stewart's Collection. It seems to have consisted of only thirty-eight lines, the same as that supplied to the Highland Society, in 1801, by the Rev. Mr. MacDiarmad, as got by him thirty years before from an old man in Glenlyon. This old man learned it in his youth from people in the same glen, and before MacPherson was born. Mr. MacDiarmad took down this "Address to the Sun," along with the "Address to the Setting Sun," the "Bed of Gaul," and some other fragments, as he says himself, "from the man's own mouth." Captain A. Morrison depond to the Committee of the Highland Society, that he got the "Address to the Sun" among Mr. MacPherson's original papers, when he was transcribing fairly for him from these original papers (either collected by himself, or transmitted to him by his Highland friends,) as it stood in the poem of Carthon, afterwards translated and published. Now it is very remarkable that notwithstanding this—notwithstanding that the poem of Carthon is included among the poems published according to the terms of his Will, by MacPherson's executors, yet the "Address to the Sun" is not in the Gaelic of MacPherson's Ossian at all. Its place in the poem of Carthon is marked by asterisks. Why was this? Did MacPherson, knowing it to be admired, actually wish to appropriate the glory of its production to himself, and so, by not publishing the Gaelic at all, try to throw discredit on those versions which other collectors might possess? Or had he lost it, as it lay loose among his papers, and found himself unable to supply it? Was its omission an oversight? At all events it is a strange circumstance that the "Address to the Sun," is not found among the poems published by Macpherson's executors, as the original of his "Ossian," and the stars which mark its absence in Carthon, point the way to some curious inquiry.

The Address, as it is now printed, consists of fifty-four lines, in place of Mr. MacDiarmad's, Captain Morrison's, Stewart's, and MacPherson's thirty eight. Following Mr. MacDiarmad's copy, and taking from MacCallum's, where the other is imperfect, I present the following as a complete copy :—

O thou! that wanderest there on high,
  Round as a chief's hard shield and bright,
Whence comes thy gloomless lustre nigh,
  O sun! enduring light?

Thou comest with lovliest might,
  And the stars their courses hide;
Hueless the moon leaves the sky,
  And shrouds in the western tide:
Then thou goest forth alone,
  There is none dare keep by thy side!

Falls the oak from the place where it grew;
  Falls the rock by age o'erthrown;
Ebbs ocean tide and it flows;
  And fades the pale moon from the view;
Yet still thy bright triumph glows!
  In the joy of thy light thou goest on!
Even when blackens the noisy storm,
  When thunders roar and lightnings fly,
Thou lookest through the wild troubled swarm,
  With thy smile of delight from the sky!

But me thou will never regard—
   Night banished from sea and from shore
Still remains in the eye of the bard—
   Thy face shall I see no more.
When thy golden bright locks, without stain,
   The fair eastern cloud have drest;
Or thou tremblest over the main
   At thy dusky door of the west.

Yet aged, and feeble, and gray,
   Thou too may'st in solitude go,
And grope through a dim sky thy way,
   As blind as myself, and as slow.

Like the changing moon may'st thou fade,
   And the morning may call thee in vain;
For then shalt thou sleep, lowly laid,
   With the heroes who rise not again.

The hunter will look o'er the plain—
   He will look in his rising fears;
His eyesight for long will he strain,
   And then, in a wild burst of tears,
Returning in sadness, will say,
   "Choice hound, no sun now appears
On our moors or our mountains for aye!"

Yes, it may be that thou, like me,
   But for a time with strength are blest,
Till our years all exhausted shall be,
   And in one certain end take their rest.

Then rejoice, O sun! and be glad—
   Thou prince, in thy vigorous noon!
For age is unpleasant and sad,
   Like the dim and faint light of the moon

> When it looks through a cloud on the heath,
>   Where the grey mists lag round the stone,
> Ere the blasts of the cold north breathe
>   On the traveller, wearied and lone.

MacCallum's and the common versions here end with,

> The light of the night will rejoice
>   When the sun of glory is gone.

Dr. Smith's version says:—

> The light of the night will rejoice
>   When the sun of glory is as Trathal.

Trathal was the great-grandfather of Ossian, and the hero of the poem in which the Address is introduced.

I will now give these passages as they were translated for MacCallum's Collection by the late Ewen MacLachlan, Rector of the Grammar-school Old Aberdeen:—"But thus aged, feeble, and gray, thou shall yet be alone; thy progress in the sky shall be slow, and thou shalt be blind, like me, on the hill; dark as the changeful moon shall be thy wanderings in the heavens; thou shalt not hear the awakening voice of the morning, like the heroes that rise no more; the hunter shall survey the plain, but shall not behold thy coming form; sad he will return, his tears pouring forth, 'My favourite hound, the Sun has forsaken us?'" There is something, it appears to me, singularly wild and impressive in that burst of the sun-lorn hunter, "My favourite hound, the Sun has forsaken us!" It is altogether a very strange fancy this of the final darkening of the day, and may be perhaps connected with some forgotten Highland superstition. It is surely very creditable to the intelligence, the taste, and the sentiment of the Highland people, that such a high-toned lyric as this belongs to their popular poetry.

The "Address to the setting Sun," probably on account of its shortness, was even better known than the preceding. This poem as given by MacPherson in the opening of Carricthura, consists of eleven lines, and so far corresponds exactly with the popular version. It is descriptive of a summer sunset; but in Dr. Smith's Cathula there are sixteen lines descriptive of the appearance of the sun in a bleak wintry day, twelve of which are generally joined to the above eleven, when the Address is collected from among the people. I have preferred dividing them, as I think they read better so, and in a slightly varied rhythm. They are both beautiful lyrics :—

ADDRESS TO THE SETTING SUMMER SUN.

HAST thou left the blue depths of the sky,
    Thou blameless Son—thou golden tressed ?
The doors of the night open lie,
    To thy place of repose in the west.
Calmly the sea-waves come nigh,
    To look on thy face bright, and best,
Raising their heads fearfully shy,
    When they see thee so grand in thy rest:
Now wan from thy side they've passed by—
    Then sleep in thy cave darkly drest,
O sun ! but with joy to the new dawning hie.

Here everything is in repose, but the rest, though usually joined to this and equally beautiful is very different. The poet in fact here seems to have been forcibly reminded of the contrast between the hopeful rest, the undisturbed peace, the glorious beauty of the scene before him, and the transitory life of himself and of all the benighted mortals around him. Heroes, perhaps, rose to his memory who had run a princely course, amid triumphs and abounding praises; but who, lying down in blood, had at last set in trouble,—slept and never woke again. The friends of his youth and his manhood, where were they? The noble and the brave, with whom he had exchanged sweet intercourse, "and whom his good strong heart had cherished in its core—the stately and the full-developed hero, fit to guide his people east and west with triumph and with joy, blessing them with his rule in peace, and plucking them, even from the extreme of peril, not merely safely, but with renown—the aged man, whose mind was like a storehouse of the wisdom of the past, and who could teach the lays in which were treasured the music and the worth of other times,—all these had shone a moment, lights of the world, and then had set as mysteriously as yonder sun; but not like him to rise again next morrow. No; nor even for a chill and wintry season to be absent, and then return once more. Alas! they were gone irrevocably. Then, what were they like?

  Like a sun-gleam in wild wintry weather
    That hastens o'er Lena's wide heath,
  So the Féinne have faded together.
    They were the beam the showery cloud sheathe,
  When down stoops the dark rain frown of heaven,
    To snatch from the hunter the ray,
  And wildly the moaning bare branches are driven,
    While the weak herbs all wither away.

  But the sun, in his strength yet returning,
    The fair-freshened wood will espy,
  In the spring-time that laugh for their mourning,
    As they look on the Son of the sky,
  Kindly unveiling his lustre,
    Through the soft and the drizzling shower.

All their wan heads again will he muster
   From their drear and their wintry bower.
Then with joy will their small buds keep swelling:
   Not so they who sleep in the tomb—
No sunbeam, that darkness dispelling,
   Shall waken them up from their gloom.

Thus then does the Highland Popular Poetry, philosophically and instructively, unite the profoundest sentiments of human hearts, with the fairest and most suggestive aspects of nature. The lofty old bard, who produced these old fragments, speaks of the glorious appearance and effect of power before him, like one who had heard, and felt, and thought over "the still, sad music of humanity," and therefore his poetry is so essentially lyrical, and overflowing with such fine emotion.

"Grian," the Gaelic word for sun, is feminine. The sun is here addressed as masculine—a circumstance which, in the opinion of some Ossianic critics, creates an odd confusion, and goes against the great antiquity of this fine fragment. The supposed confusion, however, does not appear to have been perceived by the unlettered reciters of the poem—who preserved it among them for, at any rate, several generations, and by whom it is said to be still repeated. This is something singular; for, both in Gaelic writing and conversation, the sun is uniformly represented by the pronoun *she*, and not *he*. Thus, in the 19th Psalm, we read in Gaelic—as in German, where the sun is also feminine—"*She* is like a bridegroom." "*She* rejoiceth as a hero that runs the course." *Her* going fourth is from the end of the heaven." There is nothing whatever that may be hid from the heat of *her*."

Goethe, in that most grand address to the setting sun, which he has put into the mouth of the melancholy Faust, makes his desponding hero address the great luminary as "goddess," and not "god." It certainly is very strange, then, that a Gealic scholar and poet—whether he was ancient or not—should think of calling "Grian" son, and not daughter; and spoken of it as "him of the brightest face," and not "her of the brightest face." But it is still stranger to me that the Gaelic-speaking people, who knew only their own language, should have continued repeating this fragment to one another, and should have given it unaltered to the collectors, without appearing to see the least incongruity in it, if there really is any.

In English, the sun is sometimes neuter, sometimes masculine; and in Hebrew, the word for sun, "Shemesh," is also of common gender—sometimes masculine and sometimes feminine. There may be something of this sort in the Celtic idea, though not in the Celtic word "Grian."

"The Address to the Sun," as given in Dr. Smith's "Old Lays," consists of forty-two lines. In the first twenty-six it differs entirely from what appears in the other collections; but in its concluding sixteen lines it exactly corresponds with the like number of lines contained in the Address already given. For the gratification of those of our readers who can understand the original, but who have never met with it before, we give it here:—

DAN DO'N GHREIN.

A Mhic na h-òg-mhaidne! ag éiridh
Air sléibhtibh soir le d' chiabhan òr-bhuidh
'S ait ceuma do theachd air an aonach,
'S gach caochan 's a' ghleann ri gàire;

Tha croinn uaine ro' dhrùchd nam fras,
Ag éiridh gu bras a' d' chòmhdhail,
A's filidh bhinn nan coillte fàs
A' cur fàilt ort gu moch le 'n òran.

Ach c'àit' am bheil ciar-imeachd na h-oidhche
Ro' d' ghnùis, mar air sgiathaibh an fhìrein?
C'àit' am bheil aig duibhre a chòmhnuidh?
'S uamh chòsach nan reulta soillse—
Tràth leanas tu 'n ceuma gu luath,
Mar shealgair 'g an ruagadh 'san speur;
Thusa 'dìreadh nan aonach àrd,
'S iadsan air faoin-bheanntaibh fàs a' leum?

'S aoibhinn do shiubhal, a Sholuis Aigh,
A sgaoileas, le d' dheàrsadh, gach doinionn;
'S is maiseach do chleachdan òir
A' snàmh siar, 's do dhòigh ri pilleadh.
Le seachran, 'an dall-cheo na h-oidhche,
Cha ghlacar thu chaoidh a' d' chùrsa;
'S doinionn nan cuanta gàbhaidh
Cha séid gu bràth as t-iùil thu.
Le gairm na ciùin-mhaidne bidh t' éiridh,
'S do ghnùis fhaoilidh a' dùsagdh le gean,
A' fògradh na h-oidhch' o gach àite
Ach gnùis a' bhàird, nach faic do sholus.

TRANSLATION.

Son of the young morn! that glancest
   O'er the hills of the east with thy gold-yellow hair,
How gay on the wild thou advancest
   Where the streams laugh as onward they fare;

And the trees, yet bedewed by the shower,
   Elastic their light branches raise,
While the melodists sweet they embower
   Hail thee at once with their lays.

But where is the dim night duskily gliding,
   On her eagle wings, from thy face?
Where now is darkness abiding?
   In what cave do bright stars end their race—
When fast, on their faded steps bending
   Like a hunter you rush through the sky,
Up those lone lofty mountains ascending,
   While down yon far summits they fly.

Pleasant thy path is, Great Lustre, wide-gleaming,
   Dispelling the storm with thy rays;
And graceful thy gold ringlets streaming
   As wont, in the westering blaze,
Thee the blind mist of night ne'er deceiveth,
   Nor sends from the right course astray;
The strong tempest, all ocean that grieveth,
   Can ne'er make the bend from thy way.
At the call of the mild morn, appearing,
   Thy festal face wakens up bright,
The shade from all dark places clearing,
   But the bard's eye that ne'er sees thy light.

Let us now pass from the Sun to the Ocean, and see how the Ancient Gaelic Bards treat of it. The following effusion, although in its original form it is only a kind of a wild chant—almost indeed half prose, yet it is the germ of a ballad. It occurs in many of the Tales contained in that wonderful repository of old Gaelic lore, the "Popular Tales of the West Highlands," sometimes more, and sometimes less perfect. The original of what follows, will be found in of the second volume of the "Tales," and is of course very old. We see what daring boatmen the Western Highlanders must have been, when they could encounter and speak of the dangers of the deep, in so gallant and dashing a fashion as it manifests. But it may be thought, perhaps, that the Hebrideans were thus taught by the ancient Vickings; although, surely they who lived in islands surrounded by the Atlantic, to whom all its mighty moods were as familiar as daylight—who had to contend with it manfully when they sought to leave their homes—or when they ventured to tax its prolific waters for their maintenance, needed no Vickings, nor any other people to train their hands to skill, or fortify their hearts, when they rode on the strong surges of their own immeasurable seas. The vigorous and elastic spirit that pervades the following verses, must have strung the heart of many a hardy mariner who loved to feel the fresh and briny breeze drive his snoring birlinn, bounding like a living creature over the tumbling billows of the inland loch, or the huge swell of the majestic main.

A SAIL IN THE HEBRIDES.

We turned her prow into the sea,
   Her stern into the shore,
And first we raised the tall tough masts,
   And then the canvas hoar;

Fast filled our towering cloud-like sails,
   For the wind came from the land,
And such a wind as we might choose
   Were the winds at our command:

A breeze that rushing down the hill
   Would strip the blooming heather,
Or, rustling through the green-clad grove,
   Would whirl its leaves together.

But when it seized the aged saugh,
   With the light locks of grey,
It tore away its ancient root,
   And there the old trunk lay!

It raised the thatch too from the roof,
   And scattered it along;
Then tossing it throughout the air,
   Singing a pleasant song.

It heaped the ruins on the land,
   Though sire and son stood by
They could no help afford, but gaze
   With wan and troubled eye!

A flap, a flash, the green roll dashed,
   And laughed against the red;
Upon our boards, now here, now there
   It knocked its foamy head.

The dun bowed whelk in the abyss,
   As on the galley bore,
Gave a tap upon her gunwale
   And a slap upon her floor.

She could have split a slender straw—
   So clean and well she went—
As still obedient to the helm
   Her stately course she bent.

We watched the big beast eat the small—
   The small beast nimbly fly,

And listened to the plunging eels—
The sea-gull's clang on high.

We had no other music
To cheer us on our way.
Till round those sheltering hills we passed,
And anchored in this bay.

THE BED OF GAUL.

This fragment forms the Lament spoken by Fingal over the dead bodies of Gaul and of his wife. It occurs at the conclusion of a much longer poem in Dr. Smith's "Old Lays." The argument of the whole poem is thus shortly stated:—" Fingal summoned his heroes for an expedition to the Isle of Ifrona. A flood in the river Strumon prevented Gaul from joining them in time; but he embarked in his ship alone on the succeeding day. On his voyage, however, he passed his friends, who were returning with victory, unperceived, and landed singly on the hostile shore. According to the chivalrous idea of those times he would not fly, but struck his shield as a token of defiance to the islanders, against whom he singly maintained a desperate conflict, till, fearful of a near approach, they rolled a stone from above, which, striking his thigh, disabled him, and there he was left by his enemies to pine and die. His wife, Evirchoma, anxious for his fate, embarked in a skiff with her infant son, Ogall, at her breast, in quest of her lord, whom she found in the pitiable situation described, and was able to carry him to her boat, where they were discovered next morning by Ossian, who had sailed in quest of them, speechless and dying. He was only able to save the child."

Prepare ye the bed of our hero,
   O children of music's sweet tone!
Lay his Sunbeam of battle beside him,
   Where his tomb through long time may be known.

Let the high leafy bough overshade it,
   Of the oak with its green-growing spray—
First to bud in the breath of the spring shower,
   That lasts when the heath fades away.

Its leaves, from the skirts of each far land,
   Shall summer's gay birds behold;
On Strumon's boughs, when they wearily come,
   Their joyful wing they shall fold.

In his mist, Gaul shall hear their sweet singing,
   And maidens lamenting, that say—
"Alas, Evirchoma!" Till these things shall perish,
   Undivided in thought shall ye stay—

Till this stone into dust shall crumble—
   Till with age this branch shall fade—
Till this stream run no more from its mother,
   Far off in the mountain glade.—

Till the age of the bard is lost in time,
   And his tale and his song none can sing;
No stranger shall ask, "Who was Morni's son?"
   Or "Where lies Strumon's king?"

There seems to be something like a scriptural and oriental grace about this beautiful and pathetic fragment. Whoever composed it, could have been no mean poet. Gaul, the sun of Morni, it will be remembered, was a great hero. The Ajax of the Fingalians, excelled by none in strength and courage, he deserved to have so noble an elegy spoken over him, by the ever-generous and courteous Finn.

FINGAL GOING TO BATTLE.

THERE seems to have been favourite bits of poetry floating about in the Highlands, not belonging to any particular poem, but ready to be used by the reciters in any place where they appeared to fit well. These formed an elaborate description of the dress, the appearance, the warlike equipage, or else some single great action of a celebrated hero; or, indeed, any one incident in the old traditions, common perhaps to them all, which might strike the fancy of a young and sensitive mind, that would keep brooding over the favourite passage for years, until at last it finished and refined it into such lyric excellence that it thenceforth formed a noted piece of popular poetry, and one of the famed and welcome gems of recitation round a thousand firesides.

The following very splendid description is found in Kennedy's Collection in one poem; in Dr. Smith's "Old Lays" in another; and in MacPherson's Ossian in a third place. It is a piece of popular Highland poetry. I translate this truly grand passage with the closest fidelity :—

With loud-sounding strides he rush'd westward,
   In the clank of his armour bright;
And he look'd like the Spirit of Loda, that scatters
   Dismay o'er the war-way and fight!

Like a thousand waves on a crag that roll, yelling,
   When the ugly storm is at its height,
So awful the clash of his mail and his weapons,
   While his face wore the winter of fight!

His smooth claymore glitter'd aloft—
   In his champion hand it was light;

And the snoring winds kept moving his locks,
    Like spray in the whirlpool's might!

The hills on each side they were shaken,
    And the path seem'd to tremble with fright!
Gleamed his eyes, and his great heart kept swelling—
    Oh! cheerless the terrible sight!

"The "Old Lays," collected by Dr. Smith, are not inferior in any respect to MacPherson's "Ossian." They breathe the same spirit, exhibit the same fineness of sensibility, and are coloured by a mountain-bred imagination. They speak of the same superstitions, and they look with that life-giving energy of deep and lonely nurtured feeling, so characteristic of the Ossianic poems. The following is contained in the opening of a poem called "Finan and Lorma," where the young people around him, looking upon the heavens, address the aged Ossian in the following natural and beautiful verses:—

White on the plains shines the moon, O Bard!
    And the shadow Cona holds;
Like a ghost breathes the wind from the mountain,
    With a spirit voice in its folds.

There are two cloudy forms before us,
    Where its host the dim night shows;
The sigh of the moor curls their tresses,
    As they tread over Alva of roes.

Dusky his dogs come with one,
    And he bends his dark bow of yew;
There's a stream from the side of the sad-faced maid,
    Dyes her robe with a blood-red hue.

Hold thou back, O thou wind! from the mountain,
    Let their image a moment stay;

Nor sweep with thy skirts from our eyesight,
  Nor scatter their beauty away.

O'er the glen of the rushes, the hill of the hinds,
  With the vague wandering vapour they go;
O Bard of the times that have left us!
  Aught of their life canst they show?

OSSIAN.

The years that have been they come back as ye speak—
  To my soul in their music they glide;
Like the murmur of waves in the far inland calm,
  Is their soft and smooth step by my side.

THE FOUR WISE MEN AT ALEXANDER'S GRAVE.

It may surprise some people to find Alexander the Great figuring in a Highland poem. But he is very well known to the Gaelic-speaking people, among whom he goes by the title of "Alastair Mòr," words that may be translated "Big Sandy," quite as naturally as Alexander the Great. The first time I heard this name applied to the Macedonian conqueror was by an excellent tale-teller. who offered to illustrate something or other that had just been spoken of in his presence, by giving a story about "Alastair Mòr." I thought the man was going to refer to some of his own cronies— the name he used is so very familiar in the Highlands; nor was it till, observing my ignorance, he repeated the phrase with marked emphasis, and translated it, saying, with some impatience,

"Alexander the Great," that I understood him. He then told his story, which was as follows:—

"Alastair Mòr won so many battles, and took so many cities, and subdued so many peoples, that his heart was uplifted, and he became proud; and thought his glory was for ever, and his power and majesty something more than mortal. It happened that one day, when his heart was big with these sentiments, and when his flatterers were courting him, and they told him—and he believed them—that nothing in this world had ever equalled him; lo! just then a very small fly went up his nostril, and penetrated to his brain, put an end to Alexander."

"We perish before the moth." Such was the story, and such, I fancy, would have been the moral of the Highland sage, if he had drawn it; but he did not. He left his tale to make its own impression. So Alexander the Great is well known in the Highlands. This ballad that speaks of him is a very old one—at least three hundred and fifty years old; for it is one of those in the Dean of Lismore's book, whose collection was made about that time. The poem is also found even yet among the people. A very few years ago, a version of it, almost identical with that of the Dean of Lismore, was got from a old woman in the north. The Dean's book was not then published. This shows the accuracy with which tradition can, for generations, preserve a favourite tale or ballad. The poem seems to consist of two parts—a lament in the first part, and a eulogy in the second.

> Four wise men met beside the grave
>   Where the Prince of Greece was laid—
> The mightiest Alexander;
>   And these true words they said:—
>
> "But yesterday, to serve his need,
>   The world's great hosts would rise;

And there, alas!" the first man said,
  "To-day he lonely lies."

"Proudly rode he on the earth
  Not many days bygone:
And now the earth," the second cried,
  "It rests on his breast-bone."

Then did the third wise speaker say,—
  "Not many days ere this
He own'd the whole round world; and now
  Not seven short feet are his!"

"Alexander treasured gold
  To serve his every whim;
And now," the fourth man sagely said,
  "'Tis gold that treasures him."*

"Like gold was Philip's son—the gold
  That binds the jewels bright;
Like the palm among the trees; the moon
  Amid the stars of night;

"Like the great whale among small fish;
  The lion 'mid the slain;
The eagle when she drives the birds
  From the rock of her lone reign.

"Like Sion hill amid the hills—
  The hill that holiest seems;
Like the great sea unto the floods;
  Like Jordan 'mid the streams.

---

*Alexander the Great the pupil of Aristotle, died in 323 B.C. and was buried in a golden coffin at Alexandria, Lower Egypt, city founded by himself. This explains the accuracy of the phrase:—"'Tis gold that treasures him."

> "He was a man above all men,
>   Save the High King of Heaven;
> To him were armies, towns and lands,
>   And herds and forests given."
>
> Thus o'er the great man's tomb they spoke!
>   Wise do I count their lore;
> Unlike to woman's idle prate
>   Were the sayings of these Four.

The ballad of "The Four Wise Men at Alexander's Grave" is a quaint poem—not destitute of vigorous expression, of good strong reflective capacity, or of the marks of genuine workmanlike fancy. At the same time, though it carries its years well, the poem has on the face of it the evident signs of a long bypast age. Its air and manner do not quite belong to our day. It has traces in its bearing of having been in company with the Muses when the society they cultivated differed much from ours; when the Bardic fellowship had a stated gravity, and cultivated true speaking more than the arrangement of words, or the artistic effect of sentiment, doled out by weight and measure.

THE AGED BARD'S WISH.

This poem is supposed to be one of the oldest in the Gaelic language, subsequent to the Ossianic era. It is said to be older than the conversion of the Caledonians to Christianity. I am not aware, however, that there are any other grounds than the internal evidence on which this very remote antiquity is claimed for the poem.

Judging from its contents—its train of thought and its tone of sentiment—there is certainly no reason to suppose that its author was acquainted with any of the doctrines of Christianity; but, on the contrary, every reason to think that he was not—that is, of course, granting it was really an old heathen bard, and not some one assuming such a character, who composed the verses. In the closing lines, as will be seen, the singer wishes his harp, his shell, and the shield that defended his forefathers in battle, to be laid in the grave by his side; and he speaks of his soul floating in its mist, on the breeze of the ocean, to Flath-innis—the Heroes' Isle—where Ossian and Dail reposed and slept in the house of the Bards on Ard-ven. All this is certainly quite heathenish. But all this could easily be done by a bard who lived all his life among Christian Caledonians, and merely took on himself, for the occasion, the person of an imaginary predecessor.

It is difficult to indentify the locality of the poem. Mrs. Grant of Laggan says it was composed in Skye. But the editor of the "Beauties of Gaelic Poetry," says, "The poem itself seems to furnish some evidence, that at least the scene of it is laid in Lochaber. *Treig* is mentioned as having afforded drink to the hunters. Now, Loch-Treig is in the braes of Lochaber. We know of no mountain which is now called Ben-Ard or Sgorr-eilt. Perhaps Ben-Ard is another name for Ben Nevis. The great waterfall mentioned near the end of the poem may have been Easbhà, near Kinloch-Leven, in Lochaber." Like almost all reflective poetry that extends to any length, this poem is sometimes a little obscure. It is not always very easy to trace the connection of one train of thought with another, nor is it always very obvious what the old man is turning his mind to at all. The objects of his thought, and the terms in which he was in the habit of referring to them, were both so familiar to himself that he, like other poets of his class, seems never to have suspected they might be less intimately known to his readers. "The

Old Bard's Wish," then, although a fine poem upon the whole, and very much admired in the original, does not, perhaps, bear translation so well as some others.

> Oh! place me by the little brook,
>   Of gently wandering pace and slow.
> And lay my head near some green nook
>   That kindly shades the sunny glow.
>
> At ease upon the grass I'll rest
>   Of the balm-breathing flowery brae;
> My foot by the warm wave caress'd
>   That winds throughout the plain away.
>
> There the pale primrose let me see,
>   There the small daisy close at hand,
> And every flower so dear to me
>   For grateful hue or odour bland.
>
> About thy lofty banks, my glen,
>   Be bending boughs and blooming sprays,
> Where small birds sing from bush and fen,
>   To aged cliffs, their amorous lays.
>
> Break rolling o'er the ivied rock
>   The new-born spring, with heavy moan,
> And let the answering echo mock
>   Its crowding surges' tunful tone.
>
> And let each hill and mountain steep
>   Return me back a joyous sound,
> When thousand herds with lowings deep
>   From east and west will murmur round.
>
> Let frisking calves before me play
>   By spreading hill or streamlet pure,

But the tired kid his head shall lay
    Upon my breast and sleep secure.

Then, flowing on the breeze's wing,
    Come the soft plainings of the lamb,
And let the mellowing distance bring
    The answer of its bleating dam.

Oft let the hunter's step go by,
    His whizzing javelins let me hear;
And to my cheek youth's blood will fly
    When comes the chase with tumult near.

Now marrow to my bones 'twill bring
    To hear the string, the horn, the hound.
When loud, "The stag is down," they sing,
    I'll leap to hear the darling sound.

My dog, I'll see him in that mood
    Who late and early follow'd me,
And O our dear hilly solitude
    And crags that heard my bugle's glee.

And I shall see the welcome cave,
    That saved us from the darkening night:
Its flikering flame shall wane and wave—
    Its quaichs once more shall give delight.

The sweet dear-flesh we'll roast it well;
    Treig's singing brook our thirst allay;
Though mountains roar and ghosts should yell,
    We'll calmly rest us there till day.

Then high Ben-Ard* his form will rear—
    Chief of a thousand hills is he—

---

* Ben-Ard is apparently Ben Nevis, the grandest and the highest mountain in Britain, 4,406 feet high.

His locks, where dream the antler'd deer,
   His head, where sleep the clouds, we'll see.

Sgorr-eilt looks o'er the valley's brow,
   Whence first the cuckoo's music flows;
The hill where thousand fir-trees grow,
   And green herbs for the elks and roes.

The young ducks cheerily skim the pool,
   Round which the fir-trees wave their heads,
And toss their green arms beautiful,
   Above the ripening rowans red.

With snowy breast the swan comes nigh,
   And crest the waves with graceful pride
Or, raising up her wings on high,
   Amid the clouds she'll lightly glide.

Oft doth she journey o'er the sea
   To lands where breaks the cold white spray
Where sail or mast shall never be,
   Nor oaken prow shall cleave its way.

Come to the brakes and mountain caves—
   Thy mouth full of love's plaintive sighs—
O swan! from the land of the waves,
   And sing me to rest from the skies.

O rise, with thy mild and sweet song!
   Tell thy piteous tale from on high,
The echo will spread it along,
   And send thy grief mournfully by.

Raise thy wing o'er the ocean's bound,
   Grasp its speed from the strong wind above,
For sweet to my ear comes the sound
   From thy much pain'd heart of sad love.

Whence do the wandering breezes roam,*
    That waft us thus thy grief and care,
O youth! who went so far from home,
    And left my hoary head so bare!

Are thine eyes tearful still, young maid,
    So white of hand, so fair and wise?
Peace rest with him that ne'er will fade,
    Who from his strait bed may not rise!

O winds! tell me, whose eyes have fail'd,
    The sighing reeds where now they grow,
Past which the trouts have often sail'd
    On wings that never felt you blow!

Oh raise me! raise me with strong arm!
    Beneath a new shade let me lie;
The sun is riding high and warm,
    Let the green branches shield my eye.

Then wilt thou come, O vision mild!
    That wand'rest 'mid the stars of night;
And in thy music sweet and wild
    Thou'lt bring me thoughts of past delight.

Oh see, my soul! yon maiden fair
    Beneath the oak-tree, king of groves!

---

* At this place Mrs. Grant of Laggan—who has given a translation of "The Old Bard's Wish," among her poems published in 1803—makes the following remark:—"As there is very little frost or snow in the Islands, great numbers of swans come there from Norway in the beginning of winter. Some stay to hatch, but they mostly go northward in summer. This furnishes the bard with the fine image, very strongly expressed in the original, of the north wind bearing towards him the moan of the departed; upon which he inquires of the swan from what cold country that well-known voice came. This affords him a pretence for digressing.

Her hand amid her golden hair—
    Her soft mild eye on him she loves.

She silent while he plays and sings—
    Her beating heart swims in the song!
From eye to eye his way Love wings,
    Who melts the deer their hills among.

Now stops the strain, and her soft side
    Is growing to her lover's breast,
And her fresh lips, the rose-tree's pride,
    To his are long and longer press'd.

May joy attend you both. for aye,
    Who wake my long-lost joy once more;
But on thy soul, thou fair-hair'd May,
    My warmest, dearest blessings pour!

Oh dream of bliss! and art thou gone!
    Return, return one moment still!
You hear me not; and I'm alone!
    Then, fare-you-well each long-loved hill!

Farewell, O ye youths in your prime!
    Farewell, lovely maiden, to thee!
I see not your bright summer time—
    'Tis winter forever with me.

Not far from the waterfall's swell
    That moans round its grey rock afar,
Let me lie with my harp and shell,
    And forefathers' shield in wild war.

And come o'er the sea as a friend,
    Thou mild-moving zephyr and slow,
Raise my mist on thy wings, and wend
    To the isle where the heroes go!

Where the heroes go—where they lie
   And sleep sound without music's tone,—
Hall of Ossian and Dail! open—fly
   The night comes and the bard is gone!

But ere it comes—ere my mist wings its way
To Ardven, the house of the bards for aye—
With harp and shell for the road let me play;
Then farewell to the harp, the shell, the lay!*

   The paradise of the ancient Celts, *Flath-innis*, or the Heroes' Isle—a word now appropriated to a sacred use—was supposed to lie in the Western Ocean. There was another place called *Eilean na h-Oige*, or the Island of Youth, which is still frequently spoken of in Highland tales. I once heard a long story told in prose in which it made a considerable figure. It differed, however, from the above, or at any rate, did not accord with the Old Bard's idea of *Flath-innis*. For there were not only an uninterrupted felicity and unfading youth enjoyed in *Eilean na h-Oige*, but there were also activity and consciousness—not sleep. Neither was it a place for disembodied spirits merely. The story I speak of represented a man having been carried thither by a fairy wife whom he had married, and with whom he had lived for some years in the world. He was a middle aged man when he was carried off, but his youth was renewed in even more than its early bloom whenever he set foot on the island. He stayed there, with the most perfect enjoyment, for a few weeks, as appeared to him. Then he expressed a wish to go back and see another wife and family whom he had left behind him in his own home. His wish was complied with, after he had promised his fairy wife to return with her whenever his curiosity was

---

* The measure is changed in the last verse of the original, as above.

gratified. He was carried back as he had been at first carried away, in the shape of a swan, his fairy wife accompanying him. He was set down on his own old farm; but as soon as he touched the soil he became extremely aged and withered looking—"a mere fistful of a man,"— the narrator said. His fairy wife then left him for a short time, and he wandered about, exciting a great deal of curiosity in all who saw him, but knowing nobody, and even noticing changes in the very localities he had been so familiar with, as he had thought, about a year before. At last some people that were working in a field near by gathered about him. To them he told his story; and one of them recollected having heard his grandfather speaking of a great farmer to whom that place once belonged, and who had suddenly disappeared one day, many many years ago, no one knew whither. A little after this, the old man's fairy wife returned, and carried him off, in the shape of a swan. He was never more seen in the world at all. So much for *Eilean na h-Oige.*

Of the author of the "Aged Bard's Wish" nothing is known,—not, so far as I am aware, any suspicion entertained. It was first published as an old poem, in Gillies' Collection, in 1786. It has been frequently translated,— much oftner than any Gaelic poem whatever. Other good Gaelic poems are still waiting for a translator, but of this one there have been some six or eight renderings, between prose and verse.

Miann a' Bhàird Aosda, the Aged Bard's Wish, has been admirably translated into English by the Rev. Hugh MacMillan, LL.D., D.D., Free West Church, Greenock. See SCOTTISH CELTIC REVIEW, edited by the late Rev. Dr. Alexander Cameron, Brodick.

VERSES ADDRESSED TO MR. E. LLHUYD.*

When Mr. Edward Llhuyd published his "Archæologia Britannia," in 1704, so pleased were the Highlanders with the interest with which he invested their language, that many of them addressed complimentary verses to him, expressive of their appreciation of his work, In

---

* What follows is the original of these verses, with the spelling somewhat modernized, to make them more intelligible to the Gaelic reader:—

Air teachd o 'n Spàinn do shliochd a' Ghàidheil ghlais,
'S do shliochd nam Milidh. 'n fhine nach bu tais;
Bu mhòr an sgleò 's gach fòd air cruas an lann,
Air fil'eachd fòs 's air foghlum nach bu ghann.
'N uair dh' fhàs am pòr ud mòr a bhos a 's thall
Bha meas a's prìs de 'n Ghàilig anns gach ball—
An Teanga lionmhor, bhrighmhor, bhlasda, bhinn,
'S a' Chànain thartrach, liobhta, ghasda, ghrinn.

An cùirt nan Rìgh, rè mìle bliadhn' a's treall,
Gu 'n robh i 'n tùs mu 'n d' thog cainnt Dhù'-ghall ceann.
Gach fili 's bàrd, gach lèigh, aosdàn' a's draoi,
Gach seanachaidh fòs, gach eoladhain shaor a's saoi,
Gu'n tug Gathelus leis o 'n Eiph't a nall,
'S an Gàilig sgrìobh iad sud le gnìomh am peann.
Na diadhairean mòr, bu chliù 's bu ghlòir do 'n Chléir,
B' ann leath', gu tarbhach, 'labhair iad briathra Dhé.

B'i labhair Pàdruig 'n Innisfàil nan rìgh,
'S am Fàidhe naomh sin, Calum caomh 'an I.
Na Frangaich liobhta lean gach tìr am beus,
O I nan Deòraidh ghabh gach foghlum freumh.
B' i b' oide-mùinte luchd gach dùthch' a's teang';
Chuir Gaill a's Dubh-ghaill chum an iùil 'so 'n clann.
Nis dh' fhalbh i uainn gu tur, mo thruaigh! 's mo chreach!
'S tearc luchd a gaoil—b' e sud an saogh'l fa seach!
Thuit i 's an tùr m' araon r'a h-ùghd'raibh féin,
'S na flaith' 'm bu diùth' i ghabh d' a còmhdach spéis.
Reic iad 's a' chùirt i air cainnt ùr o 'n dé,
A's thréig le tàir, 's bu nàr leo 'n cànain féin.

1707 a second edition was issued, wherein some of these verses were given. The following is a translation of what Mr. John MacLean, minister of the parish of Killninian, Island of Mull, composed on that occasion. The

> Air sàr O Liath biodh àgh, a's cuimhn' a's buaidh,
> A rinn gu h-ùr a dùsgadh as a h-uaigh.
> Gach neach 'tha fhreumh o'n Ghàidheal ghleusda gharg,
> 'S gach droing d' au dùth a' chànain ud mar chainnt—
> Gach aon a chinn air treubh 's air linn a' Scuit
> An duais is fhiach thu 's còir gu 'n ìoc iad dhuit.
> O'n Bhanrigh'nn air am bheil an tràs an crùn,
> Gu ruig am bochd 's an àit' au nochd an dùn,
> Bha 'n ainm 's an euchd, o linn nan ceudan àl,
> Tre mheath na Gàilig 'dol á cuimhne chàich:
> Nis cliù an gnìomh chluinn crìochan fada thall,
> 'S their iad le chéil', "Bha Gàidheil aon uair ann."
>
> 'S ni 's fearr, a shaoi, bidh briathran llobht' 'n ar beul,
> Làn seadh a's brìgh le 'n nochdar fìrinn Dhé.
> Cia fios an Ti chuir 'n Aholiab tùr
> 'S am Besaleel, a thogail àrois ùir,
> Nach e so féin a ghluais O Luid 's a ghleus
> Gu 'shaothair thoirt gu buil le 'thuigse ghéir,
> Bhrigh bhi 'na rùn 'ainm dheanamh cliùiteach, mòr
> Air feadh nan crìoch 's an d' fhuair na Gàidheil còir?
> Gu'm b' amluidh bhios,—'s gach neach a chi an lò
> Biodh t'ainmsa sgrìobht' 'n a chrìdh' 'an litir'ean òir,
> Agus 'na chuimhn'—a's gheibh thu choidhch' uam féin,
> Beannachd a's fàilt' le m' chrìdh', le m' làimh, 's le m' beul!

Mr. James Macourich, minister of Kildalton, Islay, addressed the following verses to Mr. Llhuyd at the same time.

> 'S e do bheatha, Fhaoclair chaoimh,
> Gu crìochaibh àrd Chlanna Gàidheal;
> Gu Innis fòs nan Cùig Còigeamh
> Is e do bheatha g' au uibhir.
>
> Gheibh thu fàilte 'an crìochaibh Ghàidheal,
> 'S e do bheatha 'n Innse-Gall;

verses are interesting as shewing the enthusiasm of a
Highland clergyman on seeing his native language duly
honoured by such an eminent man as Mr. Llhuyd was.

> When first from Spain the grey Gael hither came
> With the Melesian race,—a dauntless stock—
> Their hardy blades were not in tales more famed
> Than were their lays and lore, through every land.
> Once this fair seed had spread out far and near,
> Then honour meet and due the Gaelic gained:
> That copious, tasteful, sweet, expressive, tongue,—
> That polished, sounding smooth, well-ordered speech.
> In regal courts a thousand years and more
> It reigned, ere raised its head the dark Gall's tongue:
> Then bard, and lyrist, prophet, leech and sage,
> All trace and record of achievement brave,
> Since first Gathelus left the Egyptian strand,
> Wrote down in Gaelic with effective pen.

> Ni gach triath riutsa comunn,
> Gheibh thu moladh 'an Eirinn thall.
>
> Dhùisgeadh leat as an uaigh
> A' chànain chruaidh a bha fo smal—
> Teanga bha cian fo gheasaibh
> Do chuireadh leat an clò ré seal.
>
> Tuigseach, saibhir do theagasg,
> Soileir, saibhir, sèimh do ghlòir;
> Lìonmhor, brìghmhor do shean-fhacail—
> Sgiamhach, taitneach, ciallach mòr.
>
> Thoir mo bheannachd do Mhaisdir Liath
> A dhùisg, le buaidh, Foclair fial:
> Bheir gach Gàidheal dhuitse beannachd—
> Is e leatsa thar na dh'àirmhear.

Seumas MacMhuir, Sagart Chill-Daltan.

Thus long the clergy glory won, and fame,
And thus with native accents praised their God.
Thus Patrick spoke, in kingly Innisfail,
And sainted, mild Columba thus in *Ie*.
The polished French, from whom all people learn,
Their own first rudiments of learning got
In that fair Isle of penitential tears:
There spoke the nurse of every tribe and tongue:
For Gaelic then was not the guiding star
Of Gaelic youth, more than of Galldic too.
Now is it circumscribed,—woe! woe! and well-a-day!
Few love it now.—Alas! the weary change,—
Oh! the decline,—its authors all forgot,
Heroes who lisped it first, then cherished it;
But courtiers sold it for a poor exchange—
A modern tongue,—a tongue of yesterday:
Thus with contempt, deserting from their own.

Great fame great praise, great thanks to noble Llhuyd,
Who has revived it from the grave again.
All from the versatile, fierce Gael derived,
Each tribe in whom their language still inheres,—
All men,—the increase of the Scottish root,—
Should now requite thee with a due reward,—
Down from the Queen at present on the throne,
Even to the wandering, houseless poor this night.
Back from a hundred generations come
The memory of their exploits,—retained
In this most worthy language—slighted now.
Their deeds of fame, yet distant lands can learn;
And one to other say, "A Gaelic race hath been."
But, better still, with polished rhetoric,
We can express, with might, the truth of God.

Who knows but He who Aholiab erst,
And Bezaleel taught to build the ark,

Hath moved thee and inspired thee now, O Llhuyd
To do thy work with energy and art;
And make His own great name adored and praised
In every region by the Gael possessed.
So neither let, nor distant be the day,
When shall thy name in every heart be writ,
And every memory, in lettered gold.
And, now, a blessing, and adieu from me,—
From heart, and hand, and tongue attend on thee.

ORIGINAL POEMS.

ORIGINAL POEMS.

A FAIR DAY.*

> For it was their feist day.
> They said
> Of Peblis to the Play.
> OLD POEM.

A VILLAGE looks the keen and lucid north
Full in the blue and weather-beaten face;
Before it lies a long and winding bay,
Within whose shelter, in the gloom and storm,
When winter revels o'er the roughening sea,
Full many a coasting brig, and drudging sloop,
And tempest-baffled bark at anchor ride,
And rest from wind and tossing wave without.
Then is the village crowded with the crews,
The taverns thronged, and hard-won earnings spent,
And sometimes squabbles raised by Jack ashore.
Beyond the anchorage, a range of hills,
In mellow, undulating line, is set;
With parti-coloured culture, varied so,
They seem in Autumn as with tartan clad.
Westward, and looking from the hither side,
Down on the beach and o'er the bending bay,
A rocky eminence the village flanks,
Whose top is crested with a broken tower,
Scene of much talk and observation long.

* See Note I.

Eastward, is offered with the tide at full,
A peaceful, pleasant, variegated scene
From the green margin of the swollen loch
Deep, to the background resting on the sky,
With three high hills, its giant guardians raised,
Together standing, conical and blue.
High up the brae on which the village stands
Runs one wide street—its pride and ornament—
With its quay jutting in the sea below,
And at its head the church spire high in heaven;
Its tiled or slated houses rise between,
And in the midst of all, the ancient pump,
That mark of Terminus, the steadfast god,
Once painted blue, with freestone trough appears.
This is the scene, then, of my song to-day,
And evening is the time.

An August afternoon—blue sky—bright sun—
The village streets, that wont so quiet be,
All full of bustling life and busy talk,
And tread of men, and tramp of horses' feet;
With hundreds occupied in countless ways,
Single, together, moving or at rest,
Spreading a murmur like a cataract.
There, on one spot, are sunburnt faces seen,
With massy features and bluff hardy look,
And broad and brawny forms, all clad in blue.
The deep sea fishers these, whose luggers ride
The breezy sea that clips the Hebrides;
And these their wives, so garrulous and glad,
Who sell their hard smoked fishing by the score,
And black coarse oil, to meet the winter night.
With them their daughters come, all trig and smart,
And youngsters eager for the holiday,
Now wildly staring, for they never looked
On such a crowd of busy men before.

Leaving that scene of busy interchange,
You see the group about those horses met,
One is the ploughman in his best array ;
That broad squat man, so round and corpulent,
With dry black hair, and full brown eye and bright,
The shabby coat, and clothes that once were good,
With his hands deep into his pouches held,
And look of ready cash about his face,—
That man who, jingling, jingling, stands and looks,
Is a horse-couper. And the tall thin man
With the broad shoulders who, with out-stretched neck,
O'erlooks his comrade's round and dusty hat,
And wears a coat that reaches to his heels—
He is the friend—the friend and referee.
But that's an amateur whose brows are knit,
Who, better dressed and sprucer on the whole
Than the two dealers, sees a bargain close,
And stepping up, with calculating care
Pokes on the ribs the horse that's to be sold,—
Looking as wise as Solomon the while—
Then with one weighty sentence turns away.
These are his friends and satellites behind,
Who hang upon his skirts,—look as he looks,
Turn as he turns, and wander as he goes;
Thinking him paragon of mortal men.

See, here another ripening bargain grows,
Where the crowd severs fast from side to side,
And from its bosom rushes, at full trot,
A stalwart horse, and groom that stirs him on,
Displaying two grave figures to the view
Clad in loose clothes of no decided shape,
And darned, by'r lady, in more spots than one.
Ay, there they stand, like Damon and his fere,
Acutely watching the steed's heavy pace,
And much engrossed in cogitations deep

As any statist gives a nation's hopes—
What is his age, his quality, and breed?

Pass yet along, and see this dusty close,
With many hundred pattering feet impressed,
When, with a whirr, the flock together run
At near approach of some stray dog, or man
Who comes to choose a wether, or few sheep,
To eke his stock and bring next summer gain.
That tall stout man, in the grey homespun dressed—
Who moves about with such a manly stride,
And whose large hand, so oily and so tarred,
Picks for the buyer what he wants to take—
Is owner both and keeper of the sheep.
To all and each alike, or high or low,
He speaks sedately in his native tongue,
With easy flow of past'ral rhetoric,
And self-possessed,—in conscious rectitude
Dispenses courtesy and nice regard—
So quick to feel indignity himself.
For though his station bears no glossy show,
Yet, filled with treasured memories of old,
With deeds of valour, gentleness, and birth,
The shepherd holds within his secret soul,
A grace like David's with the pride of Saul.
And thus he feels, though poor the mode of life,
What truly makes the man may yet be great,
Although he owns not much, if he but knows
And acts in self-collected dignity
Unmoved but thus: not what the eye perceives,
But what is felt and living in the mind
Ennobles man, and doth the earth adorn
So lived the prophets in the days of old—
Long may such spirits permeate our own.

Still further pierce into the deepening crowd,
Cautious you give the frequent steeds, the while,

A FAIR DAY.

No chance to make but small bones of your legs;
Careful to steer between the talking groups
Of busy men and dressed and showy girls,
And as you slowly pass along, you note
Where, in the thoroughfare, the stands are set,
And boys with open mouth and staring eyes,
In soul devour the whole delicious stock,
They want the means one pennyworth to buy.

There, in his cart, the glib-mouthed auctioneer
Deals old, old wit, and long used up, around,
And cheats the rustics with his fluent tongue,
And much amazes them—he talks so well.
There, in bewilderment, a culprit stands,
Beneath the rattle of his brazen slang,
Who gave a bid in utter ignorance,
And much perplexed, now hesitating looks,
Hearing his opposite, with deep respect,
Quote in a breath his license and his Queen.

There, with his stand, the vendor of the nuts
Offers his bow, "Only a penny, gents!"
And eager youths come vieing for the prize,
"Sixty large nuts for him who hits the ring."
There is the draper with his goods and clothes,
All ready-made, or bundled up in bales,
And moleskin, duck, or woolen garments, ranged,
Attract the eydent housewife's careful eye;
While pen-knives, walking-sticks, umbrellas blue,
Marked with huge tickets, tempt with tiny price.

There with her plain deal table, covered clean,
A spinster stands, or pawky auld guidwife,
Who dearly loves a cheering cup of tea.
Spread are her bowls and largest cups to view,
Half-filled with comfits purchased for the fair,
Bought at five shillings, which she'll sell at twelve.

Now in the heat of rivalry she stands,
Where bold competitors, with practised wile,
On every side allure the urchin's eye.
To disappointment not unseldom doomed,
She sees the valued currency that flows
On either side, but scarcely reaches her—
Boding but ill unto the hoarded store
Devoted to her secret beverage.
Across the street there rolls a thundering drum,
And through the crowd that rush and struggle by
You have a glimpse of some gay figure near,
In cotton garment all with spangles decked:
Flitting like figures in a fairy dream.
They with their feats of rare dexterity—
Their balls, cups, cards, and strange ventriloquism,
Their matchless pony's knowing craftiness,
And Lady of the Troop, so gaudy dressed,
Who dances blindfold 'mid the rows of eggs,
And foots so featly that they cry, "O rare!"
Draw crowded houses—thunders of applause.
Did Thespis lead a life like this of old?
And thus began the comedy of Greece?
Strange what a difference a language makes,
Lagging behind, or moving with an age!

But hark! a note of music touched mine ear—
Come, we will trace it up this flight or steps,
Built to an outer wall with clumsy flags,
Whose rough ascent conducts us to the door
Now open wide, inviting customers.
Here is a loft, in winter stored with hay,
Or corn, or fodder, for the cattle kept,
Now swept and fitted for the fiery dance;
And from the gloaming, through some brisk dark hours,
A steady thumping will be heard afar,
As rattles on the sharp and sounding string
The flying reel,—the exciting curt strathspey,

A FAIR DAY.

When dainty Chloe will, or Phillis fair,
Who set so neatly, and who look so well,
Move huge affection in stout Damon's heart,
Flinging so lustily with shouts before.
'Tis yet in prelude, this hot, hasty mirth—
For still the hall is empty, save that end
Where, with the violin against his breast,
A rural amateur is showing off—
With beating foot,—bow by the middle held,
Contorted face, and wild and staring eye,
Some new-learned reel to his experienced ear,
Who sits and listens in sarcastic calm;
But when he stops, pays him high compliments,
And vows 'tis time for him to quit the stage,
Now that such fingers on the strings are laid.
The chief musician of the Fair is this,
Whose voice goes thrilling through the bungler's heart,
Who takes for gospel every word that's said.
And so the young man, moving to the door,
Nurses the praise within his flattered mind,
Till it uplifts his step upon his toes,
Like Shakespeare's Diomed, in scorn of earth.
Then touching the scraps of lively tunes,
The minstrel rolls his sightless eyes and waits
Until the hall begins to fill anon;
And the exciting motion, once afoot,
Increases furiously until the dawn.

See from that tavern pour a jolly rout,
Not yet excited with the lively draught.
Friends treat their friends, and bargain-makers meet,
And o'er the liquor talk of times gone by,
Or mention matters that obtain to-day;
The Ancient, with blue bonnet laid aside,
Fills up the glass that circulates to all.
The comely belle takes but a modest sip;

The older spinster, rising in her turn,
With glass in hand, says some appropriate words,
"To the good health of all," and does but taste,—
Protesting faintly that her head is weak,
And that indeed she cannot, dare not more,
Yet yielding most reluctantly, 't would seem,
To the warm pressure of the welcome kind,
That pours so heartily from every side.
What can she do, but sacrifice herself?
And suck in slowly every diamond drop,
Looking like Socrates, the poisoned sage,
In pensive resignation all the while.
A wringing pressure from the horny hand,
A warm good-wish to each and all around,
Then every man swigs at a gulp his share,
And forth they sally to the street again.
Meeting old faces with a tone of joy,
A quickened step, and eager offered hand,
A kind enquiry and a firm long shake,
As if the one had dropped from the moon,
The other from the planet Jupiter;
And if no further business intervene,
They will adjourn to have a dram betimes.

This jovial work makes heated heads at last,
And warms the blood that courses through their veins,
With no small ardour at the very best,
And fires the mind, and swells the excited soul,
Till whisky, talking, dancing, music's power,
Or favoured rival's envied privilege,
Or fancied insult in some careless tone,
Or pride of prowess and ambitious strength,
Or tipsy singer's loud and cheery note,
Who reels contentedly beside a friend,
With squabbles, and confused and grating noise
Close on the few late revellers the scene.

LOCHINDAAL.*

O! Thou ship-sailing Lochindaal,
   Blue is thy bracing brine,
And beautiful thy verdant meads—
   To me thou art divine;
Although perhaps to other eyes
   Thou scarcely seemest fine.

But I have trod thy pebbly shore—
   Have bathed in thy blue sea;
I've gazed on thee in all thy moods,
   And lived for years by thee:
I must forget myself before
   Thy beauties fade to me.

Those deep blue hills that rise afar,
   Like giants straight and high,
Delightedly I've looked on them
   With childhood's dazzled eye;
And now I look on thee again
   What old, old things come by.

Oh! many long past things that haunt
   Thy banks, and fields, and ways;
A thousand forms of tender things
   My heart-touched feelings raise
Around thee here, on which youth's sun,
   With noontide lustre, plays.

Old friends who now are none for me
   Still haunts thy changeless shore;
And friends, alas! who now are gone,
   Where we meet not as of yore;

* See note II.

And friends, thank God, who still are friends,
    Just as they were before.

And men and matrons—maids and youths,
    Who are no friends at all;
They too come flocking to my side,
    With or without a call:
The old, the young, the grave, the gay—
    The short ones and the tall.

They troop into the village streets—
    They stand as oft they stood,
Round the street-corners, talking long
    Of bad things and of good;
For the flippant and the wise were there—
    The civil and the rude.

Those streets and corners still are there,
    But all the men are gone;
I see the houses, hills and shores,
    And ways they walked upon;
But not the men—the sense seems lost
    That on their doings shone.

Yet all the lifeless things remain
    There in its old grey calm;
The church still stands, where first I heard,
    After a nasal Psalm,
A sermon preached by an old man,
    Who spoke of Abraham.

And there by its green hill I see
    The old and schoolboy spot,
And the scene where many a summer eve,
    My Virgil was forgot,
While lightning hours of joy I spent
    With the wizard Walter Scott.

Over the fields I see the house,
  Scarcely five minutes' walk
From where we lived, where oft we went
  To have a pleasant talk,
With friends for whose kind sake we yet
  Mark those old days with chalk.

Dear Loch! how much I've seen by thee,
  In fancy's hallowed light
On thy wan clouds the ancient chiefs,
  With Ossian took their flight;
And Douglas, Randolph, met me here.
  And Bruce, and Wallace wight.

Old Homer murmured to thy surge
  His music in mine ear,
And Burns has sung his cordial songs,
  And Shakespeare met me here;
And Thomson painted thy fair scenes,
  And Horace became dear.

Isaiah here hath wrapt my soul,
  And Job hath thrilled me through,
And David's hallowed strains I learnt;
  And all those glories threw
A charm about thy plains and hills,
  That day-light never knew.

The dark-brown hills they gird thee yet,
  The ships frequent thy bay;
The cattle low along thy shore
  At closing of the day;
And people plough, and reap, and sow,—
  All in the ancient way.

And thou art still the same thyself
  As thou wert years ago;

Thy flashing waters plunge and roll,
    And murmuring ebb and flow;
And clouds sail o'er thy lucid breast,
    And bright suns on thee glow.

While I have changed, and nobler things
    Than thou have changed with me,—
Hearts that have life, and thought, and hope,
    And yet must daily see
So much they care for join the past,
    Like my young thoughts of thee.

Sweet Loch! farewell! I love to see
    Yon sunshine gild thy breast,
For surely He who keeps thee so,
    In fadeless glory drest,
Can treasure yet for me what's gone,
    At its brightest and its best.

SIR LACHLAN MOR.*

A DISTINGUISHED chief of the MacLeans, who was known as Sir Lachlan Mòr, on account of his great size and prowess, was killed in a bloody battle between his own clan and the MacDonalds, which took place in the year 1598, on the shore of Gruinart, Islay. The story says that he was killed by a deformed and very diminutive man, named Dubh Shee, who had offered the chief his services before the fight commenced, but met with rather a contemptuous refusal. The man immediately went over to the other side, whose leader, Sir James MacDonald,

* See note III.

received him gladly. Dubh Shee was unfit to mingle in
the strife of strong men. So it is said he took up his
position on a tree which overlooked the field of battle,
though I believe there are no trees growing there now.
He was a famous archer, and he watched his opportunity
till the chances of the fight brought Sir Lachlan Mòr
within his reach, when he shot him dead at the head of
his men. The MacLeans were completely defeated with
heavy loss. A day or two after this, it is said that two
females, of whom different accounts are given—some
calling them strangers, some clanswomen, some relatives
of the dead—grieving to think that the body of so
notable a chief as Sir Lachlan Mòr should lie unburied
and uncared for on the moorland, came from a distance
in search of it. They hired a rude vehicle—the only one
to be had in the neighbourhood—and having found the
corpse, proceeded to carry it to the nearest burying-ground,
about six miles distant. The way was rough, and the
driver looking behind him saw the head of the great
chief, which extended beyond the car, nodding to him at
every jolt, as if it had life, and were giving him directions.
Boor, or perhaps enemy, as the fellow was, he laughed
when he saw this. At the next heavy rut he looked
again to please his savage soul, with the same ferocious
enjoyment. But this time the elder female, who had
watched him, acted as described in the ballad. She
killed the brutal driver with the chieftain's dagger.
Then, along with her companion, she brought the mortal
remains of Sir Lachlan to the place where they still lie
buried. A spirited gentleman of the clan recently
endeavoured to raise a sum sufficient to erect a monument
over the grave of this chief—the most famous and the
ablest the MacLeans ever had; but unfortunately he did
not succeed to his satisfaction.

  Slowly, from the field of slaughter,
   Do they bring Sir Lachlan Mòr;

Slowly, o'er the weary moorland,
    From the dank and deadly shore.

Slowly, and in bitter sorrow,
    Through a rough and rugged way,
With the yellow beams upon it
    Of the sickly setting day.

Ah! how lowly lies the leader;
    See how pale his face is now;
Never in the hall or highway—
    Never on the mountain brow—

Shall his step be laid majestic;
    Shall his stately form be seen;
Shall his voice inspire the council,
    Or the fight his manly mien.

Never shall his clan behind him
    Gather in the joy of fight;
Never draw their cold blue weapons—
    Hard and deadly—glancing bright.

Poorly now the chief's attended,
    Rudely now the hero's led;
Yet he wakes not from the slumber
    Of yon red and mossy bed.

For the sad stamp's on his features
    Which Dubh Shee's hard arrow bore;
On the moor Clan Gillian redden'd
    With their brave and boiling gore.

Only two are with the driver
    Of a rolling, rocking car,
Stretch'd whereon the dead man's carried
    From the fiery field of war.

Two that walk in silent sorrow—
    Ladies of his kindred are—
Mourning, to the field of slaughter
    Come to seek him from afar.

As they drive him slowly onward,
    O'er the bad and broken way,
His head, with all its matted tresses,
    Nodded where he lifeless lay.

Then the driver laugh'd who saw him,
    Large and massy, lie along,
Senseless, soulless—him so lately
    Foremost in the martial throng.

Laugh'd! and quicker drove him onward,
    Yet again to see the head
Nodding, without will or reason,
    With its light of manhood fled.

Nodding at the boor who jeered him
    With that mean, malicious scorn,
Nursed in secret by the envy
    In the vulgar spirit born.

Then the ladies hastened forward—
    Not a word the younger said,
While her tears rained down in anguish
    On the wan face of the dead.

But the elder damsel answered:—
    "Laugh'st thou at my fallen chief?
May thine own vile carcase, caitiff,
    Fill thy mother's heart with grief!"

Out she drew the chieftain's dagger,
    As she hurled this angry cry
At the boor who gloomed before her,
    With his dull and threatening eye.

And she struck him down, and left him
    Stretched beneath the sunbeams there,
Like a wild fowl by the falcon
    Swept from out the fields of air.

Then, alone, their dead they carried.
    While one nursed the manly brow—
Nursed, it on her bosom gently,
    Like a holy, heavenly vow.

And one—tenderly she drove him
    To the sad and solemn ground,
Where the hero's dust reposes,
    With the mouldering ashes round.

Soft and slowly there we leave them—
    Chieftain! may thine ashes rest,
Peaceful as the voice of prayer
    From a calm, untroubled breast!

Long as sound the breezes o'er them,
    Sound the voice of psalms beside;
And spread Christ's peace-speaking Gospel
    From thy green sod, far and wide!

Sir Lachlan Mòr MacLean is buried in the churchyard of Kilchoman, Islay, near the south wall of the church. This serves to explain the reference to psalms, &c., in the concluding lines.

THE PIOUS LABOURER.*

Where rolls and roars the green Atlantic wave,
That heaves and welters from the mingling sky,
Where the fresh seaweed scents the lively gale,
And rocks, and sands, and moors, and hills combine
To form, with ocean and cloud-varied skies,
A scene to love, although it be not gay,
Nor richly cultured, nor with woodland green.
There stands a heathy range, close to the shore,
Which long-tongued billows fill with hollow sound,
And frequent showers, as if they loved it, fall,
When oft the winds pass over it in haste;
Yet there the sunbeams bask in summer tide,
And autumn, with sweet odour floats therein,
While winter braces but ne'er chills the blood—
So much the sea air mellows his hard breath
Till spring, as beautiful as angel's smile,
Revives and visits its calm solitude.

Once in this place a labourer lived for long
In a small cottage, thick with heather thatched,
From youth to age, a poor but honest man.
Few were the comforts by his home supplied—
Its roof was low, its floor was beaten clay,
Its window small, its furniture was rude—
A bed, a dresser and a few plain stools,
A chest, a table, and some bowls and pans—
Things all for use and strict necessity—
No ornament I trow, nor luxury had he.
These all the plenishing his house contained,
Here had he lived, and here he thought to die—
Round it he toiled throughout the circling year,

* See note IV.

From morn to evening since his earliest youth,
Facing the task allotted him by heaven,
How unpretending was his life and poor,
And yet 't was full of something noble too,
Though passed so humbly on that lonely moor,
And I'm persuaded Angels may have caught
Themes for their praises from this cottar's acts!

The man was honest from the very first,
Although in youth he gave but little heed
To truth's great sanction and its source divine.
Perhaps he thought himself too low and mean,
And far too ignorant to turn his thoughts
Unto the cure and governance of souls;
Though in him too the eternal image lay
In lustrous fragments, as in all mankind,
But these he may have thought false, foolish toys,
Misleading men from self's more useful ways—
Thus spurning good with carnal sense away—
Thus hugging foolishness and seeming wise.
Howe'er that be, his oaths were many then,
And wild his talk, and unrestrained his wit,
And very seldom to the church went he,
Till, how it came I know not, at the last
A little seed was wafted to his mind—
A casual seed that filled his soul with fear;
Then woke he up as from a flattering dream,
And he looked onward, and around, and back
With eyes from which some misty scales had fallen,
And nothing saw but Power—Almighty Power—
Moved by a Spirit he partook not in.
Ah! then he felt an awful shading gloom;
For his past life rose like a wall of fire,
And hedged him close in his own feeble being,
With sin and terror for his visitors,
In that worst solitude man ever feels
The experienced need of sympathy divine.

Before that Mercy hath unveiled her face,
And nought but sin seems living in the soul,
He saw the course of Providence roll on,
And knew that he had always wrought against it,
And so had always God's good gifts profaned,
And God's invincible decree opposed.
Ah! then he learnt how man is God's own image—
How even creative power is reflected
By that most subtle force which never resteth,
But still debases or exalts the life—
Imagination, owned by all mankind,
Rare artist framing worlds within the world,
And much too often passing its own worlds
On every sort of man, for God's firm structure
Which foundations hath, far deeper than we know.
Imagination had deceived this cottar,
Working so humbly on the Highland moors:
He had created for himself a life,
And formed it falsely as in God's despite,
As this great truth flashed on the agony
In which he wrestled till the morning light.
There sunk a woe upon the poor man's mind,
And his heart withered like a rootless herb,
Till all he saw was coloured with his dread,
And beauty covered up with melancholy.
Without a hope, without a star he lived,
Until the Sun of Righteousness arose,
And o'er the gloom shed saving, guiding light.
Then, full of gratitude within his heart,
The poor man kept the word that raised from sin.
"Fear not, O ye of little faith! but love,"
And this he treasured till it hallowed him;
For at its sound and through its glorious power
His life grew green as at the sound of rain;
Then calm, and grave, and solemn, and serene,
And full of charity and gracious worth,
The brighter bloomed with each returning day,

In gentle happiness this rustic lived,
Thankful his Master was so good to him.
Oh! what tranquility and tender joy
Now thrilled his spirits as he trod the fields,
Where every change, each evidence of power,
Gave him fresh proof of never failing love.
What high and deep, and sacred truth he knew,
This simple peasant in these lonely fields!
How would he turn the soil which God had given
To feed his creatures in such wondrous ways!
How would he watch the waving harvest fields—
The yearly miracle on which we feed,
And touch with reverence, and hope, and love,
That offered staff of life held forth by God,
On which all creatures lean for their support!

There was a true abiding dignity in this—
A good thus lived for, and a good thus done—
A noble spirit in a lowly sphere
Was his, who lived as seeing the unseen.
There is such grandeur in a good man's life,
How poor soe'er the form that covers it,
Let but the heart be humble and sincere,
How poor soe'er the garb that covers him,
Although in homely weed he tread the earth,
And till the ground, or tend the flocks and herds:
Although he issue every morning forth
From a frail hut, and leave a humble couch—
Although his occupation be not one
That lifts the fancy, or that sways the thought—
Not one that calls for energy and power,
For knowledge, training, or for mighty care.
There is a grandeur in his life I ween—
A high nobility, a rank divine;
Though on an earthen floor he kneels, in peace,
To say with reverent devotion's power,
"Our Father" to the God that made the heavens—

"Our Father," to the God that rules the earth—
"Thy Servant" say unto the Man Divine,
The holy, harmless, undefiled with sin—
There is in verity a grandeur here.
He who perceives the mercy and the grace
That sought and suffered, and that died for men,
Stand like an angel ever at his side
To quell his waywardness, his wrath, his vice—
To check the thought that might defile the heart—
To stay the word that might inflict a pain,
And guide a cheerful and abiding hope.
Thus feeling well is taught to work with God,
And thus there's grandeur in a good man's life—
The humblest livlihood debases not;
No, nor our very sternest doom efface—
Earth cannot smother it, nor Death himself—
That dread, dark shadow—chain in its gloom!

CAPTAIN GORRIE'S RIDE.*

Still is the night—the mist is wild,
   The hour is waxing late,
The road is grey, the moor is black
   And dim and desolate.

The wind it moves, its touch is soft,
   Its breath is faint and low;
The damp of the wide waste hath flagged
   Its heavy wing and slow.

* See note V.

The moon is near its setting wheeled,
    And the southwest is bright;
Where half obscured, its site is marked
    By a dim blotch of light.

All else is dark above, below,
    And silent as the dead;
All, save the hoarse end swollen brook
    That frets its moory bed.

Another sullen stifled sound,
    Is the deep note and grand
That lulls in every hour of calm,
    An ocean-girded land.

Ten miles the road doth stretch along
    Before a house you reach;
Three miles through moor and sandhills,
    And seven along the beach.

Where, ever as you wander on,
    The sea-waves rolling blue,
The yellow sand, the bent so brown,
    And streamlets passing through.

Rocks, hills, and silent distant moors,
    Are all that you may see;
But in the night 'tis lonelier far,
    And wild as well may be.

Why then so late and carelessly,
    On trampling steed and strong,
Rides Captain Gorrie all alone,
    This lonely road along?

What boon and joyous company,
    What bien and bright fireside,

Have sent him from their jovial cheer,
    To take this cheerless ride?

'Twere better sure for horse and man,
    To hold till morrow morn,
The steaming jug, the merry talk,
    The stable and the corn.

But the Captain—it was harvest then—
    The Captain thought not so;
And though the night was dim and dark,
    The Captain he would go.

And ever as he onward rode,
    He hummed a manly strain;
In tent and field, he used to sing,
    In Asia and in Spain.

The road is long,—the Captain stern
    And sterner sings the while;
'Tis a song of Fionn Mac Cu'aill,
    The hero of the Gael.

And ever as he sings, he hears
    The massy tread below,
Of the steed that bore him safely
    Up the promontory's brow.

When the narrow rocky footway
    To the old fort that led,
Rung loud with sound unwonted
    Beneath his iron tread.

And the captain he looks round and hums
    More daringly and clear.

His ancient song whene'er his steed
    Starts at the touch of fear.

Thus far they tell the road is lost
    In the loose shifted sand,
And nearer they approach and near
    The loud and roaring strand.

What ails thy steed now, Captain, tell—
    What ail thy steed and thee—
What makes him start and snort so loud
    At scenting of the sea?

What feeling makes him toss so high
    His head, and step so light,
And seem for nervous start prepared,
    And haste and headlong flight?

A strong hand holds the bridle rein,
    The horse turns to the left,
And all along the line of waves
    Trips warily and deft.

His rider looks a moment round,
    Where o'er the wide blue sea,
Before the moon that bursts its shroud
    The misty shadows flee.

The gelding grey starts once again,
    The Captain glances back—
My God! what stalwart horseman rides
    Upon that giant black!

Dies in a cough the Captain's song,
    He spurs the gallant grey,

By slow degrees he faster flees
   Along the salt sea spray.

But ever as he glances round,
   The jet black steed is by;
Though ne'er a breath the Captain hears,
   Nor horse-hoofs beating nigh.

The motion fires the Captain's soul,
   He thinks of that awful place,
Where deep and rayless darkness hold
   The fallen angel race.

He thinks of him all suddenly,
   In his own pathway found,
So black and grim, who rides so trim,
   Without a word or sound.

And the Captain feels his heart oppressed,
   And a strange terror rise,
And with a battle shout away,
   Winged like the wind he flies.

But still his wild companion comes,
   So dark, so dismal dread,
And louder shouts the Captain,
   And faster flies his steed.

Over the hills and rivulets,
   Over the holts and hags,
O'er dyke, and rock, and beaten road,
   His wild course never flags—

Till at his stable door, in haste,
   In heat, and disarray,

His servants find the Captain bold,
  At breaking of the day.

The Captain he was weary,
  But the Captain he was well,
The gallant grey was weary too,
  For he stumbled and he fell.

And rolled away, and lifeless lay
  With a gasp upon his side,
No more his master backs the grey,
  In rough and rapid ride.

As the Captain looks in pity,
  The salt tear fills his eye,
He thinks of that dread horseman,
  Through all the night so nigh.

And swears to raise a monument,
  And dig a noble grave,
For the horse that beat Beelzebub
  Beside the salt sea wave.

THE HAUNTED WATER OF DUBH-THALAMH.*

In the Highlands, although the people are sufficiently superstitious, and tell many tales, with witches, ghosts, fairies, and water-kelpies, and many kinds of supernatural beings in them, they never introduce such creatures into their poetry; and hardly even allude, through this channel, to any of the wild and strange beliefs so

* See Note VI.

prevalent among them. I don't know whether this proceeds from a fear of offending the supernatural beings —with regard to whose existence there is indeed very little scepticism—or whether it proceeds from a notion of their unfitness for the purposes of poetry. But the fact is as I have stated. The ballad which is now given, is therefore, not to be regarded as, in its present form, a popular Highland song. The story on which it is founded is certainly popular enough in one district of the Highlands at any rate; but I am not aware that the legend is known in other parts of the country. The poem differs little from it in its incidents, though it aims at giving something of a moral tone to the legend, by bringing it as near as possible—in the midst of solitude, uncertainty, and danger—to a remorseful reflection, through means of a troubled dream, of a thoughtless and perhaps evil life. The story I have often heard. Once, especially, I recollect hearing it, on a stormy spring day, in a little barn, where three men were working not far from a roadside, and within three or four hundred yards of the place where the incident was said to have happened. After a few remarks, in a rustic Highland fashion, on the things of heaven and earth that are undreamed of by philosophy, this tale, in corroboration of something or other that occurred in the course of conversation, was told in a grave and earnest manner by one of the workers, and listened to most respectfully by the others. The narrator used, in a fine Celtic dialect, almost the equivalent of the following:—

Heavy and slow came the waves of the night,
    With a threat'ning lurch and a reel,
Ere they break with a shock on the spray-spatter'd rock,
    Like blows on a warrior's steel.

And a dreary moan from the mountains comes down
    When the roar of the surge is laid;

Then a rush whirls round, and a terrible sound
   By the wind and the water is made.

And, hark! how they breathe, like a thing that has life!
   Oh, list what the wild waves say!
"Why alone, all alone, is this mariner thrown,
   Like a waif, by the tempest away?"

He sits in the stern of his boat, and he hears
   The wan waves that beat, and the wild winds that fleet,
And the tempest that scatters the spray like tears,
   Where it treads with its merciless feet.

He sits and he groans, as the keel grates the beach
   With a harsh and a rasping sound;
And he tries to sleep till the morning steep
   In its light the stranger ground.

He tries to sleep, but soon starts and awakes;
   For a sound is in the air,
That is not the sound of the wind or the wave,
   And it raises his fell of hair.

It is not the tread of a man that he hears,
   Nor the sound of a human tongue;
He folds his arms on his breast, and peers
   The dim-dark shore along.

Now on the left, and now on the right,
   And now it comes before;
Sweet mercy! there's some vague dark thing
   Upon the stormy shore.

Oh, horror! there's a dull, deep sound,
   Like breath from a tighten'd throat—

Now on the land, and now on the sea,
    And now on the rocking boat.

And there's a form, a clouded form,
    In a shroud of misty light,
That darker makes the tempest wild—
    More terrible that night.

It rests on the gunwale and looks in his face,
    And it glares so fierce and fell;
While it breathes through its throat, with that dismal note,
    'Twixt a groan and an angry yell—

A note of pain and agony;
    A note to hear with dread;
A wrathful note—a struggling cry,
    By fear and fierceness fed!

Then at him it eagerly reach'd at last,
    And it growl'd like a beast o'er it's prey—
Till he started back with a shuddering haste,
    And the vision pass'd away.

Tenfold more wild the night became—
    Tenfold more black the sky,
With fearful leap the billows sweep,
    And the winds breathe a sorrowing sigh.

'Tis not the moaning element,
    'Tis not the wild, wild wind,
'Tis not the black, black trouble, pent
    In the sky, which moves his mind.

'Tis the vision'd form that comes once more
    To press, like a weight on his soul;

'Tis the darkening again on the lonely shore
    Of yon dim and dismal dole.

'Tis the sense that he's not alone—alone
    With the waste and the howling storm;
'Tis the sense of the ill that rises still,
    With its dark and vapoury form.

That's the wind that cries, that's the billow that roars:
    But 'tis neither that groans so near:
'Tis the shadowy form of the night and the storm
    Come to torture his listening ear.

And downward it glides, as black in the night
    As the deep thunder-cloud in the day;
And it stands by his boat, with its gibbering note,
    While he strives in his fear to pray.

Then he crouches down in the ebon gloom,
    For his sins have choked his prayer;
And above it hangs like a sorrowful doom,
    Like a poisonous mist in the air.

Forward and downward, and forward it bends,
    And it casts its embrace around,
And shuts him out from the tempest about,
    Till its roar seems a distant sound!

Away, away, his soul is drawn,
    And the darkness is more dread,
Though the storm seems hush'd as the shelter'd lawn,
    Where the hare and the fawn are fed.

Away, away, till he faints—he faints,
    And breathes one stifled sigh,
As he calls on God to save his soul
    In his parting agony!

Then high and fast away it pass'd,
  And lurid light it grew;
Oh! deep was the glow on the wave that it cast,
  And red was its fiery hue.

As it sunk with a roar far away from the shore,—
  With a roar and a wailing cry!
It sunk, and he saw it again no more
  In the place where his comrades lie!

The scene of this ballad I remember distinctly, and used to be quite familiar with as a boy. At that time, it seemed to me to possess a sort of peculiar awfulness, especially in the dusk of evening, or in the vague gloaming and deep stillness of a summer night. Then not a sound disturbed the air; not a motion was seen or felt along the earth. A beautiful Highland loch slept on the smooth stones of the sea-beach, like an enchanted princess waiting for the salute that was to restore her to consciousness and life; and, dim as the far off clouds, and silent as their own shadows, the dark brown hills looked over fields and crofts and gloomy moors, down to the little pebbly hollow through which, almost without a murmur, crept a tiny brooklet—the supposed hiding-place of the malignant genius that took the form of an old woman. There was a fascination about the place. I used to feel a thrill run through me as I drew near it in the darkness; nor am I much surprised at the Highland peasant who told me how he was disturbed and profoundly affected there one summer midnight, by what he supposed to be the wild cries of mournful and despairing spirits. In the impressive silence he had heard the soft wailings of the sea-birds on the rocks close by him; and, in the excited state of his imagination at the moment, he had made the very natural mistake, for him at least, which he mentioned.

KNOWEST THOU THE LAND?

Know'st thou the land where the herd, houseless, strayed,
When summer's night was but one gloaming shade—
Where still the billows roll in sunny gold,
And thousand moors their thousand waters hold—
Know'st thou that land? The hardy Islesman's home,
Whence oft, alas! an exile he must roam.

Know'st thou its scenes, where autumn's threat'ning shower
Now stirs scant wish to snatch the mellow hour?
Since ruins mark where houses stood of yore,
And silence yawns around the good man's door—
Know'st thou its scenes? What simple joys they've seen,—
Round them what worth, what innocence have been!

Know'st thou its hills, where wandering mists repose,
And bleach the rocks o'er which the heather grows;
Whose warmest couch the grouse and blackcock share—
Those chartered denizens of earth and air—
Know'st thou its hills whence the eye glances free
Over the measureless and western sea?

Know'st thou its lochs on which, when sunset's o'er,
The boat glides softly to the fragrant shore;
While cattle bellow and the house-dogs bay,
And hamlet noises pass with light away—
Know'st thou its lochs? On them night's sky-born beam
Welcome in peace the poorest taper's gleam.

THE ISLANDER'S GUIDING STAR.

The following verses were suggested by reading the beautiful and well-known lines, on the same subject, composed in Gaelic by Dr. John Macleod of Morven:—

    Black was the night—the waves were black,
      And black the gloom of heaven;
    Loud blew the storm, and fast the rack
      By the swift winds was driven.

    'Twas then a veil came o'er the Isle
      Of green and level lea,
    Which lies full many a heaving mile
      Out in the western sea:

    A veil that round its every bay
      With deepening darkness sped—
    And spread where lone and far away,
      One boat the tempest fled.

    Her rowers' strength was well nigh spent,
      Not yet their port they knew;
    For not a star its lustre lent
      Unto the toiling crew.

    And not a headland they descried,
      Nor rock, nor guiding light;
    While round them sank the darkness wide
      Of black and rayless night.

    Out then, and spake a mariner—
      A hardy man was he,

Who'd faced, full many a wintry year,
   The storms upon the sea:—

"My trust is yet in Him who sent
   About my mates and me,
This strong and fearful element—
   This gloom in which we be."

"My trust is yet in Him," he said,
   "Who knows to guide our way;
We have not from His mercies strayed,
   Though on these waters grey."

Just then from out the darkness broke
   A fair and starlike gleam;
The word of hope was scarcely spoke
   Ere rose its brightening beam.

And straight the rowers' strength returned—
   The rowers' hearts were cheered;
Strong with Hope's flame again they burned,
   Whene'er yon star appeared.

For well their pilot knew who raised
   Its far-flung beacon light;
He knew near whose warm home it blazed,
   To cheer the howling night.

He knew whose care had placed it there,
   Amid the tempest wild,
The whilst she breathed her simple prayer—
   His poor and lonely child.

Twas she who guarded well that flame
   From the fierce wind and spray,

Alone, until her father came
   And kissed her tears away.

Thus, on the waters wild, I ween,
   On which life's bark is driven,
The Book of God has ever been
   The beacon-light of heaven.

DEAR ISLAY!*

O Islay! sweet Islay!
Thou green, grassy Islay!
Why, why art thou lying
   So far o'er the sea?
O Islay! dear Islay!
Thy daylight is dying,
And here am I longing,
   And longing for thee!

O Islay! fair Islay!
Thou dear mother Islay!
Where my spirit, awaking,
   First look'd on the day.
O Islay! dear Islay;
That link of God's making
Must last, till I wing me
   Away, and away!

* See Note VII.

Dear Islay, good Islay!
Thou holy-soil'd Islay!
My fathers are sleeping
   Beneath thy green sod.
O Islay! kind Islay!
Well, well be thou keeping
That dear dust awaiting
   The great day of God.

Old Islay! God bless thee,
Thou good mother, Islay!
Bless thy wide ocean!
   And bless thy sweet lea!
And Islay, dear Islay!
My heart's best emotion,
For ever and ever
   Shall centre in thee!

The following extract, from Mr. Campbell's "West Highland Tales," may be read with some interest in connection with the above:—"No Highlander, if his friends can help it, is buried anywhere but at home. Coffins may be seen on board the steamers, conveying to the outer islands the bodies of those who have died on the mainland. It is a poetic wish to be buried amongst friends, and one that is in full force to this day. The curse of Scotland may occasionally intrude even on such solemn occasions; but a funeral is almost always decorously conducted. In some places, as I am told, a piper may still be seen at the head of the funeral procession, playing a dirge. There 's no want of reverence; but death is treated as an ordinary event. I have seen a man's tombstone, with a blank for the date, standing at the end of his house while he was quite well."—Vol. i. p. 235.

HOLLOW FRIENDSHIP.

The stream that's swollen by the ice,
    And the loose and melted snow,
Doth, with a swift and sounding pace,
    Down from the mountain go.

The cold of winter in its breast,
    Fast sweeps its turbid flow,
O'er stone and rock with shout and shriek,
    Like a hero through the foe.

I've seen that stream when summer's lip,
    And parched and burning throat,
Sucked in its loud and liquid strength,
    Soon lose that vaunting note.

And melt away and shrink before
    The sultry, scorching air,
Till not one whispering sound was left
    To cheer its channel bare.

And I have said, "Lo! there's the man
    Who doth our spring-time meet
With words that are extremely good,
    And very brave and sweet.

"Till the exhausting summer air
    Creates some need of him;
And then, alas! his promise good
    Grows very small and slim.

"Till, in the highest noon of need,
    Its very ooze is gone—

All self-absorbed, and swallowed up,
    With its loud roaring done!

"Methinks, beside such empty bed,
    Filled full in other days,
With many a kindly-sounding word,
    And many a noble phrase.

"I see some much relying friend
    Look down with pitying eyes,
Where manly friendship once bragged loud,
    And gallant sympathies;

"But where there's now revealed a heart,
    Hard as a stone and dry,
With greedy sands that still refuse
    A drop for passer-by.

"A scornful thought will be that friend's—
    A cutting word, I ween;
Yet, were I he, I would not change
    What's now for what hath been."

LITTLE EMMELINE.

How playfully the torrent goes—
How merrily it sings!
From out the distant hills it flows,
Afar the snowy foam it flings;

Its eddies whirl, its wavelets sweep
Away unto the distant deep.
How like our little Emmeline,-
Our dainty little Emmeline—
   Our charming little girl!

Amid the hills she too was born,
And merrily she sings!
She's joyous as the flashing Sorn,
And like its chimes her laughter rings.
With many a whirl and many a leap,
She flutters round the moaning deep.
Our playful little Emmeline,—
Our sweet, our dainty Emmeline—
   Our charming little girl.

The sun from out the storm looks forth,
The torrent foams away:
We've sought her east, we've sought her west—
We've sought her all the live-long day.
Within the wood—along the shore—
The trees they rock, the surges roar;
But no—no little Emmeline—
Our dainty little Emmeline—
   We cannot find the child.

The eddies whirl, the wavelets sweep,
The torrent rushes wild;
The wave is dark, the stream is deep;
And where then is our child?
Oh! God, her curls float o'er the pool,
Like flowers of Eden, beautiful—
She's drowned! our little Emmeline,
Our dainty little Emmeline,
   Our heaven, taken child!

OPPRESSORS AND THE OPPRESSED.
ECCLESIASTES, IV, 1—3.

And then I turned to the oppressed,
   And lo! the tears they shed—
The silent and the bitter tears,
   And the hard life they led.

Now they were scourged by bitter tongues,
   Now scorned by haughty eyes,
And shut by cold and ruffian hearts
   From fostering sympathies.

And as I looked I marvelled much—
   I wondered much to see,
That men of grace, so needful all,
   So graceless all should be.

I marvelled, when some shameless man,
   Of low and selfish ways,
I saw advanced to places high,
   And overwhelmed with praise.

I marvelled at them all, to think
   That these—and such as these—
Should have this great and glorious world
   To do with as they please.

And then I said, "Between them both,
   Hypocrisy and gold,
Sway this great world in every way—
   They sway the young and old.

"They sway the high, they sway the low—
   The learned and the lay—
They sway the high imposingly,
   The mean, in meaner way."

Yea, and I thought the dead were well,
  Or they who ne'er were born;
Since they had passed away, or ne'er
  This fleshly robe had worn.

To see the meek man trodden down,
  And the deserving lost
In the huge crowd of hypocrites,
  Who the right pathway cross'd.

To see good truths forgotten quite,
  And errors multiform
In human hearts, in human words,
  In human homage swarm.

To hear them in the pulpit speak,
  To see them wield the pen,
And point the glance, and rule the tongue,
  And darken light in men.

Making them dex'trous to o'erlook
  The glorious mint of heaven,
And quick to join the loud applause
  To counterfeits is given.

I marvelled if there ever will,
  Or ever can arise,
Some simple, blissful truths to reign
  Beneath our bent blue skies.

OLD MEMORIES.

How they o'erflow my memory,
  The sweeping gusts, the waning light,
On a bare moorland by the sea,
  Grey with the drift of the autumn night!

All lonely, but replete with thought,
   And linked to things long passed away;
By my rapt fancy thither brought
   From storied page or rousing lay.

This, this is that same solitude
   Where stooped the hern her solemn wing
To stand, like some old ghost, and brood,
   By moory loch and oozy spring.

There wailed the plover's plaintive cry—
   There wild ducks bent the heather dun,
That fringed those lines of melody
   Where secret streams still sing and run.

This, this is that same solitude
   Through which the soft sea-breathings sighed,
Like a sad soul in search of good
   From which, perforce, it wandered wide.

And still the billows' far heard moan
   Hangs o'er it like an awful doom,
Spoke in some antique Titan tone,
   Long shrouded in primeval gloom!

The hills there silent stand for aye—
   The clouds yet wander solemnly,
Through evening's weird and deep'ning grey,
   Or dreamlike on its bosom lie.

Oh! this is the old place I loved,
   When haunted by the gloaming mild,
And by the spirit-wind that moved,
   Almost to life, yon desert wild.

Then how I peopled the dim scene
   With things in climes remote and near,
And other ages that have been—
   Things that yet float like shadows here!

For now the fancies and the place
    Live both together in my mind;
No spoils which time can e'er efface,
    Because by love and thought combined.

FAREWELL OF THE EMIGRANT.

Farewell to the land where my childhood was pass'd,
And to the sweet scene these dim clouds o'ercast;
Farewell to its hills, and its dark rocky cave,
Whose shelter is music when loud tempests rave.

Thou fair green valley, sad parting to thee,
Oh! fill it, loud ocean, with wailing for me;
And, winds, the bare copses that moaningly greet,
Sad tone, ye wild singers, I ne'er shall forget.

For, fast-sweeping breezes, and thou rushing stream,
At this moment of parting, like old friends ye seem,
As now for the last time the sound's in my ear
That mov'd my young soul to a rapture so dear.

Stoop down then, grey heaven—stoop down in thy gloom;
And haste, coming tempest—haste over the tomb,
Where slumber my fathers and kinsmen, and sigh
As if mourning with me o'er the place where they lie.

Oh! land that my memory fills with delight,
On whose soil strode those fathers before me in might,
As I dream'd in my youth on thy green swelling breast
That wraps their cold dust in its mantle of rest.

Farewell now to all that embraces thy shore,
Dear land of my race that I ne'er shall see more;
Lands richer there may be before me than thine,
But no other country can ever be mine.

HASTE FROM THE WINDOW.

The words of this song are intended by the singer to convey a warning to her lover, one of the outlawed MacGregors, to flee from his enemies.

Haste, haste from the window, oh stay not, my love,
Fly swift as the breeze and delay not, my love,
Haste, haste from the window, oh stay not, my love,
Fly swift as the breeze and delay not, my love.
The pilotless ship is unmoored by the tide,
The breakers triumphant career o'er her side;
Haste, haste from the window, oh stay not, my love,
Fly swift as the breeze and delay not, my love.

Haste, haste from the window, oh stay not, my love,
Fly swift as the breeze and delay not, my love,
Haste, haste from the window, oh stay not, my love,
Fly swift as the breeze and delay not, my love,
Go quickly, but softly, for danger is near,
Oh woe, if a trace of thy footsteps appear;
Down, down by the grey copse, hide deep in its shade,
Lie hushed in the dell which the torrent has made.

Haste, haste from the window, oh stay not, my love,
Fly swift as the breeze and delay not, my love,
Haste, haste from the window, oh stay not, my love,
Fly swift as the breeze and delay not, my love,
The mist of the mountain shall wrap thee around,
Thy tread shall be lost in the cataract's sound,
Around thy light vessel the vexed waves chafe,
One bound o'er the wave and my lover is safe.

BI FALBH O'N UINNEIG.

Bi falbh o'n uinneig, fhir-ghaoil, fhir-ghaoil
'S na tig an nochd tuilleadh fhir-ghràidh, fhir-ghràidh,
Bi falbh o'n uinneig, fhir-ghaoil, fhir-ghaoil
'S na tig an nochd tuilleadh fhir-ghràidh, fhir-ghràidh,
Tha do long air an t-sàile 's i gun seòladair aice,
Tha do long air an t-sàile 's i gun seòladair aice,
Bi falbh o'n uinneig, fhir-ghaoil, fhir-ghaoil
'S na tig an nochd tuilleadh fhir-ghràidh, fhir-ghràidh.

Bi falbh o'n uinneig, fhir-ghaoil, fhir-ghaoil
'S na tig an nochd tuilleadh fhir-ghràidh, fhir-ghràidh,
Bi falbh o'n uinneig, fhir-ghaoil, fhir-ghaoil
'S na tig an nochd tuilleadh fhir-ghràidh, fhir-ghràidh,
Cuir umad do bhrògan tha'n tòir a tigh'n cas ort
Cuir umad do bhrògan tha'n tòir a tigh'n cas ort
Gur mise bhios brònach ma ni 'n tòir so cuir ás duit
Na tig an nochd tuilleadh fhir-ghràidh, fhir-ghràidh.

Bi falbh o'n uinneig, fhir-ghaoil, fhir-ghaoil
'S na tig an nochd tuilleadh fhir-ghràidh, fhir-ghràidh,
Bi falbh o'n uinneig, fhir-ghaoil, fhir-ghaoil
'S na tig an nochd tuilleadh fhir-ghràidh, fhir-ghràidh,
'Nuair a théid mi measg sloighe fear do bhòidhche cha'n
    fhaic mi
Tha faltan donn dualach air mo luaidh do na gaisgich
Gur mise bhios brònach ma ni 'n tòir so cuir ás duit
Na tig an nochd tuilleadh fhir-ghràidh, fhir-ghràidh.

THE PRAISE OF ISLAY.

CHORUS:—Oh! my Island, oh, my Isle!
    Oh! my dear, my native soil,
    Again the rising sun can smile
      With golden beams on Landy.

I see afar yon hill, Ardmore,
The beating billows wash its shore,
But ah! its beauties bloom no more,
    For me no more in Islay.
          Oh! my Island, &c.

But birchen branches there are gay,
And hawthorns wave their silvered spray;
And every bough the breezes sway
    Awakens joy in Islay.
          Oh! my Island, &c.

There eagles rise on soaring wing,
And herons watch the gushing spring;
And heath-cocks with their whirring bring
    Their own delight to Islay.
          Oh! my Island, &c.

Its mavis sings on hazy bough,
Its linnet haunts the glen below,
And O, may long their wild notes flow
    With melodies in Islay.
          Oh! my Island, &c.

The black-cock too, so glossy brave—
The ducks that cleave the moory wave—

MOLADH NA LANDAIDH.

Seisd:—Hò ro Eileinich ho gù,
Hò i rìthil ho i thù,
Hó ro Eileinich ho gù,
    Gu bheil mo rùn 's an Landaidh.

Chì mi thall ud an Aird-mhòr,
Aite 'choilich dhuibh 's a' gheòidh;
Aite mo chridhe 's mo ghaoil,
    Far 'n robh mi aotrom, ainmeil.
        Hò ro, &c.

'S ged tha 'n Landaidh creagach, ciar,
'S moch a dh' éireas oirre 'ghrian;
Innis nam ba laoigh 's nam fiadh,
    'S gu 'm b'e mo mhiann bi thall ann.
        Hò ro, &c.

'N uair a dh' éirinn moch 's an àird
Bheirinn sgrìob do cheann an t-sail'—
Bhiodh na lachain air an t-snàmh,
    'S cha b' fhad am bàs o m' laimh-sa.
        Hò ro, &c.

'S tric a leag mi air a' bhruaich
Earba ghlas a' mhuineil ruaidh;
Bhiodh an liath-chearc leam a nuas,
    A's coileach ruadh an dranndainn.
        Hò ro, &c.

'S tric a leag mi air a thaobh
An ròn ballach anns a' Chaol,—

The line of grey geese, long and grave,
   I've seen them all in Islay.
               Oh! my Island, &c.

I've heard the calf the dun cow greet,
The sportive lambkin loudly bleat—
The gentle doe trip fast and fleet
   From shade to shade in Islay.
               Oh! my Island, &c.

Though Islay's shore is rocky, drear,
Early doth the sun appear
On leafy brake and fallow deer,
   And flocks and herds in Islay.

Oh, my Island! oh my Isle!
Oh, my dear, my native soil!
From thee no scene my heart can wile
   That's wed with love to Islay.

Kilarrow, the old place of worship, and for beginning religious services in the new edifice, the good Cleric gave such offence to a few unprogressive parishioners that he had for some time to hide himself in the district of *Bruthach an Dùbhraich* until this ebullition of wrath had subsided. To continue the services in the new church was much easier than to remove the Fair from Bridgend to Bowmore. This latter struggle, which extended over a period of some years, was almost as famous as the siege of Troy. But what "Old Shawfield" could not do by persuasion, Mr. Patrick Campbell of Balinaby did by stratagem. He employed a number of pipers, who, with banners flying and pibrochs sounding, marched off at the head of the Rhinns and the Harris men, and brought them to Bowmore where Balinaby had a big banquet provided for this peaceful muster of the Clans. This incident verifies the story of Orpheus the musician of ancient Greece whose melody moved the very rocks. Henceforth the Fair found a local habitation in the beautifully situated town of Bowmore.

Carlyle the high-priest of literary portraiture finishes his pictures of historical personages with inimitable skill and power. Mr. Pattison's faithful sketch of The Fair Day shows that he was an ardent admirer of our great paragraphic biographist. The chief harper of the Fair, cheerful James Wilson, *an Dall Ruadh*, "the minstrel who rolled his sightless eyes," is portrayed with no inconsiderable skill. The blind fiddler's wife was Lizzie MacClyde, a foundling picked up on the banks of the river Clyde. Their tidy cottage at *Càrn Aithne*, Beacon Light, with its well-kept garden was a model of cleanliness and thrift. Wilson was possessed of some wit and humour. A story is told that at a party in Islay House, the sightless violinist's playing so pleased every body that "Shawfield's" generous guests proposed to collect money for each of his children. The minstrel was asked how many of a family he had got. His answer was, seven sons, each of whom has a sister. A handsome sum of money was gathered for fourteen children, Wilson's seven sons and their only sister.

II.—LOCHINDAAL.—At the entrance to this loch, there stand about eight miles apart, like the Pillars of Hercules, the Point of the Rhinns and the Mull of Oa. Lochindaal stretches to a distance of twelve miles into the heart of Islay, and forms a good roadstead for ships in stormy weather. Mr. Pattison's home was situated in close proximity to the "pebbly shore of ship-sailing Lochindaal." The reader is at once carried on the wings of bardic imagination, and placed in the very centre of Bowmore. The conical church stands, like a guardian angel, surrounded by its tidily-kept God's Acre where repose the mortal remains of our beloved forefathers. The "Nasal Psalm" has been superseded by a more melodious organ. But the "old man, who spoke of Abrahâm," is now with the Father of the Faithful in the Home above. This alludes to the Rev. James MacIntosh, A.M., who became minister of Kilarrow and Kilmeny in 1797.

III.—SIR LACHLAN MÒR.—This brave knight of Duart was one of the ablest and the greatest chiefs the plucky and enterprising MacLeans ever had. One of his great ancestors, "Lauchlayne Maklan of Dowart," is mentioned as a witness in an "obligation of the Erle of Ross," that is Alexander of Islay, Earl of Ross, and Lord of the Isles. It is dated "at Inuernys the xxiiij day of the moneth of Octobris the yere of oure lord a thousande four hundyr thyrty and nyne yeris." This obligation refers to the Marriage of Marion of Islay, the Earl's sister, to Alexander Sutherland of Dunbeath. Marion was the daughter of Donald Balloch of Islay, Earl of Ross, and Lord of the Isles. Margaret, the daughter of this Marion of Islay, was married to William Calder, seventh Thane of Cawdor. This Marion of Islay was the great-grandmother of Lady Muriel Calder, the rich heiress of Cawdor, who, in 1510, was married to Sir John Campbell, second son of Archibald, second Earl of Argyll. By this opulent marriage Cawdor passed into the hands of the Campbells. The names of the Knights of Duart and of the Thanes of Cawdor often appear in old documents passed under the seal of the MacDonalds of Islay, who till the forfeiture of "Johannes de Yla comes Rossie et dominus insularum," John of Islay, Earl of Ross and Lord of the Isles in 1475, were the Overlords of the counties of Nairn, Inverness, &c. The first Campbell of Islay was Sir John Campbell, great-grandson of Lady Muriel and of the first Sir John Campbell of Cawdor. The Sir James MacDonald mentioned by Pattison in his note on Lachlan Mòr was the son of Angus MacDonald of *Dùn Naomhaig*. He was a celebrated and able chief whose printed letters indicate thought and culture. He was long kept a prisoner in Edinburgh Castle, in order that his enemies might have time to destroy every vestige of his power in Islay and in Kintyre. His aged father, Angus, was compelled by the King and his Council, instigated by the Campbells, to write a Renunciation of Islay at Edinburgh, January 1, 1612. These illegal proceedings were considered null and void by his soldierly son Sir James. On May 24, 1615, Sir James MacDonald of Islay escaped from Edinburgh Castle, and hastening to put himself at the head of his clan, dashed through Atholl and Rannoch, crossed to Islay, surprised the Castle of *Dùn Naomhaig* and subdued the island. He wrested Islay from the grasp of the Knight of Cawdor, who, with the help of Sir Oliver Lombard's cannon, coerced Islay to show signs of obedience. The natives were delighted. They felt proud of the military prowess of their beloved Chief. He then sent out the Fiery Cross and arrayed under his banner his brave followers in his hereditary territory of Kintyre. But the King, the Council, Argyll and the Campbells marshalled their forces and speedily crushed the rising power of the lawful heir, Sir James MacDonald, who fled to Ireland, and thence to Spain. His wife was Margaret Campbell of Cawdor, Sir John's sister. After Argyll's apostacy and disgrace he, too, had escaped to Spain. But in the land of their exile, the Chief of the Campbells and the Chief of the MacDonalds dwelt together in unity! Sir James MacDonald was restored to Royal favour and died at London in 1626. To enter upon a historical outline of the sanguinary battle of *Ceann Tràigh Ghruineard*, fought in 1598, would occupy too much space.

IV.— THE PIOUS LABOURER.— This aged pilgrim who is now eighty-six years of age is still living in "green and grassy Islay." For a long number of years he acted as the honoured and trustworthy grieve of Captain Colin MacLean, Laggan, Mr. Thomas Pattison's uncle. Like Eliezer, the steward of Abraham's house, this faithful man "ruled over all that his master had." While the MacLeans increased in material wealth, the Pious Labourer, heir of a kingdom, although "silver and gold has he none," daily grew richer in faith. He does not know that he has been made the subject of one of Mr. Pattison's Original Poems: An Islay minister, in a letter addressed to me, dated March 26, 1890, says:—
"I saw —— ——, ten days ago, and I had a talk with him about Mr. Thomas Pattison, as you requested. —— —— says he knew Mr. Pattison well, and that he had a very high opinion of him. He at the same time said, that he was the first to teach Mr. Pattison to read the Scriptures in Gaelic. He also stated that his young friend frequently passed Bowmore, and went to Skerrols on the Sabbath day."

Mr. Pattison's recollections of the words and works of his saintly friend are suffused with the glow of genuine friendship. Let me quote a few lines :—

"There is a grandeur in his life I ween—
A high nobility, a rank divine;

> Though on an earthen floor he kneels in peace,
> To say with reverent devotion's power,
> "Our Father" to the God that made the heavens—
> "Our Father" to the God that rules the earth—
> "Thy Servant," say unto the Man Divine,
> The holy, harmless, undefiled with sin—
> There is in verity a grandeur here."

I shall never forget one summer evening I heard a sermon in the Pious Labourer's house beside *Loch na Crannaig*. The preacher, on this memorable occasion, was the venerable and eloquent Rev. Hugh Fraser, M.A., of the Free Church of Ardchattan. It was this accomplished country minister who wrote the interesting and instructive accounts of Ardchattan and Muckairn which appeared in the New Statistical Account of Argyllshire, published in 1845. Mr. Alexander C. Fraser, D.C.L., LL.D., Professor of Logic and Psychology in the University of Edinburgh, and the learned Editor of the works of Berkeley, Bishop of Cloyne, the expounder of Ideal Philosophy, is the son of the late minister of Ardchattan. Among those who went with Mr. Hugh Fraser to the Pious Labourer's humble home, was Mr. Pattison. In the whole audience there was not a more attentive hearer than the brown-haired, fair-visaged, large-eyed, gentle student of the Gaelic Bards. The sermon was on Blind Bartimeus. With melting tones the fluent speaker, in well-chosen Gaelic words, drew a soul-moving picture of the blind beggar rising, casting away his long outer garment and running to Jesus. My occasional reading of Longfellow's touching verses on Blind Bartimeus vividly recalls this scene.

V.—CAPTAIN GORRIE'S RIDE.—Captain Godfrey Mac Neill, tenant of Kilcalumkil, a farm in the vicinity of Port-Ellen, and laird of Ardnacross estate in Kintyre, was the elder brother of Major Bàn MacNeill of Balmony, Rhinns of Islay. Captain Gorrie became proprietor of Ardnacross through his mother's marriage with Mac

s

Donald of Ardnacross, on whom, for his memorable defence of the pass of Stirling Bridge at the period of the Battle of Bannockburn, this estate was apparently bestowed by King Robert Bruce. The gallant Captain was not only a brave and daring soldier, but was also deeply imbued with the spirit of adventure and travel. Being of a restless disposition and moved by the fascinating idea of foreign sight-seeing, he borrowed money from a Colonel Campbell of Campbeltown, in whose hands, till he should return, he left as security the estate of Ardnacross. But when he came home from his eventful tour, he had no money wherewith to repay the Colonel. However, as soon as the Major Bàn in distant lands heard of his brother's pecuniary embarrassment, he forthwith refunded Colonel Campbell every penny of the loan he had given Captain Gorrie. The wily Colonel, rather suspiciously, kept the repayment of the money a profound secret until he had heard that the Major was on his way home. This payment on the part of the Major was equivalent to buying Ardnacross. It was through him that it came into the hands of the Ellister family. It is now owned by the eldest son of the late Rev. Hector MacNeill, who was successively minister of Portnahaven, his native parish, of Hope Street Church, Glasgow, and thereafter of Lochend Free Church, Campbeltown. Captain Gorrie had a son who was familiarly known in Islay as *Dhòmhnull Ruadh a' Chaiptein*. This son, like his father, was possessed with the military spirit, entered the army and attained to the rank of a Colonel. He was knighted by the Portuguese Government. After his retirement from active service Sir Donald MacNeill resided near Glasgow.

Captain Gorrie was a keen sportsman and a famous athlete. He was a strongly built man, proud and passionate in manner, martial in demeanour, true and warm-hearted in friendship. The first time he took a fancy to the white pony was one day he watched his men trying to catch him on the hill. After that he got him trained for riding. Captain Gorrie in his day was considered the best rider in Islay. In his saddle he sat as straight as a wand, with his cocked hat sideways on his head, and in his hand a light whip which he gracefully flourished, but with which he seldom touched his high-stepping, fleet-footed Highland steed. His rash exploits, his races swift, I cannot now review. His rough and rapid ride from Kilcalumkil, four miles above Port-Ellen, to Carnbeg within a mile of Port-Askaig, a distance of about twenty-eight miles in an hour, was a riding feat worthy of "the horse that beat Beelzebub beside the salt sea wave." Like Young Lochinvar "he stayed not for brake, and he stopped not for stone," but swiftly dashed on "over bank, bush and scaur." Although "like an arrow swift he flew, shot by an archer strong," Captain Gorrie did manage his snorting steed to better purpose than did luckless Captain John Gilpin the "nimble steed," the Calender of Ware, lent him for his holiday ride on his twentieth wedding day. All this reminds me of an exciting story told me by good, honest John MacEwan, *Iain Mòr nam madadh*, who in his young days was a successful smuggler on the farm of his father, a respectable tenant in the Oa district. John had some whisky on hand, and observing the gaugers prowling about in the gloaming, he saddled his good brown mare, and mounting, hung, Gilpin like, a cask of *pure Islay* on each side "to make his balance true," and bolted off towards the Big Strand, through Duich sand-knolls, along the Iron Bridge, till after crossing *Clachan-an-tàch-air* Bridge, he turned off the main-road and dashed up the avenue that leads up to the Lonbàn farm, thereafter occupied by hospitable Mr. Duncan Blair, the father of my excellent and popular friend the Rev. Robert Blair, M.A., Cambuslang. When John thus eluded the vigilant eyes of the excisemen, hotly pursuing him on horseback, he feared that the "sparks of fire which the iron heels of his spirited brown mare struck out of the hard and flinty highway," might betray his whereabouts on the road. Honest John's "racing and chasing" was along the same route as Captain Gorrie's Ride so well poetized by Mr. Pattison.

After, at dawn of day, the grim and dark shadows had fled away, the Captain who on his fiery white charger had tried racing conclusions with the "stalwart horseman that rode upon the giant black," *Marcaiche an eich dhuibh* (Gorrie's and his pony's shadow) arrived at his stable door "in haste, in heat, and disarray," but flushed with the honours of having beat Beelzebub.

> "In the sweetest bud
> The eating canker dwells."—*Shakespeare.*

As the rose grows on the thorn-bush and the sting guards the honey, the sweetness of the gallant Captain's victory was mingled with the heart-pang of seeing that his pony *bàn* stumbled and fell:—

> "And there lay the steed with his nostril all wide
> But through it there rolled not the breath of his pride:
> And the foam of his gasping lay white on the turf,
> And cold as the spray of the rock-beating surf."—*Byron.*

The grieved Captain shrouded his faithful pony in his martial cloak, and buried him with military honours. The servants comforted the master, by maintaining that the dauntless Highland pony had two hearts. Like Ossian, after the Féinne, Captain Godfrey MacNeill lost his eyesight, and died at a good old age a man of honour and renown. His valet in his latter days was Mr. Alexander Kerr who read and wrote for him. Mr. Kerr after that removed to Bowmore and developed into a farmer, sheriff-officer, and auctioneer, and being an ardent admirer of his soldierly master's kind deeds and brave acts he used to rehearse them in eloquent words. A forgotten Islay bard, Neil MacQuilkin, Balvicar, composed a vigorous Gaelic song in praise of Captain Gorrie. I conclude these few remarks on my chivalrous and high-minded namesake who was a contemporary of my great-grand-father, and give expression to my impossible wish by quoting, after changing two words in it, the last stanza of Cowper's diverting history of John Gilpin:—

> "Now let us sing, long live the *Queen*,
>   And *Gorrie*, long live he;
> And when he next doth ride abroad,
>   May I be there to see!"

VI —THE HAUNTED WATER OF DUBH-THALAMH.—This water is a small burn running into Lochindaal, between Gartbreac and Ardlarach. This murmuring stream repeats the story of Tennyson's Brook:—

> "I chatter over stony ways,
>   In little sharps and trebles,
> I bubble into eddying bays,
>   I bubble on the pebbles.
> For men may come and men may go,
>   But I go on for ever."

Dubh-thalamh, *Buaile na h-Eaglais*, and *Bruthach an Dùbhraich* lie in the same locality, and in the immediate vicinity of Fern Cottage once the Islay home of PETER THOMAS PATTISON.

VII.— DEAR ISLAY.—This is the best known and the most popular of all Mr. Pattison's Original Poems. It is one of the bright gems that sparkle in the royal crown which her sons and daughters place upon the head of Dear Mother Islay, THE QUEEN OF THE HEBRIDES.

The Pattisons, men and women, were a talented family. The late Miss Margaret C. Pattison, one of our author's sisters, was a most accomplished lady, whose musical gifts were of a very high order, She prepared 2 vols., of music, Gaelic and English words, arranged for the pianoforte, and dedicated to J. F. Campbell, Esquire of Islay. The work was published by Messrs. Swan & Company, 4 Great Marlborough Street, London, W.

Preparing for the Press, Demy 8vo., Price 7s.6d.

ISLAY AND ISLAYMEN,

BY THE

Rev. JOHN G. MACNEILL,

CAWDOR.

Such is the proposed title of a work on this Island and its people, the materials for which are being collected and arranged.

The work will treat of Islay, its history (Secular and Ecclesiastical), Topography, Antiquarian remains, Traditions, Folk-lore, Poetry; Social Statistics, Agriculture, Industries, &c., &c. Sketches of Islaymen who acquired destinction in Science, Literature, or Art, will also be given, the whole forming an exhaustive treatise on one of the most interesting of our Western Isles.

The work will be illustrated with Portraits, Sketches, Maps, &c., and every effort will be made to make the volume worthy of "green grassy Islay," the Queen of the Hebrides.

Should a sufficient number of Subscribers be secured the work will be published.

Subscribers' names will be received by

ARCHIBALD SINCLAIR,

PRINTER AND PUBLISHER,

62 Argyle Street, GLASGOW.

JUST PUBLISHED
AN T-ORANAICHE:
Dedicated to J. F. CAMPBELL, Esq., of Islay.

THE BEST COLLECTION OF
POPULAR GAELIC SONGS
EVER PUBLISHED,
MOST OF WHICH HAVE
NEVER BEFORE APPEARED IN PRINT.

The Collection contains nearly three hundred of the most popular Gaelic Songs, forming a handsome volume of 527 Pages, Demy 8vo., printed in bold clear type, on thick toned paper, handsomely bound, full cloth, gilt. Price,—Ten Shillings and Sixpence. Postage and Registration fee, One Shilling extra.

A limited number of copies, elegantly bound Half-Morocco, Gilt Edges, (suitable for presentation). Price,—Fourteen Shillings and Sixpence. Postage and Registration fee, One Shilling extra.

ARCHIBALD SINCLAIR, 62 Argyle St., Glasgow.

AN T-ORANAICHE.

OPINIONS OF THE PRESS.

An t-Oranaiche, (The Gaelic Songster.) Such is the title of the carefully compiled, and tastefully executed volume now before us. The work contains about three hundred Gaelic songs, many of them now printed for the first time. There is much genuine pleasure in scanning the beautifully printed leaves of the *Oranaiche*, for there is not a page on which we do not find some chaste ditty or charming love-song which we had thought lost beyond recall. We find ourselves now lingering over *Mairi Bhan Dhail-an-eas, Duthaich nan craobh,* or *Gaol an t-seoladair,* or pausing to sing a verse or two of *Tha mo run air a' ghille* or *Ille dhuinn chaidh thu 'm dhith.* The songs have been most carefully selected and correctly printed, and the collection is beyond doubt the largest and best ever published. The *Oranaiche* ought to be found in the library of all who love the language, poetry, and music of the Highlands.—*Oban Times.*

The *Oranaiche* is a good book, and contains between 500 and 600 pages, beautifully printed on toned paper. There is not, so far as we have seen, one expression in the work that could give offence to the most delicate. The value of such a book cannot be over-estimated. The cost is so small, and the contents and appearance of the work so excellent, that no true-hearted Gael should be without a copy.—*Highlander.*

We have here before us a copy of the *Oranaiche*, and it gives us much pleasure to commend it very cordially to the attention of our Gaelic readers. That the power of song, so characteristic of the Scottish peasantry of the south, is no less so of the sturdy sons of the north is amply exemplified in the very tasteful and excellent work before us. The measure of the success which has crowned Mr. Sinclair's labours thus far may be judged by a simple look at the list of contents. Any work containing so many favourite lyrics cannot, we think, fail of being very popular among our Celtic friends. So far as outward appearance goes, the work is neat, correct, and well printed, thus reflecting most creditably upon Mr. Sinclair's taste and Gaelic scholarship, and being also a lasting testimony of his patriotism, courage, and enterprise. It is out of sight the best collection of miscellaneous songs in existence, and not only so, but even in point of intrinsic excellence it is worthy to take its place beside the best books of song in any language. Let Highlanders everywhere possess themselves of the work, and we have no fear that any of them will consider our praise in the slightest degree exaggerated. The work consists of 527 pages, exclusive of preface, contents, index, &c., and the price is so low that we are almost tempted to put cheapness down as the only fault which we could suggest in connection with the *Oranaiche.*—*Perthshire Advertiser.*

The *Oranaiche* is one of the best printed Gaelic words we have ever seen, and consists, with a few exceptions, of songs hitherto unpublished.—*Scotsman.*

The book is simply and beyond question the best and most complete, as it is the largest, collection of Gaelic popular songs existing. It contains all or nearly all the songs which have stood the test of popularity.—*Donald M'Kinnon, Edinburgh.*

My Dear Sir,—Allow me to congratulate you on having got the *Oranaiche* so handsomely off your hands. It is the completest and in every way the best collection of Gaelic poetry that has yet appeared; and the way in which you have managed the matter, in the face of so many difficulties, does you infinite credit.—"*Nether Lochaber.*"

JUST PUBLISHED—Crown 8vo., 270 p.p., Price 2s. 6d.,
Postage to Colonies, 6d. extra.
(Fac-simile of Title Page.)

THE
CELTIC GARLAND.

TRANSLATIONS
OF
GAELIC AND ENGLISH SONGS,
AND
GAELIC READINGS, &c., &c.

BY FIONN.

SECOND EDITION.

GLASGOW:
ARCHIBALD SINCLAIR, 62 ARGYLE STREET.

www.ingramcontent.com/pod-product-compliance
Lightning Source LLC
Chambersburg PA
CBHW021953220426
43663CB00007B/803